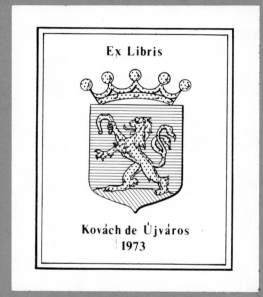

Ex Libris

Kovách de Újváros
1973

A Nervous Splendor

A Nervous Splendor

VIENNA
1888/1889

by
Frederic Morton

ILLUSTRATED

An Atlantic Monthly Press Book
Little, Brown and Company   Boston/Toronto

FIRST EDITION

LIBRARY OF CONGRESS CATALOGING IN PUBLICATION DATA

Morton, Frederic.
  A nervous splendor.

  "An Atlantic Monthly Press book."
  Bibliography: p.
  Includes index.
    1. Vienna—Intellectual life. 2. Vienna—
Social life and customs. 3. Austria—History—
1867–1918. 4. Franz Joseph I, Emperor of Austria,
1830–1916. I. Title.
DB851.M6   943.6'13   79-21306
ISBN 0-316-58532-7

ATLANTIC–LITTLE, BROWN BOOKS
ARE PUBLISHED BY
LITTLE, BROWN AND COMPANY
IN ASSOCIATION WITH
THE ATLANTIC MONTHLY PRESS

MV
Designed by Janis Capone

Published simultaneously in Canada
by Little, Brown & Company (Canada) Limited

PRINTED IN THE UNITED STATES OF AMERICA

to M. C. M.

to Felicia and Lester Coleman, for so much

and to my parents, my two dearest Viennese

ℜreface

⮜⮞

This book lifts a chunk out of the life of Vienna: July 1888 to April 1889. A limited span — but to write any history is to put limits on infinity. It seemed to me that by focusing on a brief time I might expose more of its depth, its details, its dailiness. In this dailiness I've looked for the city's pulse: small flutters no less than great poundings. I've tried to trace local tremors that began along a curve of the Danube, then echoed across the world to come thundering down into our century.

Why just these ten months? Because they seemed representative of a watershed when the Western dream started to go wrong dramatically and the very failure was flooded with genius. It was the context and subtext of a number of events that interested me — including, probably, one that goes unmentioned in my story. I will confess to it here.

On some morning in the fall of 1888 a twenty-three-year-old tool-and-die maker named Bernhard Mandelbaum shoved the last lathe into place in a basement in an outer district of Vienna and opened a factory to produce costume jewelry. I am Bernhard Mandelbaum's grandson and the idea of that fall day gripped me as a child each time I looked at the letterhead of my father's firm: *Bernhard Mandelbaum & Sohn. Gegründet 1888.*

Founded in 1888. A phrase concealing a miracle. The factory had become no more than a fair-sized enterprise in the 1930s, but under *Bernhard* it had borne up very well during the Great War. Under *Sohn* it thrived right through the Depression. For fifty years it had been the pride, the fixed star of our family. How could my grandfather have conjured it out of nothing in 1888?

Later, in grade school, I learned that the miracle was really rather commonplace. We were taught that in Vienna the decades following 1850 were called *Gründerzeit*, the Time of the Founders. In that period the Emperor had built the dream-sweep of the Ringstrasse. Other Austrians, commoners or counts but giants all, had strung the railroads and raised the chimneys which had — almost — made the baroque Empire modern.

Of course, my grandfather labored only on the fringe of that drama. Yet to me he remained a founder among founders. Later I became an American and a writer and my perspectives shifted. I saw young Bernhard Mandelbaum behind a foreground of his truly great contemporaries, the kind who create not industries but climates; men who ninety years ago brewed the very weather of our minds today, men who might have strolled past my grandfather on the sidewalks of a Vienna misted with nostalgia now, a city beyond the looking glass, shining and haunting, lilting and lost.

Do I place my grandfather in too elaborate a frame? Neither waltzer nor philosopher nor captain of cartels, he had come from Galicia to the capital to pursue an ungrandiose vision. He wanted to found with his factory a prosperous, stable, permanent place in which to be modestly dynastic. And here I am, his grandchild, looking at the Hudson instead of the Danube, writing in a language he did not know, under a name he would never recognize.

In our world, as this book tries to show, achievement must end in irony. Yet I hope that my grandfather might join the great founders of 1888 with his own small posthumous success. These pages are the seed of his seed. If he and I are lucky, they will add a little to the charting of the dark through which all of us are drifting.

F. M.

List of Illustrations

A Nervous Splendor

Chapter 1

On Friday, July 6, 1888, the price of sugar went up from forty to forty-two kreuzers a kilo in Imperial Vienna. On the afternoon of the same day, the gates of Franz Joseph's palace swung open. A carriage swept out onto the cobbles of the Ringstrasse. Many of the strollers stopped, as though they'd been waiting for the canter of these two horses.

On the new Ringstrasse one promenaded in the hope of just such spectacles. Walking, one lingered. One came here to wait, as it were, in style. The Ringstrasse itself, all four kilometers of it, stood forever on the verge of a crescendo. Its parklike malls were flower-scented, heavy-leaved with lime and plane trees. To the left and to the right rose huge, intricately wrought silhouettes: Parliament and City Hall, the Imperial Museums, the University, the Court Opera, the Bourse, all teeming with pointed arches, towers, pillars, loggias, with vista after sculptured vista in neo-Gothic, neo-Renaissance, neo-Baroque, all quite new, barely weathered and not yet, if ever, real.

Great traditions had become mock-ups here. This was a vast stage set made of concrete, poured and molded to resemble classic stone. The architecture of previous centuries had been conjured into a theatrical dream, a mirage of portals and pediments sweeping around the medieval core of the city. A mirage waiting either to dissolve or to be touched by some great hand that would give it substance. Waiting, while the price of sugar went up.

Something had to be coming. Children might shout here or horses neigh, but the sounds always fell into a peculiar and preliminary quiet. The boulevard was such a portentous backdrop. One always looked for some act in the foreground big enough to fill it. Those vaulting facades not only glorified the Empire's past but also celebrated an imminence, a transfiguring future.

Where, then, was the flesh of this future? Where the hero to animate heroic scenery? The strollers stopped and stared after the carriage. Somebody was floating away there who might justify so much splendor and so much expectation.

The carriage itself, though, was small. No herald preceded it. No guard followed. Its wheels were not painted with bands of gold. Therefore it did not belong to the coach fleet of the Imperial house. The door exhibited no escutcheon like the ones on the coaches of the aristocracy. It was just a fiacre, a private black horse cab whose cabbie held the reins. His name was Bratfisch and he was a bit more natty than most of his colleagues. He wore his mustaches longer, his cravat more artistically flowing, his top hat more fetchingly angled. And he whistled to the dancing of the hooves, the jouncing of the rubber wheels. He whistled only old Viennese songs about small, sad, dear things gone by: about the chestnut tree by the gate, the gnarled nooks of little streets, the well in the Vienna Woods; songs about the medieval walls that once had hugged the town where the "Ring" now displayed its glitter.

He whistled affectingly. But that wasn't why the strollers stared. After all, other horse cabbies serenaded their fares. But other cabbies had to obey traffic regulations; they were supposed to rein their horses to a walk at street crossings. Not Bratfisch. He zoomed right through, thanks to his passenger. That passenger, who hired him not for an hour or for a day but by the year, reclined in the shadow of the back seat.

He was a young, very slim man in a plain hacking jacket. His beard half concealed a narrow, taut, handsome face. A face conscious, perhaps, that it was being waited for. A young man's face become hollow from too much waiting.

Next month he would be thirty. The stupendous boulevard on which he rode had been under construction for as many years as he had lived. And it had been built for him more than for anyone else. He was the Crown Prince Rudolf, born by God's grace to be Emperor of Austria, Apostolic King of Hungary, King of Jerusalem, King of Bohemia, King of Dalmatia, King of Transylvania, King of Croatia and Slovenia, King of Galicia and Illyria, Grand Duke of Tuscany and Cracow, Margrave of Moravia, Duke of Salzburg, Duke of Bukovina, Duke of Modena, Parma and Piacenza and Guastalla, Princely Count of Habsburg and Tyrol, Prince of Trient and Brixen, Count of Hohenembs, Grand Voyvode of Serbia, and thirty other titles, not the least echoing of which was Duke of Auschwitz.

All these dominions awaited the slender figure in the coach. They stretched from chalets at the Swiss border to the minarets of Montenegro. Though they converged on him in a time still to come, they converged on him most specifically. Rudolf's inheritance was a spectacular oddity among the great states of Europe. His future subjects were united neither by a common language nor a common religion nor common geography or tradition. They shared only one thing: his name.

Habsburg. The Austrian Empire was a dynastic fiction, venerable, fragile, superb. Thirteen million spoke German in his babel. Ten million spoke Hungarian. Five million spoke Czech. Three million spoke Slovak, and millions more spoke diverse Slavic or Arabic languages. Only one person in those motley multitudes was really Austrian: the Emperor Franz Joseph, whose flesh magically united them all.

Rudolf waited to be the next Austrian. And Austria, that many-colored idea sprawling across the Danube lands, surrounded him as he waited, as he sped along the boulevard. Every fairytale corner of the Monarchy contributed visitors to the Ringstrasse. Visiting Vienna meant, above all, walking that boulevard, for seeing sights, for just being there. Exotic apparitions mingled among strollers in Western attire. As Bratfisch swooshed past, a Muslim — from the Imperial Protectorate of Bosnia — shuffled along in crimson fez and pointy white slippers, hawking ornate teakettles and inlaid snuffboxes. Coptic priests, with mitres and beards and violet waistbands girding dark-green cassocks, trooped beside Hasidim in black silk caftans and large-brimmed beaver hats. A Carpathian peasant took off his white fur cap before crossing the wonderful street — a form of Balkan humbleness. And few of these strangers in Vienna would ever guess who sat in the headlong carriage.

Soldiers knew, and gloves flew up in salute. Much of the iridescence on the Ringstrasse was military. The boulevard attracted officers from all over the Empire, some posted here, some on leave from remote garrisons. All jaunted in their regimentals: Hussar majors poured into pink trousers and sky-blue jackets, Tyrolean Rifle lieutenants in silver-green . . . None of these uniforms was pompous with epaulet or braid or helmet Prussianly spiked. Almost every Austrian regiment favored the Crown Prince's style, with a uniform cut along slender, beguilingly simple lines. It was not the garment of a killer or a strutter but that of a fencer, a dancer, a lover. Somehow it excised bellies, firmed chins, and transmuted soldier into leading man. At the Paris World's Fair in 1900, Austria would win first prize for the most beautiful uniform on earth (the Artillery's). Twelve years earlier, in July 1888, it was already just as beautiful in its many variations.

Such variety made a pretty picture — and difficult politics. Habsburgs (forebears of the young man in the fast coach) had long reigned over many nations. But in July 1888, *nation* was beginning to mean *nationalism*. And sore new nationalisms screamed in Parliament, groused in newspapers, growled in the taverns. Franz Joseph manipulated these tensions. Rudolf wanted to resolve them. But meanwhile he had to wait. Meantime the price of sugar rose and Bratfisch let the hooves dance to his whistle. Along the Ring they cantered, faster and faster.

On successive blocks, the promenaders stared. Wasn't that fiacre going too fast? Why was the Crown Prince always too fast? He was being waited for. But did he know how to wait? His ancestors had known. Most Habsburgs before him had been virtuosos of slowness. Patient, steady husbandmen of empire through three-quarters of a millennium. Solid, craftsmanlike majesties. Some showed glints of flamboyance. Most never outfought or outshone their opponents. Instead, they outmarried them. They were adept in betrothing princes whose marriage contracts would win new lands for the House of Austria. Habsburg's lumbering wedding processions had conquered more lands more lastingly than Napoleon's cavalry charges.

Habsburgs managed to avoid the inspirations and graces of decadence with which other dynasties danced toward their brink. Drabness was their secret. Drabness and patience. Manipulative, industrious, strangely modest, inexorable, decent, stodgy, staunch, the Habsburgs had come out of Switzerland in 1273. Manipulative, industrious, strangely modest, inexorable, decent, stodgy, staunch,

PICTURE ARCHIVES OF THE AUSTRIAN NATIONAL LIBRARY

Franz Joseph ruled in 1888. Rudolf was to carry his crown into the twentieth century.

But would he? The promenaders stared. Would he, in a coach whipped on by a whistling Bratfisch? On wheels spinning wildly while the price of sugar rose? Too fast he floated past the Renaissance colonnades of the Court Opera and then past the cupolas of the Schwarzenberg Palace.

Here Bratfisch veered his horses off the Ringstrasse, southward. In the distance stood the tenements of workers employed by the area's new textile factories. Skinny sheep bleated on meadows already half dust bowl. Left behind Rudolf were the profits of

Rudolf driving his phaeton up to the Sacher Garden restaurant in the Prater, in a painting finished in 1889. (The man sitting in back is his footman.)

industrialization, transmuted into gleaming imitation-antique on the Ringstrasse. Ahead lay the soot and weeds of progress.

"I will have it thought about," Franz Joseph would say when presented with profound trouble. Then he would order the best brains to think up a prettier facade to cover the problem. The Crown Prince, on the other hand, felt that problems must be faced and solved. "The many poor rightly see their enemy in the few who consume their substance," he'd written at fifteen to his tutor, General Latour. "A tremendous change has to come," he'd written his friend Moritz Szeps at twenty-four, "a social restructuring . . ."

Now, at twenty-nine, Rudolf had learned that the things that have to come must bide their time, perhaps until the Empire's destruction. And that it would be disobedient of him to speed changes on their way. His sonorous titles and peacock privileges did not include the franchise for doing something significant. This he had learned long ago. After a while he had also learned the pretense of accepting the intolerable.

The day of his birth his father had awarded him the Order of the Golden Fleece and appointed him Colonel of the 19th Regiment. This spring of 1888 Franz Joseph had come up with yet another hollow honor and raised his son to Inspector General of the Infantry. Only two weeks ago, the annual High Command Conference had taken place, attended by many below Rudolf's rank, and Rudolf had not even been invited. He pretended to accept that. His sovereign did not want to grant him true manhood. Very well, he would play the princely eunuch. For a while longer he would.

He was cut off from the nerve center of the Monarchy — that is, from the monarch. "Correctness" governed stiffly the relationship between father and son. Rudolf not only did accept *that* but didn't mind publishing it to those around him. Just three days before, on July 4, he'd written to his former tutor: "Do let me know when His Majesty the Emperor returns to Ischl. Surely you'll hear the news a few days before I do." He was the heir apparent. Despite that — or because of it — he had never been given any real power save the almost occult one of making heels click and hats levitate everywhere through his mere appearance. He pretended to accept that.

At last his fiacre slowed. Bratfisch stopped the horses before the Southern Railway terminal. The stationmaster's cap levitated. Policemen's heels came together. He acknowledged the ripple around him with a mild bow. He glimpsed a figure half hidden behind the coal cart. The inevitable detective, noting no doubt that His Most Exalted Imperial Highness was still alone. He accepted that as well. He let himself be bowed to his compartment.

The train moved slowly, but Rudolf riffled fast through the newspapers in his valise. Fast enough to cover all the pages during a short ride. The financial columns in the back part of the *Neue Freie Presse* reported that, yes, sugar prices had risen by two kreuzers. In the personal-advertisements section on the next page small type simmered with passion. *To my most beloved love: Have you forgotten me entirely? . . . Write! Greetings and kisses from your R.* In a neighboring column a doctor advertised his "sequestered" waiting room for patients with secret diseases. Stanley was still lost in Africa, searching for Livingston. In Trieste an American corvette had amazed the whole harbor by hoisting an electrically illuminated flag on July 4.

The Crown Prince concentrated above all on foreign news. The European picture had concerned him for years. Other empires were approaching modern greatness much faster than Austria: To the east, the Russian colossus knew how to exploit freshly emergent ethnic consciousness; St. Petersburg propagandized the Balkan Slavs both within and without Habsburg borders. In fact, Russia had just toppled the Austrophile Alexander Battenberg from his Bulgarian throne. To the south, Italy had already achieved much of its unification by reclaiming Lombardy and Venice from Austrian occupation; now Italy was going further and sending agitators into the southern part of Tyrol, the ancient Habsburg crown land. To the west, England's sovereignty over the high seas was just being reaffirmed by the Suez Canal Convention, placing management of the Canal in the hands of a company controlled by Her Majesty's Government. In Paris the dynamic shadow of General Boulanger galvanized all of France; "The Man On Horseback" — an admirer had invented the phrase for him — seemed fated to turn the Third Republic into a united phalanx under his dictatorship. To the north, in Germany, a yeasty young Wilhelm II had become Kaiser less than a month ago, impatient to start building his Greater — and ever Greater — Reich.

For Rudolf, Wilhelm was a contemporary, an allied prince, and a *bête noir* since boyhood. That weekend the papers reported a speech made by the new Kaiser of Germany. Setting sail for Russia on his yacht the *Hohenzollern*, Wilhelm had expressed much slightly condescending cordiality for the Crown Prince of Austria.

For the time being Rudolf had to accept even that.

For the time being. The phrase governed his life. For the time being he had no power to change anything, including his country's inertia vis-à-vis other lands. For the time being he must even play along with the German Emperor's airs.

The day before, he'd sent Wilhelm a copy of the freshly published Volume I of *The Austro-Hungarian Monarchy in Word and Picture*. Rudolf was not only its editor but author of the first chapter, which happened to be about the very landscape through which the train was passing — the Vienna Woods. Rudolf's personal inscription to Wilhelm ("to my dear friend and cousin") was as effective a camouflage as the banalities to which he limited his article. In it, he invoked the loveliness of the Vienna Woods, foothills to the Alps, the lyric rise and fall of forest slopes which undulated in his compartment window now. His chapter dilated on the *Schwarzföhre*, the black fir, into whose twigs the breeze stirs a hiss that is also a melody; on the woods' silence; the lonely sweetness of occasional bird songs. And on the relative absence of animals interesting to hunters.

Nowhere did the author mention that he himself had bought a hunting lodge just here, in the heart of the Vienna Woods, at Mayerling. The lodge had been inaugurated by the Crown Prince and Princess, with many Imperial huntsmen and gypsy violins attending, in the fall of the previous year. But Rudolf had many better shoots available. Gun and hound weren't heard too much after he took possession of Mayerling. "I must have a nook to myself," he said to a friend baffled by the Crown Prince's partiality to the isolated lodge. "There has to be a place to run to, when the *Krippelg'spiel* [mummery] gets to be too much." It got to be too much rather regularly. Often he "ran" to Mayerling alone, as he did on this July afternoon. Often in special company. He was not the most conjugal of husbands, nor the merriest of archdukes, nor the least devious and willful of crown princes. Elsewhere he went through the charade of acceptance. Not necessarily here. This fall his father's government had prepared a gorgeous agenda of

Imperial renewal and rejuvenation. Rudolf did not necessarily believe in all the gorgeousness. And in this corner of the Vienna Woods he could escape it. At Mayerling he did what was best done in seclusion.

Rudolf got off the train in Baden. Heels clicked, caps levitated. He allowed himself to be bowed past the view of another presumable detective, jumped into the one-horse phaeton held ready for him, drove fast, too fast, through the Helenen Valley, past the ruins of Rauhenfels and Rauhenstein, and within half an hour ground his wheels onto the gravel driveway of a rather simple farmlike building. His lodge at Mayerling.

Through the rest of the night the few servants heard little more than the rain which had begun and the hiss of the black fir.

Chapter 2

Rain covered the Empire that weekend. In Vienna a slow drizzle kept promenaders from the Ringstrasse, and the weather made drearier a raw spot still left on the most grandiloquent part of the boulevard: In the square opposite City Hall, a huge shape bulked, hooded in canvas, obscured by scaffolds.

The thing looked like a gargantuan butterfly not yet emerged from its cocoon. Workmen had been laboring on it for no less than sixteen years, longer than on any other edifice on the Ring; yet its opening, scheduled for September, had been postponed again. It was the one showpiece of the boulevard that remained unfinished. A magnificent laggard, it seemed to mirror the Austrian condition. When it reached completion, finally, sometime in the fall, then perhaps Vienna would complete its own passage to modernity.

That Austria had much catching up to do was a hoary truth by 1888. But whereas Rudolf wanted fundamental reform, his father often thought in terms of cosmetics. In 1857 the young Franz Joseph had made a characteristic concession to the need for change. By that time every other Western metropolis had long since torn down its fortifications. Now the Emperor ordered that his capital's ancient ramparts should be razed, too, at last. Their removal and replacement by the Ringstrasse had been plastic surgery on a gigantic scale. It had produced doubt at the very outset from Franz Grillparzer, Austria's most trenchant playwright:

> *Vienna's confining parapets*
> *into the sand now fall.*
> *What does it matter?*
> *We are still ringed round by a Chinese Wall . . .*

Grillparzer had died in 1872, but his skepticism survived in Rudolf and a thoughtful few. Throughout Europe and America great powers led the race toward the new century. And Austria? In Austria it was drizzling on Ringstrasse marvels still not finished after sixteen years.

In Austria contradictions danced an ornate quadrille. In Austria the Crown Prince could ride roughshod across all traffic regulations; but before the need for reform, he must stand perfectly still. In Austria the monarch could assume unlimited power over a limited Monarchy. In Austria only Parliament made the law of the land; yet article fourteen of the constitution let the Emperor make laws himself whenever Parliament did not sit — and His Majesty could dissolve any session. In Austria Franz Joseph, a "latent absolutist," could emerge from legend into politics to supersede the legislature or to sack a prime minister. In Austria old privileges began to show their age while retaining, somehow, an entirely undiminished luster. In Austria the gonfalons of a feudal Crown still flew over subject nations hissing with an unruliness that was already republican.

How long could such anachronistic confusion last?

The likes of Rudolf worried. But around Franz Joseph one hoped that many problems would give way to the season starting this autumn in the Imperial capital. Vienna's Chinese Wall — everything that insulated, antiquated, parochialized the city — would sink away before a series of progressive spectacles already announced by the newspapers. Soon the Crown Prince would help inaugurate a modern new trade exhibit. Then Wilhelm, Emperor of Germany, would come to town to pay homage to Franz Joseph in a state visit that would establish Vienna as a principal center on the international scene. Franz Joseph would celebrate the fortieth anniversary of his reign, a significant milestone. And, at the season's summit, the canvas would drop from the last important construction on the Ring. The titanic butterfly would be released from its cocoon of sixteen years: The new Court Theater would finally shine forth with a stage electrically lit and a technology worthy of the coming century. Vienna would mark that premiere with an éclat surpassing the debut of all other Ringstrasse buildings. And then, at last, the season would wreak its miracle. The Ring would be whole and Austria would be launched into the greatness of its future.

Would it not?

In the new Court Theater, which was to signify such consummation, a young man of Rudolf's generation labored. Sometimes he whistled, though not as sentimentally as Bratfisch; sometimes he cursed when a bit of paint fell onto his face. By the time of our rainy July weekend of 1888 he had been on the job for months. High above an immense staircase, so close to the roof that he could hear the drizzle drumming, he lay on a scaffold and moved his brush to the weak glow of an "electric lantern."

He was not Michelangelo painting Noah on the Sistine Chapel. He was the then obscure artist Gustav Klimt finishing a ceiling panel called *The Chariot of Thespis*.

He could not judge what he was doing. Though the mural was meant to be viewed from the staircase, the sight lines from there were blocked by the scaffold. But if Klimt could not really see his work, he couldn't really believe in it either. He didn't believe in programed grandeurs. Not in the Ringstrasse's, which rehearsed the architectural swagger of the past. And not in these ceiling frescoes representing highlights in the life of the drama muse, cliché after overblown cliché. Gustav Klimt, his brother Ernst and his associate Franz Matsch had been hired to depict thespian landmarks through the millennia, leading up, by implication, to the new Court Theater as their zenith.

It was prestigious hackwork for three unknowns in their twenties. It was also a sweaty bore for Gustav Klimt. Like the Crown Prince he was harnessed to the ornamentation of an old mode while all his instincts demanded the creation of something new.

For *The Chariot of Thespis* he had drawn a preliminary sketch that included two florally intercurved women kissing each other. Baron von Wilbrandt, in charge of the theater's decor, had put a quick stop to that. Klimt's finished panel showed the two women standing demurely side by side.

Later he would be notorious for the sexuality of his portraits, stretching the female body in sensuously skewed geometries. Now this impulse could express itself only through small mischief: he suggested slight elongations in his nudes; and he made the statues in his five mural panels more flexible than the "live" figures.

The first, still hobbled, stirrings of a giant were in the brush-strokes that touched the ceiling of the new Court Theater. Within the decade Gustav Klimt was to spearhead an assault on Vienna's art galleries and museums; to break up all the pompous gesticulation with an erotic whiplash; to stand forth as one of art nouveau's foremost, most radical exponents. His work would be central in a movement that many decades later still dotted space-age lofts with Tiffany lamps and dream-touched posters.

And there were others like him in this town, names destined to be trumpet blasts — though they gave off only struggling sounds by the Danube in the summer of 1888. Vienna, that scrollworked bastion, smoldered with more demons of the future than the most forward-minded cities of the West. Its officials were obsessed with the need to continue a great Imperial image. The true greatness gathering in these streets was often as unofficial as a guerrilla band.

Greatness was a precocious concern to the rained-on son of a small shoe-shop owner in the Jewish district of Vienna. At fifteen Arnold Schönberg paid no attention to the soaking of his Sunday-best yellow topcoat. In decades to come his audacity with chromatics and harmony would outdo Klimt's with color and line. He would not just revolutionize music but reinvent it. Atonality, as he would develop it, was to polarize the new music of the twentieth century. This July weekend of 1888, however, he was far from being a new master. He was a worshipful apprentice. He was standing just outside the covered pavilion of the First Café by the Prater Amusement Park. He couldn't afford to go inside. It would cost at least twenty kreuzer to sit down under shelter for a cup of coffee. Therefore he stood as near as possible to the rim of the pavilion so that he could discern, through the rain, the music coming from the café's bandstand. Once Beethoven had performed there in his last public appearance as a pianist. Now, in fact, the military band went from a waltz to the overture of *Fidelio*. Schönberg edged forward. He had no other way of hearing important music free. It didn't matter that he was not only listening but dripping. This was as near as he could get to greatness.

Greatness was a hypnotic ghost in Vienna that summer. Another musician pressed still closer to Beethoven — closer physically to the greatest composer of them all — though Beethoven was over fifty years dead in 1888. Anton Bruckner managed to share his pince-nez with the Olympian corpse.

Some days before our rainy July weekend Bruckner had boarded the horse-tramway to Währing Cemetery in outer Vienna. Against the protest of a policeman he had barged into a chapel where scientists bent over an opened casket. Beethoven had just been exhumed for skeletal measurements prior to removal to a belated

Grave of Honor in the Central Cemetery. Bruckner brushed past specialists at work, clamped on his pince-nez, grasped the skull with both hands. A doctor tried to interfere, but Bruckner at sixty-four still had the single-minded enthusiasm of a boy.

"Now ain't it true?" he said to the skull in his Upper Austrian dialect, ". . . ain't it true, dear Beethoven, that if you were alive today you'd allow me to touch you? And now them strange gentlemen here want to forbid me that!"

He *was* forbidden, with some mild physical force. On the way home he realized that his pince-nez now had only one lens. "It must have fallen in when I stooped over the casket," he said to his companion, Karl Hruby, and seemed "quite happy" about it.

He couldn't be sure, though. The lens might have dropped out at home. His housekeeper, the formidable Kathi Kachelmayer, conducted one of her grim searches through Bruckner's four rooms in the Hessgasse. She detested the barnlike dishevelment of the place which defied all her attempts at order. She plowed through heaps of manuscripts, score sheets, books, and God knows what else under which the piano, the organ, even the desk were buried. She assaulted similar piles in the bedroom where an ever-proliferating chaos of paper spilled across the bed, the only furniture. In vain. The lens was gone. Kachelmayer glowered. Bruckner rejoiced.

Many troubles pressed on him. He was a country boy plunged by an incongruous talent into a difficult and important city career. He could construct the most intricate of harmonies into which to pour the humble fervors of a village Mass. His compositions were admired by some, but ignored and snickered at by more. He earned general recognition — and a fair living — only as a master organist. Right now he was reworking his Third Symphony and finishing his Eighth, risking again the contempt of the city's musical hierarchy. But it didn't matter; not in a good week like this one in early July. Then he had the joy of a peasant acolyte for whom death is a mystery as superb as a young girl's loveliness. Then he thanked the Savior for His bounties. To share a pince-nez with the bones he loved! Wasn't that to partake of their greatness? And another solace: Soon he would depart for Bayreuth to commune a while with Richard Wagner, also a great friend who resided in God's mercy within a tomb.

A fellow Wagnerian, indeed one of Bruckner's few sympathizers, seemed to be an exception in July 1888. He appeared to have let up at least temporarily on the pursuit of greatness which absorbed others in town. Indeed this man might have had good reason for relenting. Born in the remoteness of a Styrian valley, Hugo Wolf had already made true a bit of the dream that drove a gifted young provincial to Vienna. No one in the city was ready yet to share the consensus of musicologists of later generations: that Wolf was the supreme master of the modern *Lied*, the peer of Schubert and Schumann. But he had already gathered a certain small following. Sponsors arranged domiciles for him, like the one at Mayerling in 1880. Hugo Wolf lived here a few hundred yards away from what was to be the Crown Prince's hunting lodge. When just past his teens, he rolled his cigarettes at Mayerling, worked his coffee machine, ate his vegetarian milk-and-groats, wandered the black-fir woods, bedded in farmhouses a girl named Wally Frank and wrote the "Mausfallsprüchlein," an exquisite song uncanny in view of Mayerling's future. "Mausfallsprüchlein" sings about a romantic idyll with a sweet little mouse — which turns sinister as a cat joins the party.

Now in July 1888, not yet thirty and just over five feet tall, Hugo Wolf was "a dancing little powerhouse of a man, stocky, broad shouldered, thick necked like a young faun, yet so light and delicate, as graceful in posture as Puck the elf."

In the months preceding he had finished the initial group of *Lieder* based on the verse of Eduard Mörike. It was Wolf's first great cycle and perhaps the first group of such songs ever which didn't just accompany lovely words with beautiful sound as Schubert had done — but used music to serve the most fragile intentions of poetry. "Wolf's Poetic Supremacy Act of 1887," a critic would one day call this approach, revolutionary for a composer. But Wolf himself suspected that in the last year he had brought about a turning point. "I have just written down a new song," he wrote to a friend. "A divine song, I tell you. What I write now, I write for posterity. . . . How far shall I get? . . . What will the future yet unfold for me? This question torments and distresses and pre-occupies me waking and dreaming. Have I a vocation?"

After the spring's tremendous spurt, though, he appeared merely to coast through July of 1888. As usual, he was very close to being penniless. A few friends put him up at the Schloss Bellevue, a frayed castle-inn on a hill in the Vienna Woods.* Wolf seemed to be busy with nothing but the repair of an old piano when it rained, as it did during the first July weekend of 1888. When the sun shone, he hiked. Even his closest friends thought he was lolling through a restful interlude.

Actually it was nothing of the kind. It was a summer dedicated to an intensity nobody knew. Hugo Wolf was conducting, and at the same time concealing, a grand passion. The woman was Melanie Köchert, wife of his most generous patron. The coded personal advertisement in the July 5 edition of the *Neue Freie Presse*, the very edition traveling with Rudolf to Mayerling, was addressed by Melanie Köchert to Hugo Wolf.

To my most beloved love: Have you forgotten me entirely? . . . Write! Greetings and kisses from your R.

R. signified Rinnbach, where the Köcherts had their country house in the Salzburg Alps. *"Write!"* was a plea he had answered through his work. He had addressed Melanie when he had com-posed such Mörike songs as "Insatiable Love": "A thousand years you'd try in vain to kiss away your passions' pain . . . caresses but augment it . . ."

But Wolf also wrote her privately. He sent Melanie a letter to a post-office box in Rinnbach. His lines from Vienna to the Salz-burg Alps crossed another extramarital missive in the rain, traveling in the opposite direction.

The other letter, written on July 5, was not carried by ordinary mail like Wolf's. A courier conveyed it on the fastest train in a pouch sealed with the All Highest insignia. After all, that letter

---

* Vacationing in the same spot exactly seven Julys later, Sigmund Freud would happen on the key insight to his *Interpretation of Dreams*. Today a plaque marks that event.

belonged to one of the most august unconsummated affairs in history.

"My dear gracious lady," wrote Franz Joseph, the Emperor and Apostolic King, from Bad Gastein to Frau Katharina Schratt, the Imperial and Royal Court Theater actress. "The weather certainly could be better. But on the other hand, it also could be worse. . . ." Then, in the same conciergelike vein, His Majesty proceeds to describe how he is fairly content in his modest rooms at the Hotel Straubinger. How he rises at 5 A.M. (much later than usual, but then he is on vacation); works on State papers till 7 A.M.; then climbs, alone, to the chalet high on the mountain where the Empress resides and where he gets his coffee; climbs down again for more State papers between 9 A.M. and lunch; climbs up again, again alone and usually in the drizzle, for some sour milk at 2:30 followed by a hike; climbs down again to his hotel at night to sleep; and how he remains Madame's most devoted and adoring — Franz Joseph.

This was the rainbow sovereign whose palaces in Vienna, Budapest and Prague totaled ten thousand rooms, who raised field marshals and erased prime ministers, who decreed the Ringstrasse's splendors, who in his working days loomed in a cloud of palatines, chamberlains, equerries, and adjutants.

Despite or because of all that, Franz Joseph maintained a paradoxical relationship with greatness. His official world moved to a steady drumroll of magnificence. And magnificence was just what he liked to exclude from his private hours. The Emperor slept on an iron bedstead, ate boiled beef, drank beer, and had a love life consisting of a hopeless petty-bourgeois crush on a lady of the stage. If Hugo Wolf required an extravagant affair to maintain his spirit and his art against a milieu of threadbare improvisation, Franz Joseph needed a homey attachment to make tolerable life on the loftiest pedestal.

What complicated the monarch's yearning for the prosy was his wife. He had married a superb sonnet of a woman, an absentee Empress. At fifty Elisabeth was still Europe's great beauty, neurasthenic and fugitive, a legendary wanderer, parsing a poem by Heine on some Adriatic shore or skipping veiled down the alleys of a Mediterranean port. Franz Joseph admired Elisabeth abstractly. Concretely she gave him nothing that he wanted.

Frau Schratt did, thanks to her attractive limitations. In her the Court Theater had a competent comedienne. Offstage she was not mesmerizing but endearingly bubbly, even in the face of majesty. When the Emperor had the sniffles, she would bake him little cakes in the form of handkerchiefs. She cooked him goulash and fed him the backstage gossip he relished. Their "soul friendship" (as he called it) was not only good therapy. It was also politically right just because it happened to be a *mésalliance*. If Franz Joseph had turned to someone more fitting — a princess, a lady of the Court — his attachment would have been interpreted as the triumph of one Palace cabal over another. Frau Schratt, however, stood delightfully beyond the pale. She was His Apostolic Majesty's beloved commoner. The actress humanized his exalted lot by reducing it to domestic proportions.

Of course he could have taken possession of her by discreet Imperial fiat. He never did; not physically. Instead he chose to adore her with all the ardors of unfulfillment. He adored her in countless letters breathing sheepish passion and homely humors. He knew he must never have the woman he desired; just as he must have known, somewhere in a corner of his mind, that the gorgeous Empire he ruled could never last.

Consecrated to two impossibilities, the Emperor and Apostolic King walked the mountains of Bad Gastein in July. He trudged up the steep meadows, alone in his plain green loden coat. He nodded at shepherds who had learned not to be amazed at greatness passing among cow turds.

On the same July weekend, one of Franz Joseph's subjects faced the same Austrian rain and experienced a rather modern uncertainty. He wondered yet again whether he deserved to be himself. That is, he wondered whether he merited greatness.

At sixty-three Johann Strauss commanded a renown even more overwhelming than the Emperor's. Second only to Queen Victoria in international popularity polls, he was the world's first pop celebrity, a composer-performer who set vast crowds pulsing, from

Bosnia where peasants imitated his mustaches, to Boston where he had directed a choir of twenty thousand to celebrate the American republic's centennial. The continents waltzed to his fiddle. It was as though he were leading a new revelry which not only enthralled the globe but expressed its acceleration. Strauss had become a mass idol without benefit of mass communications, a feat surpassing the Beatles'.

In July of '88 he summered in his country villa at Schönau in the Vienna Woods, about a dozen miles southeast of Mayerling. The "delicious" young Adele was his newly married third wife. He had just composed the Emperor Waltz, a symphonic enchantment in three-quarter time, in honor of the forthcoming fortieth anniversary of his sovereign's reign. And he was being sued for fifty thousand kronen (by the lyricist of "The Gypsy Baron") as befitted a preeminent composer. His studio was ringed with rose beds in Schönau, peacocks strutted in his garden, and like other Viennese he was jousting with the phantom of true greatness. His very name epitomized the genius enthroned in his own lifetime. And yet he resembled Hugo Wolf, that obscurely steaming spirit: Johann Strauss still struggled toward his "true vocation."

Everyone said that he was incomparable. He suspected his incomparability. What if he was incomparable in a second-rank genre? He craved the first-rank, though he had lived for over sixty years without essaying it. Now the time had come for that — now or never. In 1888 most of his summer nights were consumed in the attempt. If he succeeded he would deserve to be Johann Strauss.

By daylight he displayed a witty, charming, affable mask. After the sun went down; after the admirers, the interviewers, the fawners, his business agents and card-playing cronies were gone, he changed. He began to be his fiercely aspiring self once more. Only then did he walk to the candlelit piano.

This creative angel of lilt and light fed on darkness and rain. "Rain, nothing but rain," he once wrote to a friend, ". . . infinitely wonderful. The worse it gets the better I feel. . . . I want no sunshine while I labor." Rain at night was best. At night his hooded eyelids opened, the coal-black irises glittered, his black-dyed mustaches and his black-dyed hair rose in powerful disorder. His fingers bore down on the octaves, his pencil raged against the paper.

There must have been much such raging in July 1888. Johann Strauss, lord of the operetta, was now finally daring what he had waited to do all his life. He was writing *Ritter Pazman*, his last, his first, his only opera.

Two other Viennese escaped the rain, but not the compulsions of greatness. Both were in their late twenties, contemporaries of Rudolf, Hugo Wolf and Klimt. Both still lived in the homes of their parents. But this summer they traveled abroad, in better weather. In that early July of 1888 this pair of overreaching, over-assimilated Jewish dandies from Austria met on the fashionable English seaside. "At Brighton I had a brief conversation with Theodor Herzl," Arthur Schnitzler notes in his autobiography.

It couldn't have been a very airy encounter. Schnitzler suffered from the highest literary ambition. But to the future author of *La Ronde*, to the finest dramatist of the *fin de siècle*, all such hopes were oppressive dreams in 1888. Here he was, a custom-tailored drone whose father, the famous surgeon, financed his British tour. Here he was, an unknown physician with a whole shelf of unfinished novel drafts, unpublished stories, unproduced plays. Here he was, "unable to create for myself the necessary freedom with which to indulge my literary activities. The time for achievements had come, but I was unable to distinguish myself. . . . I gave vent in my diary . . . to all the misery within me."

What a contrast to that dazzling litterateur, Theodor Herzl! Once the two had been fellow students at the University of Vienna. But Herzl had pulled "twenty paces ahead." Schnitzler envied Herzl's "ironic dash"; envied Herzl's effortless style (at a party, Herzl had tightened Schnitzler's sloppy cravat in passing); above all, he envied Herzl's success as essayist for the Vienna papers. Hadn't Herzl already published two collections of his pieces?

Envy is a form of ignorance. Schnitzler never suspected that only a few months earlier Herzl had screamed into *his* diary against "this constant, wasting, travel-piece hacking. . . . Journalistically I have arrived. But at the same time, I fear, I am finished. . . . If I fail now, I'll be a beaten and broken man, poorer than ever because I have lost youth's courage."

Herzl felt socially stifled. By the 1890s he would emerge as the Zionist messiah. In 1888 most of his fellow Semites seemed odious. Good Jewish society was to him the slum of fashion. "Yesterday a grand soiree at Treitel's" he wrote his parents during a stay in Berlin. "Some thirty or forty ugly Jews. Hardly a consoling sight. . . ." And from Ostend beach: "Although there are many Budapest and Viennese Jews here, the rest of the vacationing population is pleasant."

No, he did not have the companionship he deserved, and his career (no matter how awesome to Schnitzler) had failed him bitterly so far. His by-line in the papers he saw as a mere stepping stone from which he should have long since leaped. His métier was to dazzle his audience on stage; to light up the world from a new, unexpected angle with the greatness of his wit. He burned to be what Oscar Wilde was about to become. But the theater managers who mattered either rejected or postponed his comedies. Only two weeks earlier he had finally received a positive letter from the Court Theater. It accepted his one-act comedy *The Refugee*; in fact it planned to star Frau Schratt as his heroine. But the Court Theater also warned that production might be far off. The Court Theater could schedule only a few one-acters per year and a number of others were already accepted but still unscheduled; besides, the Court Theater's move from the old into the great new still-unfinished building would delay everything yet further. Would Herr Dr. Herzl therefore content himself in patience? Dr. Herzl tried. Meanwhile he worked the journalistic treadmill. Three times a week he must manufacture Sunday Supplement insights out of tourist sights. The cultured middle class had developed an appetite for such products. Herzl must feed it with endless departures and arrivals and deadlines.

Yet he did not allow the strain to mar the perfection of his frock coat, the grooming of his blue-black beard, the urbanity with which he poured tea for Schnitzler at Brighton; nor the wit with which his dispatch to the *Neue Freie Presse* savaged John

Drew's acting troupe doing *The Taming of the Shrew* in London ("The actors barely missed playing badly enough to make the show amusing"). Nor did Herzl let the strain disturb the brisk, happy, good-boy genius tone marking his almost daily postcards to his parents that summer. "Dearest Father and Mother! . . . Cable me as soon as you can as soon as you see my latest article in print. . . . Your advice is very good, dear mother, I'm keeping my umbrella handy." This on July 3. And on July 18: "No, work doesn't really tire me, dearest of parents. But if I do feel fatigue, I stop writing. . . . I really feel very well."

Then and always Herzl knew much elation and much desperation. But he never felt really well. Nor did he stop when tired. He was still too far away from greatness.

The absence of greatness also gnawed at Sigmund Freud, M.D., now in his thirty-third year. But in July of 1888 he worried less about his stature than about his solvency. Every month Frau Freud found it more difficult to cope with the rising price of sugar and everything else. Her husband had done so well in graduate and postgraduate studies; the Freuds had been entitled to think that their investment in a good address would pay off. Maria Theresienstrasse 8 lay right by the Ringstrasse, a neighborhood of arrived doctors and distinguished professionals. Anton Bruckner, for example, lived opposite at Hessgasse 7 and could afford the rent, having only himself to support on his joint salaries as instructor at the Conservatory and organist at the Palace Chapel. But if the old musician ever troubled to look down from his fourth-floor clutter to the young doctor's orderly household on the second floor across the street, he would have seen precious few patients in the waiting room.

Greatness, or at least great success, hovered somewhere around the corner, but it did not enter here. Freud was as stymied as anyone else in Vienna. At the start of his career he had tried a cocaine cure on depressives — disastrously. Some patients became addicted. And though young Dr. Arthur Schnitzler — as it happened — published an article praising Freud's cocaine experiments, the medical establishment turned against him. Now he was using

PICTURE ARCHIVES OF THE AUSTRIAN NATIONAL LIBRARY

*The Sühnhaus (Atonement House) where Freud lived,
beyond his means, in 1888–89. Anton Bruckner lived
in the building facing it on the left-hand side.*

bath cures, rest cures, electrotherapy and, finally, hypnosis in partnership with Gustav Breuer.

Breuer, however, was a leading physician in town, doctor to the city's most distinguished neurotics, summer resident of a spacious house on the Gmundner Lake. Freud, younger and much less deft with patients, spent the first July weekend of 1888 in a little pension which made do as a summer resort for his family. Because of his train phobia during those years the doctor took the horse coach to the village of Maria-Schutz in the Semmering Alps, just beyond the Vienna Woods, but only twenty miles from Mayerling. He arrived drenched by the same rain as Rudolf's hunting lodge, brushed at by the same breeze that hissed through the twigs of the black fir. Among the rootwork of these pines grew large tangy mushrooms, the *Herrenpilze* which Freud liked to eat and loved to hunt during damp weather. But when could he find time? His mind was already swarming with great surmises. They all went against the dogma of the University Psychiatric Clinic. Freud was kept from an appointment there by his own ideas, though he had little leisure to explore them that summer. In the city he spent himself with his nerve-doctor chores. On his country weekends he did medical hackwork. Right now, in July 1888, he was grinding out anonymous articles for Villaret's Medical Dictionary together with a translation of a French alienist's treatise. He had (as he confessed later) the temperament of "a great adventurer, a conquistador, a Pizarro." Yet that summer he maintained a drudge's resignation and pretended to an iron fatalism.

"Life goes on tolerably well here," he wrote to his most intimate friend, Wilhelm Fliess. "We live in constantly increasing unassumingness. When our little Mathilde-baby chuckles, we think it the most beautiful thing that could happen to us. Otherwise we are not very ambitious. . . . My practice grew a little in the winter and spring and is now dropping off again, but it just keeps us alive. Such time and opportunity as there has been for work has gone on . . . matters not worthy of note. . . . In short, life goes on, and life is known to be very difficult and very complicated, and, as we say in Vienna, many roads lead to the Central Cemetery."

Freud's mood may have been colored by the inclemency of that early summer of 1888. The exact meteorological records of Iglau, a small Moravian town seventy miles northeast of Vienna, are unknown. But another man, of Freud's age, religion and talent, wrote even darker lines to *his* friend that season:

"You are right," Gustav Mahler wrote. "If this goes on I shall soon cease to be human. I am in the emotional state of my First Symphony."

By that time, though, Mahler had not only striven but risen mightily. Upward strife was in the family. His father had begun as an aggressive liquor vendor who kept in his cart a French dictionary for cultural improvement. Mahler senior ended with a distillery and a couple of taverns in Iglau, and an ambitious brood. His son Alois once rode through the streets costumed as a medieval

German mercenary, one trouser leg blue, the other red, to announce to his parents: "One day I shall ride past the Imperial Palace in Vienna like that, and the Crown Prince will see me and say, 'Who is this handsome horseman?' and will summon me to give me a great position."

Among the Mahler boys, though, it was not Alois but Gustav who went off to Vienna, toward glory. The pursuit left little room for *Gemütlichkeit*. Only for a little while did he take time out to be young. During his Conservatory days he'd joined a raucous, Socialist-tinged, German-nationalist vegetarian society where he thumped out "Deutschland über Alles" on the piano while Hugo Wolf barked out the lyrics. Soon afterwards he embroiled himself in his career.

Socks drooping, sloppy, hurried and harrying, scurrying about with an oddly jerky gait, satanically intense, he grated on musical tempers in the pit or on stage. Mahler stormed in and out of a succession of increasingly important opera houses in Hall, Laibach, Kassel and Prague. In July of 1888 he had just broken with Leipzig. Few singers and hardly any orchestra members could keep up with the demands and visions of the pince-nezed little fiend up at the lectern.

Often the dislike was mutual. Mahler hated "this hell of a theater." Hated it not only because of the insufficiencies all around him but also because it kept him from composing, which was a more satisfying agony and therefore his proper mission.

The summer of 1888 had already seen the successful production of *Die Drei Pintos*. This opera, though, wasn't really *his*, being the uncompleted work of Carl Maria von Weber which Mahler had only finished. He had already written his haunting *Songs of a Wayfarer*, yet they were very rarely sung. Most painful of all, he had composed his First Symphony to very little avail. Its intensities and vehemences surged far beyond the bounds of the respectably romantic. It thundered, fluted, trilled and wailed the anguish of a soul stretched to its farthest limits. The *Titan* symphony (as Mahler titled it) was ablast with the demonology of greatness. This work contained most of his future ideas, and no established orchestra would play it.

So much for his composing. But 1888 did not seem to be a good conducting year either. After his bitter divorce from the Leipzig Opera, Mahler could not count on a single promising prospect. His "subterranean" problem, piles, already afflicted him. He had just gone through an operation, very discreetly, in Munich. He felt better. But what next? What nincompoop music managers would he have to battle next? And where?

"Things are bad with me," he wrote a friend in July 1888. "I see no chance of finding an engagement elsewhere and I must confess in all honesty that this worries me terribly. I now need a very absorbing activity if I am not to perish!"

He did not perish. He saved himself by making out of perishing a poem. In the first July week of 1888 Mahler sat down in his childhood room at his father's house in Iglau and worked out great sound-metaphors of perdition, the first movement of his Second Symphony. He would call it *Totenfeier* or *Death Celebration.* And to this same friend he would confess: "It is the hero of my First Symphony I carry to the grave here. Immediately arise the great questions: Why hast thou lived? . . . Why hast thou suffered? . . . Is it all nothing but a huge, terrible joke?"

ᏋᏉ Chapter 3 ᏉᏂ

On Saturday, July 7, 1888, the
Crown Prince returned from
Mayerling. He arrived at the
Vienna Southern Railway terminal sometime in the late afternoon, observed by a detective
and met by Bratfisch who drove
him whistling through the rain.
At the gates of the Hofburg —
the Imperial Palace — Bratfisch
jumped from the coachman's
seat, too late. Too late the guard
stepped from his yellow-and-
black striped sentinel box. Rudolf had already opened the
fiacre door himself, slipped
through the gate, hurried up

marble steps and down parquet corridors, past spurred boots click-
ing and hands saluting, to his apartments facing the inner Palace
courtyard. He carried a small valise. At journey's end he put it
down on his study desk, next to a paperweight — a polished, snow-
white human skull.

Why dost thou live? The question had been flung publicly at
Rudolf the day after he was born. Three hundred yards away from
the death's head on his desk stood the old Court Theater, not yet
superseded by the new Court Theater where Klimt was still
painting. The old theater had celebrated Rudolf's birth with a
gala performance of allegorical scenes: Among mighty ruins, Clio,
the Muse of History, had sat onstage and with a gold stylus had
incised on a golden slab the heir's birth date: August 21, 1858.
"Here I inscribe the year and the date," she had said to an
audience of the Empire's foremost dignitaries. "But the rest of the
tablet I leave empty. There must be room for his deeds — and I
divine greatness — which I shall record here yet!"

Why hast thou lived? Why hast thou suffered?

Of course it wasn't just Rudolf's bafflement. It was the soul-
bray of the times, of the new ego. Man believed himself emanci-
pated from the limits of custom and station — therefore he was
also estranged from their shelter. Man had become An Individual,
born for his unique great purpose, for which he must quest and
under whose pressure he must justify his life through every moment
until death.

How could men meet this superb demand? Some, like Mahler,
managed to give it eloquent voice. Others, like Freud and Herzl,
would see much of it fulfilled while they still walked the earth.
Most labored in vain and chafed out their days in inadequacy. But
at least they could chafe in private. Not Rudolf.

Rudolf was wriggling in his first diapers as History pronounced
him a titan before the world. Twenty-seven years of expectancy
later, on New Year's Day of 1886, he wrote his friend Moritz
Szeps: "To make a few speeches which aren't so bad, to write a
few fairly good articles and books, to have a modern education —
those are things which are still a long way from a great success

in the course of world history. Who knows what the new year will bring? Perhaps one will have to show what one is worth."

The year 1886 had brought him no "great success." Nor had 1887. Yet to a degree he'd shown what he was worth. His slim, quick presence could make a personal gesture out of an official hand-wave. He entranced crowds and leaders alike. Queen Victoria's crustiness dissolved at the sight of him. At her Golden Jubilee in 1887 she particularly asked for his attendance. No sooner had he arrived than she awarded him the Order of the Garter and not just with routine courtesy either, but with such caressing tenderness, "tickling me as she did so, that I could hardly keep myself from laughing." In fond violation of protocol she asked him to escort her to her state dinner. Leading her on his arm, he preceded all attendant kings.

But he never escaped the hand of his own sovereign. He was an extraordinarily graceful stylist, but at Buckingham Palace as at all official functions, he had to give his toast in the clumsy tropes concocted for him by his father's Foreign Minister. Rudolf's personality was displayed abroad as an advertisement of Austrian charm. But his opinions? His ideas? If His Imperial Highness insisted on indulging himself in such, His Imperial Highness must not indulge himself in public.

For a man who lived intensely through his thoughts and words this was a throttling restriction. He could not violate it head-on. But he could evade it indirectly. For some years now he had been speaking in a roundabout but effective fashion to some fifty thousand Viennese newspaper readers unaware that it was their Crown Prince who was addressing them with such subtle polemics, in such accomplished language.

The path from writer to reader was labyrinthine. On the day of Rudolf's return from Mayerling to the city, Saturday, July 7, 1888, he sent his manuscript on its usual route. He rang for his old servant Nehammer and pulled from his valise the pages written at Mayerling. Nehammer then left the Palace. It was the end of his day's work, but he did not go home to his little apartment in the *Lerchenfelderstrasse*. He did not head for his true destination

*Rudolf with his wife Stephanie, daughter of the King
of Belgium, called "the Flemish peasant" by many at
the Viennese Court*

either. Twice he changed horse-tramways to throw any hounds off the scent, but he could never be sure he wasn't followed. Apparently old Nehammer never worried either. For a quarter of a century, since the Crown Prince had been a tot, he had helped his master into coats and out of scrapes. Service was service, even if it meant zigzagging through Vienna.

Finally arrived at a mansion at Liechtensteinstrasse 51, old Nehammer announced himself as the masseur for Fräulein Szeps. He was admitted into Fräulein Szeps's bedroom where not only Bertha Szeps was waiting, but also her father Moritz, editor and publisher of the *Wiener Tagblatt*, one of Vienna's leading liberal papers. To him the old man gave his master's manuscript. Herr Szeps immediately copied it in his own hand, gave it to a messenger standing by who then sped the copy to the paper's editorial offices at Universitätsstrasse 4. Szeps returned the original to Nehammer along with some late information from *Tagblatt* correspondents, foreign and domestic, much of which the censor would not allow in print.

"I belong to the people least informed by official sources," Rudolf had once complained. Well, through Nehammer, who came to work the next day with dispatches inside his jacket, he was well informed unofficially. And that same day, July 8, 1888, the *Wiener Tagblatt* featured an unsigned lead article, presumably by Szeps. But only Szeps knew that the Crown Prince had written it. The article discussed Kaiser Wilhelm's current voyage to Russia on his yacht *Hohenzollern*. It paid tribute to the might and honor and youth of the Prussian Empire as personified by the new German monarch. But it also could not conceal the fact that there sailed on that ship "not only the pride of Prussia but also a question." Why, for the first stop on his Imperial travels, had Wilhelm chosen the retrograde Tsar's realm, which seemed unwilling to compromise on its anti-Austrian policies?

It was as fine a diatribe against Rudolf's enemy as could slip through the meshes of censorship.

Why hast thou lived? Why hast thou suffered? . . . To what purpose?

In July 1888, more than ever, Rudolf wanted to budge the Monarchy from its friendship with Wilhelm, that bumptious reactionary. He wanted to move toward an alliance with a forward-minded republic like France. More important still, he wanted to encourage everything that might modernize and liberalize Austria. On July 10 he appeared at the Vienna Trade Exhibit, opened rather perfunctorily by his father the Emperor a few days before. The Crown Prince allowed himself to be photographed with all the new developments advertised there, the trends in interior decorating, the new methods in carpentry, the latest building techniques and new-fangled sports gear like bicycles and metal skates.

For a while the Crown Prince's personal interest drew more attention to the show. Then attendance dropped again — way below that of similar exhibits in other lands. Rudolf was the city's Prince Charming; and it kept stalemating him charmingly. He exhorted his Viennese to progress. They loved the lecturer all the more for the peculiarity of his lecture. They adored his arm, the comeliness of its angle, the fashionability of its sleeve, but adroitly ignored the future to which it kept pointing.

How long it had been pointing by 1888! How often had he encouraged technical exhibitions in Vienna, had sponsored, funded and inaugurated! Five years earlier he had opened the International Electric Fair in Vienna with the phrase: "Let an ocean of light and progress pour forth from these streets . . ." This happened to be one of the rare speeches he'd been able to write himself without some Lord High monocle peering over his shoulder. His "ocean of light" had become a byword. People also remembered — not knowing that the Crown Prince was here the source as well — a particularly striking unsigned article in the *Wiener Tagblatt* called "A Thousand and One Days." It coincided with the start of the Electrical Fair and combined a paean to the liberating potential of modern science with an assault on the dead hand of the aristocracy:

"Here is the difference," Rudolf had written, "between the old fantastic fairytale and its realization in the nineteenth century. The magic light streaming from the enchanted castle could once be seen by only one individual whom a fairy princess rewarded with her favors. But what one man creates out of the soil of facts today does not belong to him alone, it becomes the property of all people. It belongs to the use, advantage and enjoyment of all mankind. The fairytale is an aristocratic dream. Its realization through research and invention is democratic reality. . . ."

Thus spake the Crown Prince, nameless but eloquent in the *Tagblatt* of 1883. Yet "democratic reality" still brightened very little of Vienna in 1888. Oceans of light already poured forth from other capitals, but within Vienna's Chinese Wall one still relied on gas lanterns. True, even in this respect a change had been promised for this year. The great season ahead was to be illuminated by bulbs shining not only in the new Court Theater but in Parliament and in a number of other Ringstrasse buildings. So far, however, the electric current expressed itself most emphatically through electrotherapy dispensed at insane asylums and at the Prater Amusement Park.

At the Prater it had become fashionable for young bucks to buy themselves jolts at "electrocution extravaganzas." There was supposed to be a safe limit on the voltage, but the extravaganza managers had discovered that safety wasn't good box office. That summer many young men, literally overcome by modernity, had to be carried off in ambulances.

If his subjects' electrical frivolities frustrated the Crown Prince, so did their attitude toward the telephone. Rudolf admired the telephone's use abroad, not least its facilitation of stock-market business between widely separated cities. Particularly in America this let more and more of the common people participate in transactions heretofore limited to millionaires.

In Rudolf's own country, though, the telephone could not seem to become a democratic utility. Austrians treated it like a rococo bauble. This summer long-distance service began between Vienna and the suburb of Baden near Mayerling. Calls were limited to ten minutes, of which at least six were taken up by delicious arabesques of protocol.

"Fräulein Operator in Baden?" said Fräulein Operator in Vienna. "Might I have the honor to wish you a good morning? It is my privilege to establish a connection on behalf of His Excellency, the Privy Councillor Alfons Baron von Wieck, who presents his compliments. His Excellency would be grateful for the pleasure of conversing with . . ."

In Austria people just couldn't seem to take efficient advantage of progress. It baffled Rudolf. Perhaps he would have been less baffled if his fervor for the future had allowed for some interest in the past. A speeding driver, he bent forward too keenly ever to look back. Yet only such a look would have revealed why his Viennese subjects lacked every instinct for the up-to-date; why they could not assimilate the middle-class utopia of technology or the entire middle-class enterprise of modernity — why, for that matter, they couldn't quite manage being middle-class at all. The fact was that their class structure had failed to crystallize a viable middle. It was a failure integral to the town's character and to its history.

Chapter 4

What vexed the last Rudolf Habsburg had really started over half a millennium earlier with the first. The perverseness of the Viennese genius was, among other things, a consequence of an act of the original dynast. When Rudolf I founded the Habsburg Empire in 1273, he made a choice that was literally eccentric, i.e., off-center. He picked Vienna as his capital though it lay on the precarious eastern rim of his possessions.

Geography is destiny. Henceforward Vienna had to be both throne room and fortress. There was a good reason why the Imperial Palace was called Hofburg, "Court Fortress." More than once the battering ram of the Turk drove at Vienna's ramparts. Through a long historic stretch the town was, simultaneously, traumatized by war and exalted by intimacy with the crown. As a result it never went through normal urban development by way of a gradual unfettering of the middle class. The sword of the knight and the flourish of the courtier marked its streets, not the common sense of the tradesman. There was little physical or psychological room inside these ramparts for bourgeois growth. Sometimes the guilds managed to assert civic independence, but in the end the Imperial overseers always carried the day. In other, comparable, Western capitals burgherdom thrived along with practicality, efficiency, industry. Not in Vienna.

The principal manufacture of the city was the grandeur of its monarchs. In this outpost Habsburg maintained an immense, brocaded court through which the sovereign (usually drably and inexorably) manipulated the feudal levers controlling his diverse dominions — often by setting one against the other. An old joke went: "The King of Croatia declared war on the King of Hungary, and Austria's Emperor, who was both, remained benevolently neutral."

Other large states generated a bureaucracy that could keep pace with technics and with the times. Habsburg still preferred to govern by legend; by the loyalty of its princely vassals; and, as the years passed, by an intricate, picturesquely costumed backwardness. That is, "by a standing army of soldiers, a sitting army of officials, and a skulking army of informers."

A more substantial business society did, after all, develop in the capital, often in the form of craftsmen displaced by factories from industrially advanced provinces like Bohemia. But these artisans tailored and carpentered and wove and troweled mainly for the monumental Imperial household. They acted as free-lance domestics to the Imperial family, to equerries and ladies-in-waiting, to the cupbearers, lord marshals, seneschals and chamberlains who made up the resident aristocracy; to the lord high ministers, the noble judges and titled generals, with their palaces, their subsidiary establishments and their attendant retinues. The total Court amounted to a multitude, escutcheoned, exalted and rarefied, of over forty thousand.

The Court absorbed the products and the services of the middle class. The Court also consumed the middle-class soul. Even when that class attained some political power, it never turned fully bourgeois. Hypnotized by the Court, Vienna's burghers became like the city's fountains, squares and churches — irretrievably baroque. Not only in the salon but in the counting house, manner overtook substance. Theater overtook reality.

As the nobles, shut out from their political roles by the Crown, retreated into their estates, the moneyed commoners appropriated their airs, their avocations and their amorality with a grace unmatched by townsmen elsewhere. "I kiss your hand, dear fellow," one aristocrat would say to another in eighteenth-century Vienna for the loan of a horse with which to chase the fox. "I lay myself at milady's feet," he would say if he wanted to give the countess his regards. He did not care to chat about annoyances like the Jacobins or death or poverty. But he would discuss, with finesse and feeling, the music of a dead pauper like Mozart.

"I kiss your hand," a nineteenth-century butcher would say to the owner of a slaughterhouse in thanks for the extension of another month's credit on that wagonload of hogs. "I lay myself at the gracious lady's feet," he would say to convey greetings to the slaughterhouse owner's wife. He would drop such words naturally and easily. Furthermore he was as lithe as an aristocrat in the evasion of Heavy Topics. The rising price of sugar? The expensiveness of bread? The confiscation of a too-liberal newspaper? Of such things one acted elegantly unmindful. One let play a spirited wit and an informed eloquence on arguments considered truly important: What was superior — Mendelssohn's classic chords, or the romantic nocturnes of Chopin?

Yes, Rudolf had an urgent purpose in making Vienna more seriously modern. London, Paris, New York — they all bristled with engineers and pragmatists. On the sidewalks by the Danube sauntered nothing but cavaliers, courtiers, epicures, estheticians, attitudinizers.

That had been all right for a few hundred years. But now truly new times were coming down on the city. Industrialization was tearing up the villagelike outer districts. Textile plants had opened, and the smoke of piano factories and paper mills smudged back-yard gardens. Soon workers might discover that they were the proletariat. As for the capitalists, they often faced deprivation of a peculiar internal kind. It showed most in their sons. Many scions, unable to find meaning in their fathers' factories or mansions, sought it vainly in coffeehouse broodings or by the betting window at the races.

The bourgeois were troubled at home now. There were also international frictions, bruised national egos, and pent-up new talents famished for release. To cope with it all the city had built the theatrics of the Ringstrasse and cultivated the dramaturgy of pure gesture.

Would that be enough of a defense? Enough to cope with the unease seeping even through the affluent Inner City districts? Or to contain the slums sleazing through the town's south and west? Or to face the sleek new might of other empires? Would Vienna be able to assume the modern greatness that was demanded and that the fall season was to bring?

"Fräulein Operator in Vienna?" Fräulein Operator in Baden said. "The party whom I have the honor to serve at this end of the wire, University Professor Dr. Dr. Alois Zechner,* would like to convey to you and to your party a hand kiss for the courtesy of awaiting the completion of this connection. Fräulein Operator, if it is still convenient for His Excellency the Privy Councillor Baron von Wieck to entertain the connection, Herr Professor Dr. Dr. Zechner would be only too deeply pleased . . ."

The rococo kept rolling over the telephone during the warm months of 1888. Not everybody shared the Crown Prince's im-

* (*sic*) In Austria, to this day, in addressing an academician, each of his doctorates is separately mentioned.

patience over it. Why hurry? This new season ahead, this new-fangled autumn wasn't here yet. In fact, right now fall seemed further off than ever. The rain stopped, the sun shone, and July flowed so radiantly into August that one might think that August would, with the same ease, flow back into July. One floated through a summer of reprieve.

It was during this reprieve that Dr. Freud added a day to his Alpine weekends with his family at Maria-Schutz. He picked mushrooms, climbed past fragrant dwarf larches to the Schneeberg peak, enjoyed the view of the Vienna Woods, and for once let the Grub Street deadlines for that medical dictionary go hang.

During this summer of reprieve Hugo Wolf took a leave of absence from the passion play with Melanie Köchert. *Melanie 66* read his furlough notice in the personal-advertisements column of the *Neue Freie Presse: With heartfelt wishes a letter is sent to you today, sweet friend.* By the time the message was published, Wolf had already left with the Wagner Society charter train for the Wagner Festival in Bayreuth.

Anton Bruckner boarded the same train, and for him the departure from Vienna was a still more distinct summertide relief. He could get away from the persecutions of Eduard Hanslick, Chief Critic and Grand Inquisitor of Music in the magisterial *Neue Freie Presse.* He could escape from his housekeeper-harpie Frau Kachelmayer (who caught up with him at the Western Railway terminal, irate because he had forgotten his snuffbox). He could arrive in Bayreuth and kneel and cry to his heart's content at the grave of the "High One," as he called Wagner; he could have his gray fringe cut by Herr Schnappauf, the late High One's barber; and he could indulge in another of his frequent young-girl crushes, this one on Henrietta Samet, the daughter of Herr Samet who owned the café where the High One had once sipped mocha. And then he could take the train back to Austria, to his native village of St. Florian. Here he could sit down at the organ of the local monastery and close his eyes and touch the keys that sang under his fingers as they would sing under no one else's. This bumpkin Bruckner was, among other things, the world's greatest organist. But he could compose here too, in this summer of reprieve. He settled in the abbey's music room to revise the Third Symphony. In the beer garden of his youth he could sit at a weathered table with old friends who tried to understand his bewilderment at his own beleaguered eminence. The village tailor could fit him another suit with the too-wide, too-short trousers at which city children would hoot in the fall. But it wasn't fall yet. It was the summer of reprieve.

Anton Bruckner in an 1889 portrait: Court organist, genius composer, country bumpkin lost in the Imperial capital

45

It was a moment of reprieve even for Viennese away from Vienna.

In England Theodor Herzl drew fitful enjoyment from his role as the *Neue Freie Presse*'s new ace travel writer. His constant chatty letters and cards to his parents (vacationing in Bruckner's Upper Austria) speak of bits of fun between the deadlines: He savored the elegance of the famous Goodwood races and basked on the shores of the Isle of Wight. "I am beginning to be satisfied with this trip," he wrote on August 3, "and even with myself. . . . My dear, good parents, so far I've written ten feuilletons on this trip, and may raise the total to fifteen by my return. . . ."

It had turned into a summer of reprieve for young Dr. Schnitzler. He had sailed with the Channel ferry from Britain to meet his parents in Belgium. On the beach of Ostend (much favored by Vienna's *haute bourgeoisie*) he simulated being just the son of Europe's leading laryngologist, the illustrious Dr. Johann Schnitzler. Schnitzler Jr. became all princeling, fop, flirt and flaneur; tried to give up his literary hungers, intrigued with a married coquette on the boardwalk, and wrote long letters to Vienna to the mistress he cheated on — that is to Jeanette Heger, the model for the Sweet Girl who would not only invest his best plays, but enter the German language as the essence of milkmaid vulnerability, as the plucked rose of summer ripeness.

The Crown Prince himself found reprieve in the summer. He left for Hungary and Poland to inspect garrisons and to observe war games. True, he suffered from the dog days' heat; in 1888 he seemed especially frail. On the other hand he loved nothing better than to be with troops on maneuvers. He particularly enjoyed a regiment — and he made sure to pick the right one — whose officers were not vapid aristocrats but of the intelligent middle class. The colonels and majors with whom he sat around the mess table might be awed at first, but he quickly charmed away the gap in rank. Talking freely about politics and culture, he felt (and he didn't feel that often) that he was among his own. What relief from the hollow pomp imprisoning him in Vienna! To his wife Stephanie he wrote of marching through stifling dust. But to Moritz Szeps he reiterated a thought he'd expressed before: that the Army was "the single central thread which in this chaos still stands for the Empire." With him moved a young, pleasant-looking woman named Mitzi Caspar, registered as "household assistant" in his retinue. When not with the Crown Prince, she lived quietly with her mother in the suburbs. Princess Louise, Rudolf's sister-in-law, once caught a glimpse of her. She was, in Louise's words, "a sweet girl."

Meanwhile the milkmaid among Court Theater actresses enhanced the midsummer reprieve of the Monarchy's First Drudge. Katharina Schratt took the train to Ischl in the Salzburg Alps where the Emperor had just arrived. Now Franz Joseph could hike past cowherds in the company of *his* Sweet Girl.

At the same time the Johann Strauss ménage made its customary midsummer move. The Emperor's annual stay at Ischl attracted to that resort many of the Monarchy's fashionables. It was therefore incumbent on a Johann Strauss to leave the manor at Schönau and open the villa at Ischl and, with it, the round of resort sociabilities — the corso in the Kur Park, the promenades to and from the Café Walther, the candlelight dinners and soirees. Which is another way of saying that Strauss temporarily suspended work on the opera *Ritter Pazman*, and was thus freed for a while from his life's hardest chore.

As for Gustav Klimt, he wasn't only reprieved that summer from his endless daubing, but released. He and his two co-muralists climbed down for good from the scaffold on the Court Theater ceiling. They were done with their frescoes. But since their scaffold remained standing for the use of various craftsmen, they still had no way of judging their own paintings. They hadn't seen them yet in their totality with an unimpeded look from below. And Klimt was happy to be spared the view. Indeed he ran as far away from it as possible into the mountains of Salzburg and Tyrol and Bavaria.

The only artist left in the Court Theater neighborhood that August was a certain Johann Pfeiffer, "King of the Birds," as he billed himself. The sidewalks he played for were now largely deserted but he played on through the August emptiness. He played "previews" from classics the new Court Theater would present after its great opening. His fellow actors were parrots he kept in a huge baroquely domed cage. "Romeo, Romeo, wherefore art thou Romeo?" his leading lady's beak would squawk, and he would respond using the bells of passing horse tramways to punctuate his speeches. He would bow whenever a coin fell into the upended plumed hat that was his collection box; he would pick up a new mask for a new role, from a box on which in golden letters a sentence was imprinted. The sentence expressed the spirit of his city, especially during the summer of reprieve: LIFE IS SERIOUS BUT ART IS GAY — VIENNESE SPECIALITIES.

Chapter 5

During the hot months of 1888, while Vienna was waiting for its autumn greatness, a coach rolled into the leafy driveway of a villa in the Vienna Woods. It belonged to Count Walter H., as the newspapers would refer to him later. A gentleman stepped out, excellently cravated, and handed a footman his calling card. It said, *Philip H. Elkins, Esquire, New Jersey, USA.*

Admitted to the Count's presence, Mister Elkins introduced himself as the chief European representative of Thomas A. Edison Enterprises of New Jersey. He admired the Count's salon and said he had heard much praise of the Count's extraordinary baritone. The Count, who was the principal performer in the amateur musicals given in his house, smiled. To what did he owe the pleasure of Mister Elkins's visit?

Mister Elkins replied that Mister Thomas Edison was planning a phonographic gallery of famous great voices of the nineteenth century. At Mister Edison's request he had therefore brought along an Edison machine in the hope that the Count might be kind enough to let the machine record the art coming from the Count's throat.

The Count was most cooperative. With the help of two of his footmen, a heavy American-looking machine, bristling with tubes and wires, was dragged out of the coach, over precious carpets, into the music room. Here the Count sang feelingly his favorite aria, "Se vuol ballare," from *The Marriage of Figaro*, while Mister Elkins kept adjusting levers to accommodate the remarkable volume of the Count's voice.

At the end Mister Elkins applauded most appreciatively and packed up his machine. However, the Count requested that his aria be played back before its shipment to America. Alas, Mister Elkins could not comply. This recording machine was so delicate that it required a very special playback apparatus which he, Mister Elkins himself, had perfected from Mister Edison's blueprint. Unfortunately the only such apparatus existing so far was with Mister Edison in New Jersey, though Mister Elkins had plans to produce some in Europe as well.

Here the Count, most eager to hear his "Se vuol ballare," had a thought: Why not build a playback apparatus in Vienna? Mister Elkins seemed struck by the idea, but warned the Count that it would cost five hundred florins and take at least three weeks. Whereupon Count H. gave him two hundred and fifty florins to get the work started, plus a fifty-florin licensing fee to Mister Edison.

Mister Elkins then carefully guided the footmen as they heaved the wires and tubes out of the house and into the coach, climbed into the coach himself, waved his hat, and was never heard of again.

Count H. was by no means the only one to succumb to the New World's siren song that summer. Throughout the Monarchy not only the rich but the poor, the young and the old, all dreamed America. America fascinated because it had leaped with such ease to modern greatness, the kind of greatness Vienna would essay in the fall. Rudolf himself was not immune to the dazzle. In a recent memorandum on the European scene he had stated that the best solution for the Hohenzollern Empire would be to change it into a republic "and then not a centralized republic like France but a federal republic like the United States." On another occasion Rudolf saw the Habsburg realm ideally as "the miniature form of Victor Hugo's dream of a United States of Europe."

To the Viennese, America's greatness lay not only in its political structure but in its glamour, its adventures, its riches. The America fever mounted during the Danubian summer of 1888. Little boys kept running away to the Wild West even after they discovered that it didn't lie just beyond the last tramway stop. Old men discussed the Last Chance Gold Rush in California. During the hot-months doldrums, when not much happened domestically, it was America-time in the newspapers.

In a front-page story datelined New York, the *Wiener Tagblatt* reported that possession of a mere million dollars was no longer enough to make one a true millionaire in the United States; over there being rich started with *two* million. And the *Salonblatt*, organ of the socially ambitious, described the ineffable wealth of American summer resorts: One single Saratoga Springs night surpassed the jewelry and silks of a whole season in Karlsbad.

No wonder that His Majesty's Minister of Education threatened to prosecute printers whose pamphlets seduced laborers into emigrating to the U.S.A. Brochures showed the Statue of Liberty glittering in solid gold and skyscrapers edged with diamonds. But threats or not, the temptation of America continued.

And yet and yet. There was another side to this, with a reverse dynamic. Vienna, for its part, exerted a magnetism on the Anglo-Saxon West, though it was a pull of a quainter kind. To many a Britisher it was the roofs by the Danube which formed the golden never-never city. This view almost seduced a correspondent of the London *Times*. His paper had dispatched him in view of the excitement scheduled in the Austrian capital for the fall. He was to probe the ambiance of the city beforehand. He did, and found Grillparzer's dictum confirmed: Here indeed glistened the Cathay of Europe.

At first the *Times* man found nothing but marvels behind the

Chinese Wall. Even the off-season everyday Vienna of the summer dog days was gorgeous. Its women were piquant, combining the tasteful with the provocative. Its military music exhilarated. Its uniforms were dashing, its fiacres original, its pastry irresistible, its coffee superb, its environs, the Vienna Woods, without peer, its manners charming, and the most common details of life sweetened by effortless grace. But life here was also so encrusted with strange quirks and traditions and such peculiar philosophies that foreigners found it difficult to settle down permanently. Thus Vienna was not likely to become an international center like London or Paris. The Viennese themselves, though they would not live anywhere else, knew something was missing. They were not happy with the city they loved. The London *Times* man concluded that only if these aspects were changed, would the town deserve to be called a great metropolis.

There was the problem again, weighing on the Crown Prince and his liberal allies, the problem to be engaged this fall. Before that, however, Franz Joseph's birthday loomed. Its celebration would be a rehearsal for the crescendoes to follow.

On August 18, His Majesty would be fifty-eight years old, after no less than four decades on the throne. And this year the Empire tried to mark the date with reverberations that would be heard across the borders.

Every class prepared to join the party, including people from the bleakest walks of life. If the *Times* correspondent had bothered to investigate Ottakring, the largest proletarian district, west of the Ring, he would have been amazed both by the poverty and the loyalty prevailing there that August. Most workers bent over lathe and loom eleven hours a day. By the time they reached home they had little time or energy for anything but sleep — and they slept in houses of which more than half lacked plumbing of any kind except the pump in the courtyard.

Yet on all the peeling doors of all the dank corridors there were glued naive votive posters of the Emperor. Children had made them in school for the Imperial anniversary. And when their parents left for work early in the morning, the men pinned on

*Franz Joseph — sideburned, third from right in
foreground — receiving at Court. He holds his sword.*

their lapels, the women on their babushkas, the two-kreuzer discs on which the Emperor's profile has been printed together with the number 58.

The Ottakringers were set to rejoice in their monarch even though their life in his capital did not exactly warrant celebration. Most of the thirty thousand apartments in their district consisted of two narrow rooms which often must accommodate more than one family. More than ten thousand of the residents here could afford to rent no more than the use of a bed; they had to share the night table with another tenant. In balmy August the nights meant cramped rest in Ottakring; the days, smoky toil; but the prospect of the Emperor's birthday — a festival.

"Hatred for the rich," Rudolf had once written in his notebook, "becomes as demoralizing for the poor as the struggle for their own survival."

A thought true of the Western world in general; but not necessarily of Vienna in 1888. Not yet. The Crown Prince writing in that notebook was more of a Jacobin than many slum dwellers in ugliest Ottakring. It so happened that in 1888 the Austrian Social Democratic Party, a tremendous force in later years, was being organized. But who was its founder? Dr. Viktor Adler, living comfortably in his father's apartment house close to the Ringstrasse.* Few of the workers on whose behalf Adler was framing a program saw themselves as the masses unified by the need to revolt. Though large factories had begun to spring up, many of the city's laborers were still separated into small sweat-shops. Often they were also divided linguistically — Czechs, Slovaks, Slovenes and others come to the city only in recent years.

And Vienna itself, its Imperial presence, narcotized the poor past their troubles. The very tenements in which they slept were embossed with flourishes outside. Each window had its corniced dignity — never mind the dank bedding that hung out of it each morning for fresh air. The plaster goddess supporting a fake

---

* The actual address was Berggasse 19, and Adler's apartment was the very one Sigmund Freud was to occupy later. Both psychoanalysis and Austrian socialism began in the same rooms.

balcony ignored the laundry drooping from her stucco limb; she only looked at the monarch's birthday banner that already glittered from the flagstaff.

Here was poverty spiced with panache, with the capital's royal flavor.

Even hard work was different in Vienna, especially in the fine, not overly hot August of 1888. Street harpists would materialize here and there, all ancient men of a storybook calling. On a good summer morning an old troll caped in loden might shuffle into the mossy yard around which most workshops were built, and lean his cane against the wall and sit down by the well rim and prop his harp on it, and twine his gnarled fingers through the strings to sing *Das Lied vom Augustin* and *I bin so gmütlich heut*, and by the time he got through *Der Weaner geht net unter* (You can't get the Viennese down), to end — in view of the great birthday ahead — with *Gott erhalte unsern Kaiser* . . . why, by then the boss had tossed a fifty-kreuzer piece into the hat and told his workers to forget about work for a minute and gather round and join in the hymm. And perhaps he even took time out to explain to the Czech apprentice just arrived from Brno what the words meant and why Vienna was so wonderful and unique. Afterwards the quarter of an hour thus lost had to be recouped by working deeper into the evening. Still, if the harpist lengthened the work day, he also leavened it.

The city had other such leaveners, particularly during the warm months. At the start of their lunch break — thirty minutes — the workers went out into the street. They'd settle down on the curb stone; they'd bite into the black bread and cut into the lardy, meatless side of bacon that was cheaper than the leaner stuff. And they watched incarnations of grand Vienna that were not a whit less grand on Ottakring's dingy cobbles. Even here an imposing personage would pass in a uniform reminiscent of the Foreign Legion, cigarette dangling under a curvature of mustaches, shouldering something like a rifle and accompanied by something like a chariot. The rifle was a birch broom; the chariot, a wheeled dustbin; and the street cleaner himself not so much a remover as a curator of the city's dust; he gathered it up in one place and deposited it in another, executing a scheme of slow, grave, subtle precision. Indeed the imminence of the All Highest birthday seemed to have lent his design a particular intricacy directed by some high councillor in the Emperor's own Palace.

On the street corner the *Dienstmann* or public porter conducted his office with kepi and epauletted jacket, his medal gleaming on his chest. Actually it was not a medal but a tin badge indicating the number of his license. License for what? For being the nerve center of the neighborhood. Especially in districts like these, where many services were not professionally available, the *Dienstmann* acted as a one-man moving firm, private security agency and message-delivery business. Usually his hair style resembled that of the Emperor who was also a universal genie; but the *Dienstmann* was cheaper and as a rule older, with silver sideburns. Regardless of age, he possessed a strength as great as his discretion. If the master baker Herr Pfandl had a new trough delivered, it was the *Dienstmann* who got it down the steps into the basement shop without a single scratch. If Fräulein Oberhuber (just off the train from Lower Austria to start her urban life as salesgirl) needed someone to watch over all her worldly goods for a moment, it was the *Dienstmann* who would extend his protection, one foot dramatically propped on the papier-mâché suitcase. And if Herr Pfandl ever needed to send a gallant, if extramarital, note to Fräulein Oberhuber, the *Dienstmann* would accomplish that in a way nobody much noticed.

Well, almost nobody. The workers sitting on the curb would poke each other, grinning. But then they seized on anything piquant during their thirty-minute lunch. Anything that would see them through six more hours of sweat.

The week ground on to its toilsome end. Sunday, however, was a deliverance. If workaday streets could produce spectacle in an Ottakring, Sunday was a bonanza around the Palace in the Inner City. Of course on Sunday the Ottakringers would first go to Mass, which unrolled even in small parish churches with cathedral colors — and never more so than now, what with extra devotions performed in advance for the Emperor's birthday.

Yet on a good summer Sunday even the pious poor would hurry from church toward the Palace. A family would wear the best-darned trousers and the least-frayed skirts; they would provision the children with a slice each of the Sunday raisin bread that was the week's great gastronomic treat. To save tram fare, they would walk the two miles to the Inner City. They were off to watch the changing of the guard.

The Franzensring part of the Ringstrasse was our family's first goal. Here they stopped and congregated at a respectful distance from the regimental band of the relieving troops. After it had assembled they marched behind it, often together with thousands, all faces rigidly at attention. They knew that at this time of the year the Emperor's ears must be offered the Army's best music — and there was none better in the world. The bandmaster's fretted silver staff rose: twelve beats of base drum (drawn by a most darlingly uniformed pony); six beats of snare drum; five echoing cymbal blows and *boooorrray!!!* . . . the entire Ringstrasse fifed and fluted and tromboned and danced with the "Radetzky March" written by Johann Strauss Senior, not for infantry slogging but antelopes leaping.

The band always stopped when it reached the outer Palace yard. In the sudden silence, what fine staccato of commands! What flurry of white-gloved salutes and shining sabers! What a fierce chorus line of boots and rifles! And most exciting of all, the actual changing of the guard that took place during those moments. The entire enormous mansion of Franz Joseph's was transfigured. It came to life everywhere. All of its eighteen wings, built over the centuries, had doors, portals, gates, posterns and portcullises; and at each of these, two or more sentinels relieved each other with martial and yet childlike pantomime. It was as though the Palace had turned into an infinite cuckoo clock where dozen after dozen of bright-carved figurines popped in and out of innumerable niches. . . .

Twelve beats of bass drum, six of snare drum, five echoing

cymbal blows — and off the relieved guard regiment marched down the Ring with flutes and fifes and French horns blazing.

Most Ottakringers would have preferred to stay and feast their souls on Vienna's grandness. Our family too. But they didn't linger. They knew that the Ring, being elegant theater in itself, must not be blemished by too many of their own kind; the Ringstrasse — littered with threadbare gawkers and children trailing crumbs of raisin bread — would no longer be the Ringstrasse. They knew it was important to keep its splendor shined during the Emperor's birthday month.

They must return to their part of town. Only no one in the family felt like *walking* back. The father decided to splurge on the horse tramway. It would be easier to relinquish the wonders around the Emperor's precincts if you could leave in comfort, sitting. And so the horses pulled our Ottakringers away, down the brilliance of the Ringstrasse, past solid burgher houses in the Alsergrund district — and then back into the dismal tenement landscape of their own grounds where there were no Hussars and no palaces, no bandmasters with silver-fretted staffs; just barracks hidden under laundry lines and the crumbling of pseudo-classic stucco.

The father made another decision. He told his family not to get off here. They rode on, for three more stops to the end of the line. Here they disembarked and discovered once more the dream Vienna. Their own dreary region was just an interlude, however sprawling, between the glory of the Inner City and the idyll of the Vienna Woods. Here was the village of Alt-Ottakring after which the desolation of Neu-Ottakring had been named. Here they found the simple, shapely steeple of the parish church, a flock of homey whitewashed Biedermeier houses, and some wine gardens set into the first soft roll of the Alpine foothills.

They walked into one such garden to sit down by a table dappled with salt sticks and leaf shadows. They ordered a strawberry phosphate for the children, and for themselves two glasses of the new wine. They munched the salt sticks costing only a kreuzer each and decided to call that their evening meal. The salt made them thirsty and they ordered two more glasses and then two more, already spending the money meant for a chicken dinner the following week. They ordered two more, spending the replacement of the wife's old stockings. The wine was miraculous and they drank and ordered still more, having drunk up by now the amount planned for the warm coat their oldest would need in the fall.

But by then it didn't matter any more. By that time they were singing together with others from the next table, a wonderful song about their marvelous city, about the one little drop it takes, the right magic drop squeezed from the right Viennese vine, to cure a world coming to an end. . . .

Chapter 6

In Vienna the world was often coming to an end, usually to wine-garden songs. But the Empire would go on forever; and so would the Emperor, who had already been on the throne for generations though he was about to complete only his fifty-eighth year. Mid-August had come: the entire realm gathered itself up to celebrate his birthday. Not only on the Ring-

60

strasse but on the boulevards of all principal cities, barricades were erected for the parades to be held by day, for the torchlight processions by night. From the Carpathians to the Tyrolean Alps, peasants dragged logs up high slopes so that three thousand bonfires could be lit on three thousand mountain peaks. Gala performances were rehearsed once more in many theaters in all the Monarchy's languages. Aviators tried out balloons from which to trail congratulatory messages. No park or square was without workmen setting up candle illuminations. Every child readied its Japanese lantern glowing with the sovereign's sideburned ikon.

Yet nothing happened on Saturday, August 18, except disappointment.

Hardly any of the festivities planned for the Emperor's birthday took place on that date. It had begun to rain the night before. It poured throughout the Imperial and Royal dominions. All the public open-air commemoration, set so nicely for that Saturday, had to be canceled on short, wet notice.

The Emperor himself observed his birthday on time with accustomed simplicity, attending a Mass in the Ischl parish church and then dining with his family and the sweet Schratt in his rooms. But not until the twentieth could the fireworks go off, the drums start rolling for the great processions. By then it was Monday, though, a hastily appointed holiday, still moist, still blue from Monday-ness.

And in Vienna something flawed even the delayed festivity.

At the Western Railway terminal a crowd of four thousand gathered, with faces much too grim for birthday celebrants. They had come not to honor Franz Joseph but to cheer Georg von Schönerer. Schönerer led the small but zealot anti-Semitic pan-German Party. In Parliament he represented a district in Upper Austria whose constituents included not only Anton Bruckner but the customs inspector Alois Hitler and his wife, Klara, who had just become pregnant.

Which was of no importance on August 20, 1888. For the crowd milling by the railroad station in Vienna, Schönerer was important. They gasped when he finally stepped from the train. His mustache and his beard were gone. He had shaved them in compliance with a regulation of the jail awaiting him that day.

A few months earlier, Schönerer had stormed into the offices of the *Neues Wiener Tagblatt.** With twenty companions he had beaten up the "Jewish pig scribblers," broken typefaces, hacked up the desks and pulverized the lighting fixtures. He had been arrested, tried, and sentenced to what his followers considered martyrdom — three months in jail. Now four thousand pan-Germanists surrounded his coach as it rumbled slowly toward the prison on the Landesgerichtsstrasse.

Down with Habsburg! . . . Down with Austria! . . . Down with the Jews! . . . Long live Germany!

A shouting, howling caravan tramped along the streets, scarring the Emperor's birthday.

The incident also marred the good wishes tendered to Amalie Freud, Sigmund's mother. She had transposed her vital statistics from the Jewish to the Christian calendar in a way that made her birthday fall on the same date as Franz Joseph's. The Schönerer demonstration shook the whole Freud family.

It even touched Theodor Herzl. In 1888 he lived and wrote on an esthetic elevation far above politics and at a rather careful distance from all matters Jewish or anti-Jewish. But in the third week of August he had been jarred by something unexpected. The week brought not only Franz Joseph's birthday but a special day for the Herzls. On August 20, Father and Mother Herzl celebrated their wedding anniversary as well as their reunion with their son. The family sat around a festively decked table in the dining room of the Hotel Hirsch in Bad Gastein. From his travels in England young Theodor had brought gifts for his parents and a smartly tailored London frock coat. Passing through Germany on his way home, he had acquired something else. A shock, a pallor in his cheeks. Written rudely on his face was the discovery that he was nothing but a Jew pig to some people.

---

* The *Neues Wiener Tagblatt* had been founded by Rudolf's friend Moritz Szeps. Szeps left it in 1886 to start the *Wiener Tagblatt*, the newspaper which figures frequently in this book.

A couple of days earlier, in a music hall in Mainz a crowd of students had pointed at his nose and beard. "Hep! . . . Hep! . . ." came the jeer immemorial in German lands. Herzl had known the more ideological kind of anti-Jewish prejudice before. In Mainz he'd had a new experience. Street anti-Semitism had exploded directly in his face for the first time.

On the day following the senior Herzls' anniversary, on August 21, another family passed a milestone, also not entirely smoothly. The Crown Prince's thirtieth birthday was observed at his summer residence, the Castle of Laxenburg in the Vienna Woods. It appeared to be a rather idyllic ceremony.

The castle chapel had been decorated with pine branches. Court Chaplain Mayer conducted Solemn High Mass. Afterward Rudolf's tiny daughter Elisabeth presented him with a bouquet of roses as snow-white as her crinoline dress. In her little voice she recited a birthday poem and read aloud congratulatory telegrams from the Emperor and Empress. For once the Crown Princess Stephanie did not look like "the Flemish peasant" as nasty Palace tongues called her behind her back. She couldn't help the puffy jaw peculiar to the Royal House of Coburg (her father was the Belgian king). But her latest slimming diet had obviously taken and she moved with animation.

The Crown Prince himself was at his beguiling best. When his retinue filed past him with their bows and curtsies he had a different pleasantry, a special individualized word for everybody, down to the lowliest beater of his hunts, down to the most junior mess boy from Ruthenia. He seemed gracefully unaware of any lingering glances. At the Emperor's birthday dinner in Ischl only seventy-two hours earlier, he had still worn a beard. At his own red-letter day only the mustache was left. His exposed face looked handsome but also disturbingly haggard, and his blue eyes were hard — harder than eyes should be in a great prince who was only turning thirty.

To Moritz Szeps he wrote that week: "The age of thirty marks the dividing point in life and one that isn't very pleasant either. Much time has passed, spent more or less usefully, but empty in

*The Crown Prince early in 1888, wearing the Order of
the Golden Fleece, and with one of his many uniforms,
and with an already spectral gaze*

real action and success. We live in a slow, rotten time. Who knows how long this will continue. . . . Each passing year makes me older, less keen and fit. The necessary daily routine is in the long run very tiring. And this eternal living-in-preparation, this permanent waiting for great times of reform, weakens one's best powers. . . ."

Rudolf's mood seemed to touch the city's as it approached its great season. One overture to that season was the Congress of Austrian Rifle Clubs in Vienna. It started on a macabre note. On September 3, before an assembly of nine thousand marksmen from all over the Monarchy, the heir apparent raised a glass "to our most gracious Emperor beloved by us all."

Whereupon fifty-two bands from fifty-two of the biggest clubs began their parade by marching across the Reichs Bridge. A man in an officer's cape, ostensibly a parade official, led the procession. Briskly he stepped to the trumpet's blare until, just as briskly, he scaled the bridge rail and jumped into the river.

Pulled out half drowned but alive, the man would not give a motive. Documents on his person identified him as one Albert Last, owner of the first large lending library in Vienna. The Crown Prince had witnessed the scene and asked if he could help. Herr Last just shivered and bowed deeply and requested permission to drive away wet in a fiacre.

The incident left its mark on Rudolf. In recent times it had not escaped his staff how closely he followed press accounts of people who had killed themselves. And the year had been rich with suicides in Vienna; this summer the newspapers had reported some spectacular instances. A few weeks ago, for example, an elegant young woman had boarded the Budapest express, taken a small suitcase into a toilet, emerged in bridal gown with veil and train, opened the car door and leaped out of the speeding train. She was found dead by the rails, her snowy lace brilliant with blood.

Then there was the recent case of the courting couple who picnicked on capon and champagne outside the gate of a cemetery before going inside. Here the young man placed a pistol in the girl's mouth. After exploding her skull he blasted his own. The pair had permission to marry; they were attractive and rich and members of the *jeunesse dorée* — and they had chosen to blow out their brains. Was it because they lived "in a slow, rotten time . . . empty of real action and success?" It seemed as if these people tried to overcome an uncontrollably failing life with a controlled, willed, carefully shaped death.

Chapter 7

Vienna had not only more suicides per capita than most European cities, but a particularly high incidence among the upper bourgeoisie. Yet Rudolf felt that this very class would be decisive for the survival of the realm. "The true basis of a modern state," he had written a few years earlier, "is the great bourgeoisie."

Where was that greatness in his country? Vienna's middle class had enjoyed much economic growth but gathered only very little emotional substance. We have seen that its baroque nature kept it from developing a more modern idiom or a distinctly modern soul. It never acquired the toughness of other Western burgherdoms. Politically it could not seem to come into its own. Austria had no counterparts to bourgeois statesmen like France's Gambetta or the Whig dynamos of England. Despite their numerical strength, Austrian Liberals were ineffective in Parliament. In 1888, in fact, Rudolf had not been able to prevent an alliance directed against them from strata above and below. Some aristocrats had begun meeting with leaders of the Catholic proletariat. Nobleman and working man were about to form a huge joint power, the Christian Socialist Party, which would soon outnumber the Liberals. And of course there was that other soon-to-be-born giant, the Social Democratic Party. Together those two forces would endow the worker with a combativeness, a self-respect far transcending that of the middle class. Toward the end of the century Vienna's entrepreneurs discovered that it was easier to found a factory than to establish a social identity.

It had been better earlier. The successful artisan of the 1830s enjoyed an understanding with the universe which the successful manufacturer of the 1880s had lost. In 1830 a master carpenter, fashioning an escritoire for the Duke under His Grace's super-vision, had lived in a personalized world with his customers, his apprentices, his family. Like the Duke, though on a lower scale, he practiced the give and take of a small face-to-face hierarchy.

But the manufacturer of the 1880s never saw the Duke except from a humiliating distance at the opera. In a city where Court and courtier modeled most social images, the industrialist received no access to courtliness. The Crown just threw him some glorified scraps. He was allowed to purchase certain plots of the Ring-strasse; outrageous sums paid by eager *nouveaus* like him financed the Court Opera in which he could be snubbed. And the Ring-strasse palazzo he raised for himself was a pseudo-Florentine futil-ity. Aristocrats flew past it in their coaches without even bothering to sneer. Austrian nobility was ancient, exclusive, rigorously pedi-greed. It treated the mushrooming burgherdom — like a fungus.

Earlier and more conclusively than elsewhere, a piece of bad news came to the arriviste in Vienna: he would never really arrive. Worse yet, he found himself cut off from his point of departure. The human contact a master craftsman had once had with his men and his clients dissolved for the manufacturer into the abstractions governing factory efficiency. He could line his living room in satin. He could not give his life organic texture. Yet, outside the Austrian borders, his confreres gave the nineteenth century its middle-class tone. Just before the French Revolution, Bourbon courtiers had already exchanged the aristocratic sword for the bourgeois walking stick. During the Napoleonic Wars, Wellington had to reprove his British officers for carrying umbrellas. And Beau Brummel, a shopkeeper's grandson, became the tyrant dandy who took English fashion from courtier's breeches to business-man's trousers and from the tricorne to the top hat.

A painter named Hans Makart was Vienna's reverse Beau Brummel. Born in 1840, the year Brummel died, he preened his way through the capital in a direction opposite to Brummel's: away from bourgeois self-authentication. In England, Brummel had retailored the nobleman in the image of the smart banker; in Austria, Makart managed the contrary. He ended the popularity of the Biedermeier style, the bourgeoisie's own mild vogue, and decked out the uncertain banker's house as a fustian baronial hall. Though Makart was four years dead by 1888, the salons of Vienna's rich were still heavy with his plumes and silks and drapery and historicist surfeits.

And vainness. In 1888 several good London clubs catered to the merchant prince. In Vienna only the Jockey Club counted, and it was hermetically restricted to nobility. Merchants entered and left by the tradesmen's door. No matter how high the pile of ducats on which a Viennese burgher squatted, he squatted there at an altitude far below the blueblood's. He never came to possess the feistiness of the cockney millionaire, the smug spirit of the Parisian *haut bourgeois*, the go of the Yankee trader. Vienna's feudal aureole was too brilliant and too constant — it seared any flowering of a middle-class life-style.

Let a plain man labor greatly, accumulate greatly, succeed greatly; let him ride the crest of industrialization, control vast wealth and even procure a baronetcy; let him build the machines and the organizations generating a great Austrian potential in times to come. Let him do all that — and where was his own greatness? Where could his heart and soul connect to the forward swell he himself had powered?

Even paragons of their class like the Wittgensteins foundered in their very splendor. Hermann Wittgenstein, originally a Jew of unspectacular means, became a rich Protestant in the mid–nineteenth century by practicing farming as a large-scale enterprise. His pursuit of culture was similarly efficient. To be more precise: he seeded *Kultur* with his money, he sired *Kultur* in his children. Joseph Joachim, the renowned violinist, was related to him by marriage, and he financed Joachim's apprenticeship under Mendelssohn. His daughter Anna studied the piano with Johannes Brahms.

But the chief phenomenon among his children turned out to be Karl. Running away to America in his teens, Karl taught not only the violin but also Latin and Greek at the Christian Brothers School in New York. At twenty he returned to Vienna and kept playing sonatas through the nights while preparing by day for one of the most gigantic business careers in history. With little help from his family, it took him less than two decades to become the Empire's premier industrialist. He was forty-one years old in 1888 and controlled a vast complex of factories, including virtually all Bohemian steelworks, the industrial hub of the Monarchy.

This peer of Skoda and Krupp followed his father and made his mansion a temple of the arts. His children immersed and exhausted themselves in creativity. Daughter Hermine Wittgenstein would be midwife to art nouveau through its embattled beginnings. Daughter Margaret Wittgenstein would support Klimt by commissioning portraits of herself; in her later years, a champion of Freud, she would help the doctor's escape from the Third Reich. Her brother Paul Wittgenstein would lose his right arm yet reach such eminence as a concert pianist that Maurice Ravel would write the Concerto for the Left Hand for him. His brother Kurt Wittgenstein played the cello with exceptional skill while Hans, the eldest, was a virtuoso on several instruments. And through the youngest boy, Ludwig (in his mother's belly in 1888), the family name would spread as an intellectual byword. Ludwig Wittgenstein would haunt the philosophy of the next century as Mahler would its music.

Did the Wittgensteins live the Viennese *haut bourgeois* triumph? They illustrated its tragedy. Karl Wittgenstein's daughters suffered from manageable neuroses. His sons were blighted. A number of Ludwig Wittgenstein's letters are ruminations on suicide. Three of his four brothers — Hans, Rudi and Kurt — killed themselves.

They had ordered things better in the aristocracy. The founder of a noble line might have swashbuckled his way into a princedom. His descendants, open handed and self-indulgent, had loved the arts the way they loved the fox hunt. They bought the child Mozart chocolates and hired Haydn to compose symphonies for their private orchestras. These patrons of earlier times had been genuine dilettantes, i.e., delight-takers.

Not so the *fin-de-siècle* manufacturers who imitated the mode. In evening clothes their diligence was no less than in a business suit. Startling talents and great coups might mark their lives, but only rarely a happy flair. Grimly they perfected their avocations. The Wittgensteins, who were business corsairs of the first order and whose cultural gifts matched any clan's — not one of them could take delight. No matter how great their boardroom prodigies, how heroic their cultivation of things esthetic, they did not truly savor either their cartels or their salons. To their children they left an opulent joylessness, a hothouse of silk blossoms without breath, without roots.

And there was something ultimately unsatisfying even about liberalism, the bourgeois public stance. Liberalism wanted to eliminate any unfair privileges the Church still enjoyed, whether in the tax structure or the school system. Yet once upon a time religion and ritual had provided the burghers with an inner buttress for which their progressive politics now were no substitute. As liberals they wanted to change a governmental scheme weighted to favor the aristocracy — yet their hearts beat faster before the feudal gleam their parliamentarians attacked. In principle they favored electoral reform. Yet in practice they opposed universal suffrage. Retention of the five-gulden poll tax kept the full, dread force of the working class away from the ballot box.

No, the Viennese bourgeoisie didn't come off well in the class struggle. In the fall of 1888 Viktor Adler was already discussing with Europe's other socialist leaders the idea of an annual world-wide workers' festival, to be proclaimed in 1889 and to be organized fully in the year following. The first May Day in 1890 would produce an orderly march of laborers in Vienna and a great deal of much less decorous cringing on the part of their employers. "Soldiers are standing by," the *Neue Freie Presse*, grand organ of the bourgeoisie, would report on the occasion. "Food is being hoarded as though for an impending siege, everybody's mind is weighed down by grave worries. . . . This fear is humiliating and would never have arisen if the middle class had not sunk so low, if it had not lost all confidence. . . ."

But how should it have discovered confidence in the first place? In Vienna one's identity was molded by the past. The nobles, of course, anchored their rights in immemorial usage. The workers would soon call on the fraternal solidarity left over from the guild system. But the manufacturer? He was a noisy arrival from nowhere in particular. Confidence was hard to come by for a man with a silk hat but no roots. Yet he had to confront historic castes above and below — and, in addition, he must maneuver against his own kind in "the free competition of the marketplace" that was the one article of his faith. What tints and shapes of the past justified his stature? What hallowing precedent sustained him? What culturally grounded emotion fortified his politics?

None. Politics was a puzzle to Vienna's bourgeois of the 1880s. But esthetic and neurasthenic introspection — those were their métier. They were always trying to find themselves individually since, unlike other classes, they couldn't do so collectively.

Why hast thou lived? Why hast thou suffered?

Somewhere they had misplaced their souls in a world they had changed. Of course they tried to be proud of this novel world while, at the same time, trying to overcome embarrassment over their own newness. They were irremediably new in a city where only old families had the self-confidence to look ahead. Being new, they were *ipso facto* sweaty, coarse, raw. All around them exemplars of accomplishment wore ancient quarterings.

The bourgeois's problem was the opposite of Rudolf's. For him, centuries of cachet were only a heraldic encumbrance. He hoped to liberate himself and the aged Monarchy through the fresh skills of the middle class. Yet just these skills had led many of the middle class toward a vacuum. Some did a convulsive about-face. Since it was so strangely empty to be new, they must head for something old, that is for an artificed antiquity.

An example of just that was the Schönerer clan. The father of the leading anti-Semite of the day had risen from civil engineer to chief executive of the giant railway lines founded by the Rothschilds. In 1860 Franz Joseph had raised him from commoner to baronet. Promptly he'd purchased a fourteenth-century Lower Austrian estate in Rosenau complete with Maria Theresia castle.

Technically, Schönerer Senior had become the member of an aristocracy for which he had neither the psychological conditioning nor the social standing. An appointed nobleman, he'd found himself invisible to those whose grandfathers had been born with titles. But he was old and died before too long. His son Georg and his daughter Alexandrine inherited social vulnerability along with wealth. This ambivalence drove the prominent careers of both brother and sister.

Georg von Schönerer became the violent pan-German politician who helped spoil the Emperor's birthday in 1888. The manifesto of his party assailed the same Jewish capital which had generated his father's millions. Young Schönerer attacked it in order to glorify a pre-capitalist, pre-bourgeois ideal: he worshipped the idea of Germania as it had been two thousand years ago, ancient and pure. Germania restored would reunite once more all true-blooded Teutonic tribes in Europe. And he, the Knight of Rosenau, as he liked to be called, would be the leader of that homecoming. He would slay the dragon Jew, that capitalist demon of all subversive change. He announced a new calendar whose Year One was the year of the battle of Teutoburg Forest in which Hermann, the great Germanic hero, had defeated the Roman legions: Now Schönerer would defeat the Semitic polluters and restore the German nation to its clean and noble simplicities of old.

In the 1880s his crusade never attracted more than a coterie of fanatics. But in the next decade his rantings still echoed through the campaign promises that helped elect his more moderate fellow traveler, Karl Lueger, Mayor of Vienna.* And in the end Schönerer found the ear of the perfect heir. *Mein Kampf* rings with praise for the visions (if not for the political ineptitude) of the Knight of Rosenau. The Knight in turn would have seen his program fulfilled in the chimneys of Auschwitz.

During the fall of 1888 Georg von Schönerer sat in jail for beating up Jews. At the same time his sister Alexandrine embarked on a vocation that seems surprisingly different from her brother's. Four years earlier, in 1884, she had purchased the Theater an der Wien, the city's leading operetta house. Now she prepared to take over as its Managing Director. Late in 1888 she began her career as the Ziegfeld of operetta. A former actress become entrepreneur — the class her brother Georg despised — she was a lifelong liberal on the friendliest of terms with many Jews.

Still, Alexandrine's light muse played on emotions exploited by Georg's ideology. In their very different ways both used the nostalgia of a bewildered middle class — nostalgia for the romantic yesteryear it had never had. The typical libretto of an operetta produced by Alexandrine von Schönerer sang of some princely glamour which would, despite scoundrels conspiring against it, triumph in three-quarter time. In *The Gypsy Baron* the gypsy child regains its escutcheon after many a tuneful adventure. In *Die Fledermaus* the machinations of hero and villain revolve around the prospect of a prince's soiree. What tripped across sister Schönerer's stage with lilt and humor was snarled through brother Schönerer's clenched teeth: a marvelous nobility will be reclaimed against all vulgar resistance — and he, Schönerer himself, will confirm his knighthood with his heroic mission.

Another parallel to the brother's savage politics was the waltz on which his sister's operettas surged — the wild and giddy Viennese waltz that had superseded the reasoned measures of the minuet. Indeed, the waltz with its despair hidden deep inside the gorgeous vortex, the waltz whose rhythm overwhelmed the quadrille as today rock has overwhelmed the fox-trot — the waltz was

* After he assumed high office, Lueger's anti-Semitism became largely rhetorical. His excellence as an administrator makes him Vienna's best-remembered mayor.

dark whirligig intoxication engulfing the hopeful, target-happy, progressive straight line.

"African and hot-blooded, crazy with life," an observer said, not of the Rolling Stones but of nineteenth-century Vienna swept up in the waltz, "restless . . . passionate . . . the devil is loose here."

Yes, perhaps in Vienna the devil was loose first. Here the energies of alienation built up fastest. Elsewhere the shopkeeper lands of the West continued to do business more securely blinkered by burgher certitudes which had never hardened by the Danube; elsewhere the middle class, believing in debit-credit truisms, remained shielded a bit longer from its own rootlessness. But in Vienna its distress could already be manipulated by a von Schönerer. And soon it would be diagnosed by Freud, the first specialist in bourgeois *Angst*.

In Vienna, as the rewards of modernity became uncertain earlier, its psychic risks were thrown into relief sooner. Progress from feudal to bourgeois, from provincial to urban, turned out to be a dubious good — and doubts that cloud the faith of an era will excite its geniuses.

Freud's, Mahler's and Schnitzler's grandfathers had been artisans or merchants in small-town Jew Streets. Bruckner's grandfather was a village schoolteacher; Hugo Wolf's grandfather a tanner; Klimt's a tobacconist. Now all their grandsons had broken through into competitive middle-class status in Vienna. Which is another way of saying that they had completed the process of breaking away from organic ties and breaking out of traditional frameworks; and that they had achieved such ruptures in a metropolis where the grace period between emancipation and a resulting erosion was all too brief. Consciously or not, these grandsons used their gifts to ask, through insight or esthetic instrument, the alpha question: Why dost thou live in such a glitteringly corroded world? Why suffer in it? How can we see, or hear, or paint, or understand, what we have lost and what we are aching to regain?

Anti-Semitism, operetta, psychoanalysis: three contributions from Austria's *fin de siècle*. One impulse motivated them all, namely the quest for a way out of present-day bourgeois frustration into a magic and revelatory past. A great searching sprang from the neurasthenia of a class with which Rudolf was prophetically concerned. It seems fitting that the Crown Prince's death drama should have started during the fall of 1888 with parvenu ferment as embodied, seductively, in the person of Mary Vetsera.

 Chapter 8

Sometime in September of the year Count Georg von Larisch and his wife Marie were invited to dinner at the Vetsera Palais in the Salesianergasse in Vienna. Only the Countess went. Her husband, being old nobility, preferred not to share a table with a family so new. The widowed Baroness Helen Vetsera was extremely *nouveau*. She was also known for her strong social aspirations, many of which were considered ungratifiable.

Countess Marie Larisch, then, ran into a surprise. At the Vetsera soiree she found a genuine duke, Miguel de Braganza of the Portuguese royal family no less. It piqued her still more to learn that it was he who had sent the magnificent roses displayed on a mantelpiece — an offering from His Grace to Mary, the Baroness's seventeen-year-old daughter.

Most startling of all, however, was young Mary's insouciance after dinner, when the gentlemen had withdrawn to the smoking room. Countess Larisch congratulated the girl on her conquest. Whereupon Mary said, not quite nodding, "Oh yes. He's nice. He wants to marry. But I suppose one could do better."

Decades later the Countess still had not gotten over that remark. "It was amazing," she would say. "Of course Mary was adorable. And she was already a lady of fashion. But the nerve!"

She shouldn't have been so startled. It was just "nerve" which characterized a certain female expertise in the Vienna of the late nineteenth century. "Nerve" was a hallmark of adepts like Mary Vetsera.

Women in this redoubtable category were anything but Sweet Girls whose appeal lay essentially in their vulnerability, in the fact that they were born to be betrayed. Nor were they demimondaines content to know their (deliciously indispensable) place. No, a girl of the Mary Vetsera sort was quite different. She satisfied the surface requirements of respectability while remaining tactically mobile in her attachments. A man could leave her, just as he could leave the Sweet Girl, but *this* girl he always left at a place higher than where she had been found. This newly prominent woman was the Lady of Fashion.

In earlier centuries high fashion had been yet another aristocratic privilege. It separated blueblood from commoner. But then, more and more, ambitious burghers began to emulate what hitherto they had only admired. Gradually fashion became commerce, professionally created, cannily merchandised, widely broadcast, tensely practiced. It was as widely reported on, as greedily read about, as any interesting war.

The wealth of the upper middle class and the columns of the

daily journals made "taste" a challenge for the upward-minded tens of thousands. Now the newest in bodices and bustles became important; as decisive a clue to self-advancement for the female half of a newspaper's readership as stocks and bonds were to the male. Through fashion a woman mobilized her personal attributes for conquest. Through fashion she hinted at the social altitude of the suitors to whom she might be receptive.

How lofty were the stakes in this arena! Played in Vienna's otherwise still highly stratified society, the fashion game had become intoxicatingly open ended. The right lovers could be rungs on a ladder for the right woman. Therefore the contest was fierce no matter how melting the waltz, how softly glowing the chandeliers. Gliding across the parquet floor, the Lady of Fashion was the social outrider of the higher bourgeoisie, ever wary of her own kind, ever covetous of the fields ahead. Never mind her piquant smile. She was a dead-serious modern strategist. Every silky gala was another secret battle.

Among such warriors the very young Baroness Mary Vetsera began to make history in the fall of that year. Mary — her official name was Marie, but she used the chic English form — Mary had all the martial skills; could make more of a petite figure and a retroussé nose than other girls could of lusher assets. She could float, sort of helplessly, in a flamboyance that was unforced and thus doubly magnetic. She knew it wouldn't do to arrive at costume balls as a Bourbon princess (accountants' wives were known to do that). Instead she'd come as a saucy chambermaid (the favorite disguise of duchesses). She could deploy the frill, the lacy hem, the fan and the parasol with a sureness and an effect already perfect in her teens. She knew at what Hussar major's arm to appear at the races in the Freudenau and how to smile while spooning sherbet at the Sacher Garden in the Prater. She knew how to stand out, incidentally but unforgettably, at the *cercles* of Princess Pauline Metternich, the only gatherings in Vienna which sometimes mixed good titles with big money. One could hardly guess that this lovely thing represented the second category.

Ambition had been bred into Mary Vetsera's genes. It had begun

Mary Vetsera, dressed as a peasant for a costume ball.
At seventeen the darling of the fashion columns, the
"Turf Angel" of the horsey set . . . adorable and
relentless.

with her maternal grandfather, Themistocles Baltazzi, a commoner grown rich on the collection of bridge tolls and other government franchises. Later he had, like Schönerer Senior, involved himself with the Rothschild railroads, though on the money rather than the engineering end. And like the Knight of Rosenau, this toll-bridge baron ached for true nobility. His means toward that end was not anti-Semitism, nor the Wittgensteins' *Kultur*, but the wedding ring and a tireless siege of the *beau monde*. He had married his three daughters to diplomats, that is, to needy younger sons of the lower Austrian aristocracy. As for his own sons, they had turned to England's much more open society where dukes were known to accept good Havanas gladly from bankers. In London the Baltazzi boys invested in horses long enough and well enough until they had a Derby winner, and thereby purchased the nodding acquaintance of the Prince of Wales.

With this coup they returned, determined to storm the innermost bastions of social Vienna. And to at least one eye that saw them from a rung below and watched them dine at the Sacher Garden after a day at the Freudenau races, these Baltazzis seemed enviously upper-class. "The race track played an important part in my life," Arthur Schnitzler would write in his autobiography. "The unattainable ideal: Henry Baltazzi . . . became the prototype of the Count in 'La Ronde.' . . . In the Prater [I saw] Baltazzi at a nearby table, looking summery in a gray hat."

Seen from the top, however, the Baltazzis made a much less seignorial spectacle. They might mime casualness at a luxury restaurant, but they were hell-bent on being introduced at Court. A potential shortcut was the favor of Katharina Schratt. Therefore Hector Baltazzi sneaked his way into a horsy set frequented by the actress. In his eagerness he offered Frau Schratt one of his thoroughbreds for her morning rides. The importunity was so bald that Franz Joseph had to warn his lady. "First of all I am not sure these horses are safe for you to ride," he had written her on June 7, 1888, ". . . and then . . . the gentleman's reputation is not entirely correct."

The gentleman's niece, Mary Vetsera, committed no such mistakes. During her ascent to society's mortal summit she never made one wrong step. And she never paused on the way up.

It had to be up, up all the way. Having the Duke of Braganza was all very well, as conducting was all very well for Gustav Mahler. But Mary Vetsera wanted better. She willed the ultimate as the genius wills the masterpiece, as Mahler willed the symphony. "He is mine," she told her maid. "I know I have no right to say it. He may not even know I exist. But he is mine. I feel it in my heart."

He was the *ne plus ultra* of catches for any girl in Europe. *He* was Rudolf, heir to the Empire.

He presented a long-standing target for the Vetsera women. *He* was greatness. Mary's mother, that weathered social climber, had done a bit of Rudolf-chasing herself. A decade earlier her pursuit of the Crown Prince, years younger than she, had been stopped only by the irritated intervention of the Emperor himself. Now in 1888 the Baroness Helene Vetsera turned forty, and her daughter Mary seventeen. It was time for Mary to inherit the hunt.

And Mary took it up with an intensity that frightened even her mother. In the summer the Rudolf mania in her had become such that the girl had to be packed off to England. The idea was to distract her with some earls. At first the plan seemed to succeed. Mary returned to Vienna in time for the great season and did talk less about the Prince. Sessions with her dressmakers kept her busy. She plunged straight, unerringly, into the tournaments of fashion.

At the first race meeting in Freudenau her ensemble — a black cape with gold insets — carried the day. The *Salonblatt* gave more space to her than to the Princess Montenuovo. Since Vienna read the *Salonblatt* as a weekly score sheet of chic, this was quite a coup. A little later the *Wiener Tagblatt* ran a feature on the furs being worn this fall. Inevitably Mary Vetsera's name stood out on the front page. "Look who's become unfaithful to her favorite dead animal," the article said with the jeer behind which society reporters liked to hide their admiration.

> Baroness Vetsera no longer favors the fox. But after all, the sable, too, was born in the Garden of Eden. This precious little animal clung to her neck all through the afternoon at the races. Under Baroness Mary's renowned round chin lay the beastie's tiny head, its legs looped behind her nape. The creature must have been happy there because it did not stir once throughout the races; its black-pearl eyes vied with the gleams of its proprietress's proverbial pearl teeth.

At the age of seventeen, when other girls still giggled at the lycée, Mary Vetsera was an established cynosure. And soon more than that. In the fall of 1888 it wasn't just the press that focused on the "Turf Angel," as her friends called the young Baroness at the Freudenau courses.

That fall Edward, Prince of Wales, made a prolonged Austrian visit. In Vienna he inevitably attended the races. Somewhat covertly too. Early in October the first big track day was a crisp and sunny Sunday. Reports of Queen Victoria's son cheering on horses on the Lord's Sabbath would not sit well with the English. But it was such lovely weather for the sport of kings and the entries were so attractive, particularly Count Esterházy's steed Etcetera, and the Prince of Wales had a good friend in his Austrian counterpart. On Wales's behalf, Rudolf called Moritz Szeps's office at the *Wiener Tagblatt* to ask a favor. Could it be arranged that Viennese newspapers refrain from mentioning the presence of a certain British personage at Freudenau?

It could indeed. In fact, it was the discretion of the press which indirectly catalyzed the indiscretion of the century. On Sunday, October 7, Rudolf and Wales appeared at Freudenau. They watched Etcetera win the steeplechase. Afterward the two imperial heirs strolled to the tea pavilion where Baroness Mary Vetsera sat sipping at a front table. Wales almost recognized her from previous encounters in London. Here was some glittering little minx mixed up somehow with a Derby winner. That sort of sight always stimulated the Prince's memory and activated his manners. Yes, this little morsel was the niece of the horsy Baltazzi brothers. He greeted her and introduced her to the young man at his side. The Baroness curtsied deeply. The Crown Prince bowed and walked on.

Nothing further came to pass between the two during the next weeks. Rudolf's agenda was now dominated by the imminence of Vienna's most splendid season in many years. After all, the Prince of Wales's stay had only begun. The King of Greece was expected. The appearance of Wilhelm, Germany's new Kaiser, would be spectacular and difficult if the Prussian ran true to form, but also potentially important to Rudolf. The Kaiser's authoritarian strut could be used against him to make Austria recoil toward the left, domestically as well as internationally. When the Kaiser left, the new Court Theater — after too many postponements during too many years of construction — would open. Just a little later the globe's most prima, prima donna would alight: Sarah Bernhardt would come to Vienna for the principal engagement of her European tour. After that, in December, the Empire would rejoice in having lived under Franz Joseph for exactly forty years and with that celebration revenge itself on the rain that had dampened the All Highest birthday. And the pre-Lenten carnival with its myriad balls would round out the jubilee season.

For Rudolf this schedule meant mostly dressed-up theatrics along with a few genuine opportunities to shore up the realm. His contribution would consist of frequent changes of uniform. But couldn't he break beyond gold braid and shako into reality? Couldn't Vienna? Along with others, similarly worried, he hoped that by the season's end the city would start moving from its mythic seclusion into the mainstream of progressive greatness.

Wasn't it time at last?

Chapter 9

The weather tautened all anticipations. Summer thinned into a fall of tightly stretched lucidity. The sun throbbed out of the blue, but each day the warmth drained faster from the golden light. On such a day a woman walked singing to the window of a villa in Döbling, at the lovely edge of the Vienna Woods. Singing, she jumped from the third floor. She kept singing the Imperial anthem right up to the thud. A rosebush broke her fall, and the ambulance brought her to the psychiatric retreat of Professor Leidesdorf close by.

She was not the only one. Another woman in the news at this time (whose name was also withheld by the papers) entered a church in the elegant Hietzing district. Dressed in the latest style, quite in the vein of the fashion report starring Baroness Vetsera, she waited for Mass to begin. Then, to the solemnity of the organ, she began to remove her clothes. While she stripped, she preached.

The sable fur dropped onto her pew, then her jacket, her lacy blouse, her petticoat. The nave echoed with her shrieks about the coming Christ and the catastrophe that would precede Him. She, too, ended the day at the Leidesdorf retreat.

So did a Herr M., a director of the Danube Steamship Company. Suddenly, while playing billiards, he accused his opponent of being an anarchist plotting to gun down the King of Greece. He tried to stab "the assassin" with his cue stick. Police officers took him into custody until attendants from the Leidesdorf retreat took over.

They also had to come for Emil W., as the *Wiener Tagblatt* identified him. This twenty-six-year-old son of one of Vienna's richest manufacturers had always been a habitué of Freudenau. In the fall of '88 a series of betting paroxysms seized him. The only means by which he could cope with the uncertainty of the future was to wager on its outcome in all situations, trivial or important, be it the date of the Emperor's death or the location of the next dropping left by the horses of the Ringstrasse trams. He must bet his way through the day. Anybody refusing to gamble with him would risk his rage. The Leidesdorf retreat had to rig up a "casino" for him, complete with roulette table, jetons, and an attendant playing the croupier.

Professor Leidesdorf, as may be gathered, ran a socially elevated establishment. The professor's reputation, extending far beyond the Empire's borders, acclaimed him messiah to all the disordered regions of the mind. The fall of '88 was just another season in which illustrious patients flocked to the Leidesdorf Clinic in Vienna to be relieved of their devils.

Proudly the press reported that the Prince of Wales himself had recommended the Professor to Mrs. Bloomfield-Moore, a multimillionairess from Philadelphia whose daughter had sunk into the blackest depression. That thousands of gulden a week had been paid for treatment and board of the heiress. That a healing machine had been specially built for this case, emanating ether together with an esoteric sequence of noises and blue rays. That an American, a Dr. Keely, had constructed the machine at the staggering cost of 435,000 gulden, but that Professor Leidesdorf had found it wanting and stuck to his customary methods of electrotherapy, water im-

86

mersion and drugs. That a glamorous international custody fight had ensued between the young woman's husband, a high Swedish diplomat, and her dowager mother in Philadelphia — a contest in which Professor Leidesdorf's testimony would figure prominently.

All of Vienna devoured the story. Dr. Sigmund Freud must have read it with some rue. Three years earlier he had been on the staff of the Leidesdorf Clinic as a twenty-eight-year-old nerve doctor. He'd worn white gloves and a silk hat while administering hydrotherapy to schizophrenics from good families. He'd also drawn quite a pleasant salary — until he'd quit. He'd wanted to be free to go to Paris and study under Charcot, the famous neurologist. Now in 1888 he was free to envy and to worry: a free-lance practitioner unable to attract much of a practice. During the autumn of Vienna's great season, Freud's mind was on money.

"In the summer things were very bad," he wrote his friend Fliess. "This left me . . . with cares enough to sap the inclination [to creative work]. . . . The whole atmosphere of Vienna is little adapted to steeling one's will . . . or fostering . . . confidence in success."

The problem was that in Vienna the accomplishment of actual success did not count for as much as the accomplished gesture. A physician, for instance, was expected to make house calls in a two-horse fiacre. Freud could not afford a fiacre — not even a one-horse *Einspänner*. One hour a week he lectured at the University to a scant audience of eight or nine (sometimes eked out by friends for the looks of the thing). The honorarium was a few pennies above nil. Yet the gesture let Freud call himself *Universitätsdozent* on his shingle.

Three mornings a week he spent at the Vienna Pediatric Institute, a long-moribund facility which its director Dr. Max Kassowitz was trying to rebuild. Its entire premises — a few rooms — consisted of Kassowitz's former apartment in the Tuchlauben alley. Unaffiliated with the University, it was ineligible to draw on any University resources and Freud was not even permitted to use clinical material gathered there for his University lectures.

At the Pediatric Institute, Freud functioned as "Head of the

Department of Neurology." His staff consisted of a single student assistant. His "department" occupied corners here and there in whatever space happened to be free. Its equipment was virtually nonexistent, and since most patients were penniless, his salary amounted to zero. Still, in title-happy Vienna, Freud could now pronounce himself Department Head of a clinic as well as University Lecturer.

His own apartment-office was itself a gesture printed on his visiting card; the place was impressively beyond his means. Maria Theresienstrasse 8 constituted a prime address on the Ring. The very house had come into being as a gesture from none other than the Emperor. On this spot the famous Ring Theater had stood before it burned down on December 8, 1881, killing hundreds of Viennese, including an uncle of Mary Vetsera's. Anton Bruckner and Freud himself had had tickets for the performance that night. Both might have been among the three hundred and eighty-six charred bodies if they hadn't been separately — they never knew each other — diverted to other engagements at the last moment.

Over the ashes of the disaster the monarch had ordered the construction of a stately new building. It contained a memorial chapel as well as some choice commercial and residential units. This had attracted Freud when he had looked for a "married" apartment. Vacancies were frequent at Maria Theresienstrasse 8 because of popular superstition surrounding this *Sühnhaus* (atonement house). The Freuds hesitated, too, but for a different reason. The rent amounted to no less than sixteen hundred gulden a month. In the end they decided to pay it. The sound of the location — in other words, the gesture — was the thing.

Indeed, residing here paid some very flossy fringe benefits. The Freuds' first child, Mathilde, was also the first baby in the building. Two days after the birth an adjutant in plumed hat called from His Majesty's Palace. He presented the gift of a vase from the Imperial Porcelain Works together with a signed letter from the sovereign himself. It conveyed the All Highest's pleasure that new life in the form of Mathilde Freud had arisen on the spot where death had claimed so many.

Unfortunately the Emperor's congratulations did not reduce the rent by one penny. And in the great fall of 1888, the pennies came in such trickles to Dr. Freud. He knew that the weather would soon turn raw. Four large and noble rooms would have to be heated. He still couldn't afford to furnish them fully and their bareness made them look cold already. The prices of coal and kindling wood as well as sugar were going up. Every kreuzer counted. He didn't have to pawn his gold watch again (as he had, soon after his honeymoon two years earlier) but life was awfully tight and getting yet tighter.

The doctor kept the habit he'd begun right after his engagement to Martha: he turned his income over to her for deposit in a cash box. Freud "borrowed" from the funds in the box, giving his wife a detailed written account of his expenses to curb what he considered his extravagance, especially his "scandalous" outlays for cigars. They cost him only about ten cents a day, but there was so damnably little in the funds box.

The smallest expenditure had to be weighed. He had long wanted to give Martha a gold snake bracelet, a status symbol distinguishing the wives of University-affiliated physicians from those of lesser doctors. In 1888 she still had to make do with a merely *silver* one — a minor but real humiliation. He owned all of two good neckties and was fortunate in his tailor, a family acquaintance indulgent about tardy installment payments.

Since the arrival of the baby, much more money seemed to be leaving the household than entering it. Freud's waiting room attracted fewer patients than ever. The method of hypnotic suggestion he now liked to try on nerve cases produced interesting results but dour reactions from referring physicians, fewer and fewer new referrals and hence a diminishing income. The few gulden he'd received for his dictionary articles were gone and he received no new assignments. He did make something extra with medical translations from the French and with private lectures on neural pathology, occasionally held in English for visiting American students.

The only original work he squeezed in was on his paper about hysteria. But as it went on it focused less on anatomy and more on emotion. In other words, it trespassed beyond prevalent dogma.

Psychiatric theory was still firmly based on malfunctions of the physical brain. A challenge to those axioms would only endanger Freud's already precarious career. Certainly it would do nothing to advance him. His ornate address, too, turned out to be of small help. He hustled from one chore to another. Had he held on to the white gloves and silk hat which went with his job at Professor Leidesdorf's, he would have been much more in tune with Vienna's splendid season in the fall of 1888.

Johann Pfeiffer, street clown and King of the Birds, did better in his particular field. He was still performing on the Schottenring, a block and a half from Freud's doorstep. Professionally he was more facile and more flexible than the doctor. He and his parrots in their turretlike cage had changed their repertoire. Now they did scenes about the encounter of great kings — the like of which Vienna was to see soon. But there was always a court jester's line thrown in to amuse the strollers on the Ringstrasse who were waiting for greatness to happen and who laughed and threw coins into the upended lid of the mask box whose gilt letters said: LIFE IS SERIOUS BUT ART IS GAY.

The mounting excitement in town also affected Gustav Mahler. Toward the end of September he received a sudden, electrifying summons. It was a telegram from Baron von Bernizcky, master of Franz Joseph's Court operas and Court theaters in both halves of the Austro-Hungarian Monarchy. Would Mahler meet the Baron's representative in Vienna, at his earliest convenience?

Actually von Bernizcky had been flirting for a while with the idea of appointing Mahler opera director in Budapest — risky as that idea was because of the man's odd intensities, his already notorious quarrelsomeness. But Budapest, sister capital of the Empire, suffered an understandable case of sibling rivalry that fall. A great shining season was being prepared in Vienna; Budapest needed to be given some spark of its own. The Royal Opera House there, fading away placidly for years, could use a new glow, a new powerful director, no matter how complicated his personality.

On September 24 Mahler checked into the Hotel Höller in

Vienna. On the twenty-fifth he met von Bernizcky's envoy there. No doubt he stirred his coffee with his cigarette. It was a habit apt to emerge during intense conversations. The very next day Gustav Mahler left for Hungary. At the incredible age of twenty-eight he was the Director of the Budapest Royal Opera. His unfinished Second Symphony in which he demanded of the heavens why he struggled, why he strove and suffered — it would have to wait until after he had started his great embroilment with the Magyars.

Gustav Klimt had his own confrontation just then: the moment of truth about his frescoes on the new Court Theater's ceiling. One day at the end of September he walked into the building with his two fellow muralists, his brother Ernst and Franz Matsch. The theater was still closed to the public but, alas, open to participating artists. The staircase scaffolds had been removed.

Klimt hesitated to look up. On the ceiling his work of the past two years would now be visible as a whole for the first time. For the first time the view from below and the light from the windows were unobstructed.

He looked up. He hated it. Here was the saga of the theater, from Greek myth to Shakespeare's Globe, daubed in all the historicist grandiloquence of the 1880s. Here was the only self-portrait he would ever paint — himself as a member of The Globe Theater audience. It didn't help either.

"*Dreck! . . . Schweinsdreck!*" Klimt said — "Pig shit!" (Matsch would remember his precise words many years later.) And at that very moment guards announced the entrance of the Emperor.

"Let's get the hell out of here!" Klimt hissed. Too late. His Majesty, retinued by his First Lord Chamberlain, by von Bernizcky and the architect Hasenauer, had arrived. Franz Joseph, too, wanted to see the ceiling murals. But first a problem had to be overcome. His Majesty's stiff gold collar prevented him from looking up in comfort.

Klimt muttered something about it being better if the Big Chief didn't see a thing. In the meantime, though, an attendant had rushed up with a mirror. With its aid the Emperor could inspect the ceiling without straining his neck.

PHOTOGRAPHED FOR THIS VOLUME BY FOTO HELMUT KOLLER, BURGTHEATER VERLAG, INC.

The only self-portrait Gustav Klimt ever painted: second from the left, the face haloed by the dazzling white ruff. The portrait is part of the ceiling mural Klimt was working on, disgustedly, above the right-hand staircase of the new Court Theater in 1888.

He inspected thoroughly, for minutes. He stared at the paintings stretching above the great staircase — the five done by Gustav Klimt, the two by his brother Ernst, the three by Franz Matsch. The artists stood by waiting, petrified. At last the Emperor turned to the architect Hasenauer. He said something softly.

"*Wonderful!*" Hasenauer called out to the Klimt group. "You people are just wonderful! I am to convey the All Highest appreciation!"

To bows and scrapes and whispered obeisances the sovereign departed. "Did we go bats while working on this thing?" Klimt said in Viennese dialect to his partners. "Or is it them that got a screw loose?"

Gustav Klimt's engagement at the new Court Theater ended in official praise and private fury. Theodor Herzl's had not even begun, to his great impatience. The theater would make its debut in a few weeks. High time to honor a vow spoken years earlier. With Arthur Schnitzler he had sauntered on the Ringstrasse, past the new Court Theater when its walls were still going up. "When that opens," Herzl had said, "I am going to have a play in it!"

Now the opening loomed close. Herzl's featured by-line in the *Neue Freie Press* left his other, loftier ambition unfulfilled and palpitating. His accepted one-acter *The Refugee* was still unscheduled. He inquired. He remonstrated. He was told once more that the delays in the opening of the new Court Theater had delayed everything, especially the production of one-act plays, of which there was an oversupply. Herzl's might not be done at all in the foreseeable future.

He couldn't wait. He had to burst forth with *something* sooner than that. Therefore he had begun to collaborate on a full-length comedy with an already successful playwright and essayist, Hugo Wittmann. Wittmann, however, didn't want it known that he was working in partnership. His condition: their play, if produced, must remain anonymous. Herzl's worst foe was anonymity, yet he agreed. The project would help him toward greatness. He couldn't wait.

For his friend Arthur Schnitzler — also not one of your con-
tented loiterers — autumn appeared to end the summer's drought.
During his travels abroad in the hot season Schnitzler had to endure what was, for him, relative continence. Now things changed
for the better. Reunion with his Sweet Girl Jeanette in Vienna
relieved him of even intermittent chastity, as proved by the first
item in his diary after his return to native grounds.

> *August 25th, Saturday, Baden, near Vienna. Evening with*
> *Jean. (5).*

In his diary the digit between parentheses always kept count of
precisely the number of sex acts performed on each occasion.
Hence (5) measures the multiplicity of welcome he received on
the twenty-fifth. After that it's

> *August 26th. Sunday. Afternoon. Jean. (2)*
> *August 27th. Monday. Prater. Jean. (4)*

. . . and so on until the thirty-first. Here the diary in its iron
arithmetical conscientiousness added up all previous parentheses;
it recorded that Arthur and Jeanette had, on completion of the
eleventh month of their relationship, tumbled to a climax exactly
three hundred and twenty-six times.

That wasn't all, either. The fall promised to fulfill still another
of young Schnitzler's desires — literature. One day he was conducting a laryngological examination, mirror strapped to his forehead; he was acting as one of his father's numerous assistants at the
Polyclinic. Professor Schnitzler entered the room; in his hand he
held his son's deliverance. It was a letter from *An der schönen
blauen Donau*, the literary supplement of *Die Presse*. It informed
Herr A. Schnitzler that his story had been accepted.

This was Arthur Schnitzler's first such triumph. Yet weeks passed
and "My Friend Ypsilon," as the story was called, did not appear.
Great names and high events began to ripple through Vienna.
Schnitzler read of them, but not a word of his story. Indeed he

began to read more and more about and by his father while still searching for a word of his own.

Schnitzler Senior, full University Professor, Chairman of the Department of Laryngology, head of the Polyclinic, Editor-in-Chief of important medical publications, physician extraordinary to the city's theatrical lights — Schnitzler Senior rode the crest of the news. He was always either at the bedside of celebrities or at their balls, apparently indispensable at both. When Vienna's first actress, Charlotte Wolter, came down with a fever — an indisposition threatening the debut of the new Court Theater in which she was to shine — the *Wiener Tagblatt* became impatient. "Frau Wolter is silent but Schnitzler speaks," it wrote in October. "We respect the prose of the excellent professor. He has a wonderful baritone, yet we confess that we might prefer a single word from the lovely actress to all those beautifully phrased bulletins of the famous doctor that are being published everywhere on her condition."

La Wolter recovered, with much credit to her healer. Schnitzler Senior's bulletins on other patients kept brightening the public prints along with his social scintillations. Meanwhile drought had once more befallen his son. Schnitzler Junior chafed against being a lackey in Papa's clinic, searched vainly for his story in *An der schönen blauen Donau*, reduced his lust to parenthetical numbers in his diary. The pomp and ceremony which had begun to trumpet through Vienna that fall were not for him.

They were not for Anton Bruckner either. But he was sixty-four. His exclusion from greatness seemed much more final than young Schnitzler's. True, he had some encouraging news on his return to Vienna in September. His mail brought him two issues of the Parisian magazine, *Guide Musicale*, which were both wholly devoted to him: "*Un symphoniste d'avenir, Antoine Bruckner.*"

But that was from the friendly distance of Paris. The same mail contained a blow from enemies closer by. He found his Romantic Symphony rejected by a Mainz conductor without even the courtesy of an explanation. In Vienna the Philharmonic halls remained inhospitable. From the heights of the *Neue Freie Presse* the sovereign critic Eduard Hanslick decreed that Bruckner was still unworthy of performance. The old man walked the streets in his country togs, lonely and dazed, like a stranger. Even the chaos of his bedroom in the Hessgasse was no longer familiar.

"Dear Sir," he wrote one of his far-away supporters, W. L. van Meurs in the Netherlands. "It is a mystery what you can do (for me) . . . as it is a mystery what Hanslick, Bülow and Joachim do against me. . . . Till 1876 Hanslick was my greatest supporter and friend, and then became my greatest enemy because I accepted the Lectureship for Music at the University. Brahms is full of jealousy . . . therefore nobody dares to perform anything of mine . . ."

He felt abandoned in his Hessgasse flat, at the onset of the fall in Vienna. His sometime ally, Gustav Mahler, was away, struggling to reorganize the Budapest Opera. Hugo Wolf, another occasional friend, was engrossed in his surreptitious love affair and in his own work. Bruckner abided in isolation, just like Freud across the street. But he was more than thirty years older than these others, a rumpled, vulnerable village creature in the big city, bullied by his housekeeper for misplacing a slipper.

Still he kept working. A new draft of the Third Symphony was almost finished. In his low mood he feared more than ever Hanslick's anti-Wagnerian wrath and removed most of the direct Wagner quotes from the score. Saturday evening and Sunday morning he played the organ in the chapel of the Imperial Palace — not even Hanslick could take that away from him. He enjoyed his pilsner, his roast pork and cabbage at the restaurant Zur Kugel. At home, snuff from his silver box was a solace, even if Frau Kachelmayer growled about brown stains everywhere. He also had the memory of Fräulein Martha Rauscher, "a very nice, lovely girl" he'd met during the summer in Upper Austria; she'd sent him a duplicate of the photograph he'd lost on the journey back to Vienna. And the organizers of the Industrial Fair in the Prater asked him to display his virtuosity on an organ there.

It was the only public occasion to which he was invited. The great things happening that autumn passed him by. And yet

Bruckner had a sort of season of his own: On the first day of fall this wrinkled mystic from the Upper Austrian meadows received a state visit in the dimension special to him.

On September 22, at noon, he began to get himself ready to meet his visitor. He put on his best black suit with its trousers too short and too wide, his Sunday St. Florian jacket, and his top hat which Frau Kachelmayer refused to brush because, she said, it was no use, the Herr Professor had let it get wet again the night before.

So he brushed it himself at great length. At three P.M. he boarded the horse tramway out to Währing, to the district cemetery there. A number of officials from musical organizations had already gathered at a graveside together with some doctors and anthropologists. Bruckner took his place in the front row.

At 3:45 sharp the cemetery workers started digging. Within minutes the vehicle of the visitor rose into view: A crane lifted the heavy sarcophagus from the tomb, and transported it to the chapel where only Bruckner and a few officials and scientists were admitted. In the chapel the coffin lid was opened. Anton Bruckner stood face to face with Franz Schubert, now sixty years dead.

As in his earlier confrontation with Beethoven, Bruckner started forward, but was restrained. First others had their turn. The Mayor's representative delivered an address praising the bones that had produced such beautiful melodies. Today, he intoned, these exalted remains had been exhumed not only to give them a more dignified resting place in the Central Cemetery but also to afford scientists a chance to examine the physical evidence of genius.

Everything proceeded with characteristic Viennese ritual. On a small table covered by black velvet, Schubert's skull was placed, as ceremoniously as though it were a priest's monstrance. A Dr. Langl photographed it four times, especially the profile on the right side, which was much better preserved. A secretary in top hat took down minutes of the event. It was noted that Schubert's head was a deep yellow; that his teeth were still in excellent condition (much better than Beethoven's as observed in the similar procedure in June) and that only one molar was missing; that the face was strongly developed in proportion to the skull top; and that some clothes and hair were still present.

Now came the anthropologists. Their calipers ascertained curvature and depth of the brain cavity. Whereupon another commemorative appreciation was pronounced by the Mayor's representative. At half past five the officials wanted to replace the remains in the coffin, when Bruckner pressed forward, greatly excited, and insisted on touching the head "of the master." With both hands he grasped the forehead. He clutched it until the Mayor's representative had to dislodge his hold gently. But he was permitted to put the skull into the coffin. Thus Bruckner became the last man to touch Schubert. Finally he went home again in the horse tramway while Schubert wended his way toward the Central Cemetery in a black coach. It was hard to say who was more fulfilled.

❧ Chapter 10 ❧

By late September, high guests who were very much of this world had begun their travels to Vienna. The great season would begin with an arduous first act. Kaiser Wilhelm's descent on the city cast a long shadow in advance, gothic and spike-helmeted. "Wilhelm II is making waves," Rudolf wrote to Moritz Szeps on August 24. "Probably he will soon create much confusion in old Europe. By the grace of God he is dumb, but also energetic and stubborn, and considers himself the greatest genius. I imagine that in a few years he will bring Hohenzollern Germany to the pass it deserves."

Words eerily prophetic. But Rudolf was wise enough to know that prophetic is not politic. He despised Wilhelm for his Prussian saber-happy presumption; his anti-liberal Junkerism; his addle-headed bombast about German tradition, blood and honor. He suspected that Wilhelm's posturings in Vienna might unleash the Teutonic furor for which von Schönerer had been jailed. In fact he shared these thoughts with one of Wilhelm's employees —

99

Bismarck. The aged Iron Chancellor had not yet been fired by his new young master. But he, no less than Rudolf, looked ahead to the ultimate consequences of Wilhelm's demagoguery: What would happen if Wilhelm were to succeed in taking Austria's German-speaking areas for the Reich? Hungary apart, the Habsburg Empire would then consist of twenty-odd million Slavs who might well leave the remnant Empire to join Russia. This would compound, not lessen, the danger to Germany from the East.

Of course none of this could be uttered aloud in Vienna. Rudolf was aware of that. The government maintained a delicate ambivalence about Prussia. Franz Joseph might partly agree with the Crown Prince's opinion, but Franz Joseph's censors would not release such an opinion into print — at least not in so many words.

Therefore other words would have to be found. Again Rudolf went to Mayerling to think and to write. Again he returned with sheets covered by his bold, curving script. Again the old servant Nehammer zigzagged from the Imperial Palace to arrive at Moritz Szeps's doorstep as the "masseur for his daughter."

Soon a piece in the *Wiener Tagblatt* described the friendship between the German Kaiser and the Austrian Crown Prince: They were both of the same generation and had the same great vitality and the same high level of ideals, all of which bound together two quite different and yet allied temperaments. This article protected the paper from any charges of obvious bias. It was followed by an editorial, also unsigned, which hoped that the enthusiasm shown to Wilhelm on his arrival would have an Austrian character. To pervert the welcome into a pan-German demonstration would insult Emperor Franz Joseph and "presumably distort the Kaiser's purpose."

Rudolf was cooking up a careful climate for the arrival of His Prussian Majesty.

Before that arrival, however, Rudolf found more companionable company: Edward, the Prince of Wales. Wales would be the right diversion before the trials to come. The Englishman had just met the Emperor in Croatia to watch Austrian army maneuvers and to do some hunting. Rudolf gladly joined them. Edward was the opposite of Wilhelm and therefore in some ways like Rudolf: he breezed past protocol, evaded ceremony, favored liberal politicians, snubbed the stiffer bluebloods, fraternized with the more enlightened millionaires. He couldn't match Rudolf's intelligence nor the Austrian's ethical and social acuity. But he did radiate a bonhomie that was depression-proof. It worked like balm on the Crown Prince, whose frail nerves were tested still further by the prospect of Wilhelm.

"I would invite Wilhelm only to get rid of him in some elegant hunting accident," Rudolf wrote his wife that fall. ". . . but I like to invite Wales. He's in fine fettle and wants to see everything, take part in everything. He's indefatigable, he remains his old self. Nothing seems to tire the old boy."

Franz Joseph didn't always take to Wales's loose ways, yet he found himself almost helplessly amused by the Britisher. The Emperor got into one of his rare playful moods and teased his guest with his own superb horsemanship. "The weather is still excellent and the riding enjoyable on maneuvers," he wrote Frau Schratt on September 16. "I tried hard to shake off the Prince of Wales by continued hard trotting and then by sustained gallop. But I didn't succeed. This chubby man kept right up with me. He showed incredible endurance and esprit, even after he grew a bit stiff. He wore through his red Hussar's trousers, which was pretty uncomfortable since he had nothing on underneath . . ."

Nothing daunted Wales's jolliness. Shortly afterward Rudolf took him to Vienna, to see *The Gypsy Baron* at Alexandrine von Schönerer's Theater an der Wien. For this occasion Johann Strauss rushed out of his sequestered palais in the Igelgasse to conduct his operetta in person. By 1888 this was a very unusual sight. Even more unusual was his reward: a summons to chat with Their Highnesses in the Imperial Box during intermission. As a rule members of the All Highest Family did not ask commoners (however famous) to sit with them in public. Afterward the Crown Princes drove to the Prater for supper in the Sacher Garden. Here Wales invited the leader of the orchestra to the table, again to Rudolf's delight and to the narrowed eyes of other archdukes present.

The following day the august twosome again blithely violated royal protocol. They lunched on the terrace of the Sacher midtown restaurant with Baron Hirsch — and Vienna gasped. The Baron was a Jewish banker of near-Rothschild caliber. With Rudolf's encouragment he had financed Austria's Eastern Railway to Turkey and thus completed the route of the Orient Express which began to run this year. Again through Rudolf, his capital infusions had saved Austrian shipping lines in the Adriatic from collapse. And he had helped launch — once more through Rudolf's good offices — newspapers like Moritz Szeps's *Wiener Tagblatt* in which the Crown Prince so often ghosted.

All this did not keep Baron Moritz Hirsch from being a Jew. He had conferred with kings before; usually after slipping into some palace's side entrance. But here he was on the Sacher terrace, in the blatancy of the noonday sun, sharing champagne and laughter with royal bloods.

Ordinarily Rudolf was no ready laugher. That mid-September week was one of the last truly happy ones in his life. Shortly afterward the First Lord Chamberlain in Berlin addressed a message to the First Lord Chamberlain in Vienna. Amidst a padding of amenities came a steely hint: "As soon as His Royal Highness, the Prince of Wales, has made his dispositions, His Majesty, Kaiser Wilhelm, will make his own concerning His Majesty's visit to Vienna." In plainer words: Wilhelm would not set foot on the Austrian capital unless Wales left it first. Wilhelm wanted to shine in Vienna as its only high visitor.

Wales was jolly even about that. Nothing else could be expected from a man like his nephew the Kaiser, a man consisting almost entirely of boots and spurs and epaulettes. Wales announced that he would like to go hunting in Rumania for a while before returning to Vienna later. Now the Junker's dispositions could proceed.

Franz Joseph had been away from his capital for weeks. He had vacationed in Ischl (working daily, though, from dawn to noon); had attended maneuvers all over the Balkans, and stalked deer in Hungary with such rustic passion that he scratched the knees left bare by his leather shorts. "After these beautiful days," he wrote his wife Elisabeth, "I must go to Vienna to start preparing myself for the arrival of the German Emperor, an event whose sole enjoyable element is the fact that I'll be able to see you at last after such a long time."

But it was also an event that would prove the importance of his capital. Back in Vienna, he first inspected all the changes made in the Imperial Palace on behalf of his guest. In the so-called Leopold Wing, dozens of apartments were being refurbished to accommodate Wilhelm, his *Kaiserin*, his retinue and the numerous officers of his guard. Next, the Emperor's protocol gestures had to usher out all other majesties sojourning in the city.

"Today at ten minutes before 10 A.M. the Emperor called on King George of Greece at the Hotel Imperial," stated a Palace communiqué on September 27. "The monarchs exchanged greetings and then repaired to a reception salon. After twenty minutes the Emperor took his leave, being escorted by the King to the vestibule. Immediately thereafter King George of Greece was driven to the Imperial Palace to reciprocate with a visit of his own to the Emperor."

A day later the King of Greece left Vienna.

"This morning the Emperor paid a fifteen-minute call on Albert Edward, Prince of Wales, at the Grand Hotel," stated another Palace communiqué on September 28. "Immediately after the conclusion of the visit, the Prince of Wales called on the Emperor in the Palace."

Within twenty-four hours Albert Edward, Prince of Wales, entrained for Bucharest to kill boars.

The stage was set. On October 1, the flags went up on the Ringstrasse. From roofs and towers they waved, from pediments and cupolas: the black-and-white of the Kingdom of Prussia, the black-red-gold of the German Empire, and, of course, the black-and-yellow of Austria. On October 2, the police finished putting up barricades behind which the crowds could watch the spectacle. On October 3, Wilhelm arrived.

That day the entire Vienna garrison was called out "to gratify Kaiser Wilhelm's military inclination," as the official *Wiener*

Zeitung put it. The malls of the Ringstrasse and the roadway of the Mariahilferstrasse (a thoroughfare leading from the Western Railway terminal to the Ring) were sky-blue with row upon row of crack infantry regiments standing at attention.

Gold-caped and crimson-trousered, the Hussars set on horseback, facing the station from the east. White-tunicked Dragoons on black steeds faced it from the south. The sun gleamed on silvered helmets, tier after tier. Baroque Vienna knew how to stage a show; it enlisted the very sky. Not the puniest cloud dared blemish the perfection.

In the station itself the Friedrich Wilhelm Infantry Regiment (named after the Kaiser's father) had taken up position in their carmine trousers, their blue coats and silver sleeves. In front of them stood Franz Joseph wearing the uniform of the Prussian Grenadier Regiment of which he was "Proprietor" and Honorary Colonel. On his head rested the helmet whose bronze eagle on top was swathed in a snow-white plume made of bleached buffalo hair. He was waiting, silent and motionless, along with the rest of the Imperial Family, at the precise spot where Wilhelm was to leave his car.

At 1 P.M. sharp the Kaiser's private train blustered slowly into the station. The locomotive bore a huge shield with the Royal Prussian arms. To a solemn great hiss of steam it stopped at the proper mark. There was silence — and a moment of confusion. It turned out that the Kaiser had changed the sequence of railway carriages designated in the protocol. His saloon car had come to a halt sixty yards away from where the Austrian Emperor expected him. Franz Joseph was therefore forced to run to meet his guest.

It was the day's one mishap, quickly overcome by the Emperor's fleetness. At fifty-eight he was still light of foot and met the young German Emperor in time. Wilhelm descended with his renowned slow swagger, splendid in the uniform of his Austrian regiment, his withered left arm propped on the hilt of his sword.

Franz Joseph stepped close to him, saluted, removed his hat. The two sovereigns embraced and kissed each other three times, sideburns against mustaches. Crown Prince Rudolf, also embroidered in a Prussian uniform, followed suit. Introductions and greetings

Four Imperial Highnesses in 1884. Standing: Crown Prince Rudolf and the future Kaiser Wilhelm II of Germany. Seated: Crown Princess Stephanie of Austria and Princess Auguste Victoria of Germany.

between the highest dignitaries of both entourages. Heels clicked. Spurs jingled. All over the capital one hundred and twenty cannon thundered twenty-one times in echoing, re-echoing salute.

Then trumpeters on the platform blew a fanfare that was taken up by other trumpets outside the station, then by still others on the Mariahilferstrasse. Like lightning the signal leaped from shining brass to shining brass, all the way to the Imperial Palace.

Meanwhile the two Emperors had entered the street. Commands rang out like whipcracks. In a thousandfold flash of polished rifles and braided sleeves, the regiments presented arms. Massed bands began to heave with the anthem whose music both Empires had in common. The Austrian lyrics were "God protect our Emperor . . ." while the Prussian Reich's, not yet notorious, were "Deutschland über Alles . . ."

From windows and roofs and sidewalks the throng roared out its cheer. Then the Emperors boarded the Imperial Coach of State, a gilded, scrollworked baroque mountain on wheels. The hooves of escorting cavalry began to clatter. Stately, the procession flowed eastward toward the Palace. The sun, golden and unclouded still, moved the other way, toward the west.

During that first week in October Jack the Ripper stalked through the world press. Nearly every morning dawned over a new mutilated whore's corpse in Whitechapel, and the Viennese newspapers reported the horrors. But Vienna's eyes were elsewhere. It even paid less attention than usual to the fact that October 4 was Franz Joseph's name day. All heads turned to the Kaiser; his presence straddled the city. Used to Franz Joseph's simple deportment and Rudolf's subtler charms, Vienna was astounded by an All Highest boor. A cloddish emperor — what grandiose scandal!

To begin with, Wilhelm managed to vulgarize his own state of mourning. Because of his father's recent death he could not attend the opera. Hence the opera attended him. That is, the Court Opera orchestra trooped to the Palace on October 4, to play for what was essentially an audience of one. And that one, the Kaiser, talked and laughed noisily throughout the performance — despite the fact that the selections were mostly from *Tannhäuser* and *Parsifal* to please the Kaiser's professed taste for Wagner.

This concert was followed by a reception where the Kaiser awarded the Black Eagle Order with Diamonds to Count Kálnoky, Franz Joseph's Foreign Minister; the Black Eagle Order to Koloman Tisza, Prime Minister of Hungary; the Red Eagle Order, Second Class, to lesser notables like Herr Uhl, Mayor of Vienna — and nothing, nothing whatsoever to Count Eduard von Taaffe, Prime Minister of the Austrian half of the Empire. The omission expressed not only Wilhelm's dislike of Taaffe's reliance on Slavs in his government coalition; but also harbored a hint that the "Austrian half," being really German, did not merit separate recognition.

Rudolf, for his part, disliked Taaffe's reactionary bent. But the affront to the Prime Minister was an affront to his native region of the Habsburg patrimony. Wilhelm's rudeness recalled an even more egregious snub four months earlier. At that time Wilhelm had sent a special representative to Vienna to announce his accession to the throne. The envoy carried individual messages for most members of the Imperial House. For the Crown Prince there was none. From the first Wilhelm had made it clear that he considered Rudolf an intellectualizing sissy who would never be able to make Austria strong. Franz Joseph's heir would be lucky to keep the Danubian crazyquilt together. And Rudolf, as *this* man's host, would now have to smile for days! For *his* health he'd have to raise glass after glass!

October 4 ended with the state dinner in Wilhelm's honor. Franz Joseph, who gave it in the *Redoutensaal* ballroom of the Palace, did not have a very smooth time of it either, as his letter to Frau Schratt confessed: "I was terribly afraid of the toast I had to offer, but I managed to get through it without getting stuck and without needing a prompter. . . . Luckily I am surviving the current festivities . . ."

For his son the evening must have been much more painful. Once Rudolf had published an anonymous pamphlet which called on the Austrian aristocracy in rather peremptory terms to do more working and learning, and less idling and attitudinizing. As if by way of answer, Rudolf's cousin Otto had appeared amid the red plush of the Sacher Restaurant one night, his Imperial and Royal person entirely nude except for the Order of the Golden Fleece gleaming on a hairless chest. On October 4, dozens of such elevated drones pranced in the *Redoutensaal* all too fully dressed, on their meticulously best behavior. To Rudolf it compounded their inanity. They took such pains over this of all occasions.

They tripped on parquet covered with Oriental rugs for this one night, postured against Gobelin tapestries brought specially from Imperial storerooms. More than three thousand candles flickered from chandeliers, from sconces and candelabras. The flames lit up all those archdukes, grand dukes, princes and miscellaneous highnesses curvetting about the Prussian and his gracelessness. They were like gazelles thrilled silly by a gorilla. They loved the way he sat with his arms akimbo; or poured down *mineral water* between sips of champagne; or tapped his foot so cockily out of beat with the "Simplizius" waltz conducted by Edi Strauss, Johann's brother; or how he adjusted his monocle baldly at the cleavage of a simpering comtesse. . . . "Herr Uhl, the Mayor of Vienna," reported the *Wiener Tagblatt*, "did not succeed in thanking Kaiser Wilhelm for the decoration he had received. His Majesty was too closely surrounded by aristocrats."

From the Vienna populace Wilhelm aroused a much thinner response. Rudolf upstaged him. He hadn't been able to budge Franz Joseph from belief in the necessity of this state visit: it would display the continued solidarity of the Central European powers. But he had managed to persuade his father of another need as well. The Kaiser must be kept on a tight leash in Vienna.

Wilhelm was dying to do a solo strut that might easily provoke a pan-German riot. Rudolf intervened. Rudolf's own popularity was so potent, the sight of the Crown Prince would bring on Habsburg cheers to drown any Teutonic dissonance. Hence he did what was personally repugnant and politically paramount. He stuck to Wilhelm like grim death — with his father's permission. "The Emperor wishes me to tell you," he wrote Count Kálnoky, the Imperial Foreign Minister, "that he is in full agreement that I should take part in the déjeuner given by Reuss (the German Ambassador), but he was of the opinion that the matter must be done with extreme care, so that the real intention, not to let the German Emperor walk about alone in Vienna, cannot be discerned."

And so a slim shadow accompanied all of squat Wilhelm's postings. Most of the cries the Kaiser heard were "Long Live the Crown Prince!" Again and again the liberal press ended its description of a round of appearances by the German Emperor with the same phrase: "It was a beautiful Austrian day."

Of course Wilhelm realized damn well who was obscuring his magnificence and didn't wait too long with a counterblow. It came out of the blue at a reception in the Palace. Walking up to his Habsburg hosts Wilhelm suddenly rapped out a series of pronouncements: He was Austria's military ally. As such he was obliged to draw Franz Joseph's attention to a mistake made by the Austrian Army. It had ordered several hundred thousand Mannlicher Repeater Rifles with a caliber of eight millimeters. This ammunition was much too heavy to be carried by soldiers in quick-firing quantities! Responsibility for this rested squarely on the Inspector General of the Austrian Infantry!

Rudolf stood among the group to whom this declaration was made. *He* was the Inspector General. But since he had assumed his office less than seven months ago — when the Mannlicher decision had already been made — he could have defended himself easily. He said nothing, however. He bowed and left. Franz Joseph limited himself to observing that he was aware of the matter. His wife, the Empress Elisabeth, turned her back on Wilhelm and followed her son. A Russian diplomat (St. Petersburg's Ambassador to Brussels) who witnessed the scene found it mortifying.

Somehow the surface of the incident was smoothed over. On the night of October 5, Wilhelm departed for a shoot in Styria, and Franz Joseph escorted his guest. The King of Saxony joined the party. Rudolf came along, too, after a day's delay. There was no "elegant hunting accident" to dispatch Wilhelm. Still, the Austrians obtained another, though smaller satisfaction. Soon the newspapers reported that the Emperor, the Crown Prince and the King of Saxony bagged a stag each. The Kaiser scored zero. He was getting wet for nothing. It had begun to rain and to freeze.

"While sitting in my blind in the storm," Franz Joseph wrote his wife on October 7, "my beard and the entire left side of my face became encrusted with ice . . ." Three days later his lines to Frau Schratt reported worse woe. "It is snowing higher up, storming everywhere and yet we hunt daily. In the very early morning while everybody else is sleeping, I work by lamplight, and at night at dinner and afterwards I must keep up my amiability . . . horrible . . ."

It was no pleasure for Rudolf either. The rain kept raining and the Emperors kept hunting because protocol demanded it and because Wilhelm's martial ego would have it so. He finally did bring down *his* stag. Yet the rain would not let up until he left Austria at the end of the week.

Chapter 11

The Prussian was gone, and had left behind him a city which, as Szeps put it in a letter to Rudolf, "suffered a hangover without having first enjoyed a spree." Habsburg had performed well against Hohenzollern during most of the ceremonial joustings, and yet the aftertaste of the visit was bitter. Wilhelm had not come as a junior emperor deferring to his senior. He had descended on Vienna as a generalissimo descends on some outpost in Graustark, allowing himself to be entertained by the native chief — and finding the bayonets of the garrison sheer marzipan. Nothing great had come of the experience. Only a whiff of contempt.

Whiff became gust after the Kaiser returned to Germany. Here Wilhelm's press began to close in on one Viennese in particular. Two German journals, the *Norddeutsche Allgemeine Zeitung* and the *Neue Deutsche Kreuzzeitung*, outdid each other in stabbing, without naming, Rudolf: The Reich could not tolerate a comrade-in-arms rotting at the center. The Reich deserved better than an ally corrupted by highly placed bleeding hearts, by liberal sermonizers and questionable financiers. The Reich could not allow this clique — this Golden International — to foment trouble between two German nations.

"The Golden International" was a not-so-oblique spit at Rudolf and his Jewish friends Baron Hirsch and Moritz Szeps. Naturally Rudolf decided to fight back. But he thought that the answering salvo would be fired more effectively from a source other than Szeps's *Wiener Tagblatt*. Toward the end of October a new weekly in Vienna, *Schwarz-Gelb* ("Black-Yellow," the Austrian colors) carried a cool polemic against "the peculiar overconfidence" prevailing in Berlin. "We ought not to risk the bones of one of our soldiers to defend Prussian domination . . ." The unpronounced but unmistakable target of the article was the German Emperor. Wilhelm counted on Austria's obedient support for any of his military ventures in pursuit of a greater Reich — and *Schwarz-Gelb* was sniping at this presumption.

Only one culturally prominent voice in Austria spoke in Wilhelm's defense — and then in private. It came from a German resident in Vienna. "This young man [the Kaiser]," wrote Johannes Brahms to a friend, "who has surely prepared himself for his high office with seriousness and dignity . . . should not be unfairly attacked."

But it was Rudolf who suffered the really unkind cut. It came from an unexpected direction: Paris, where in October an anti-Semitic tract called *La Fin d'un Monde* was published. In the preface the author, Edouard Adolphe Drumont, described Austria's Crown Prince as a dissolute, shiftless libertine, a marionette whose strings were pulled by Jewish fingers.

It stung. After all, Rudolf had long been the champion of the French in the Imperial Palace. His dream was to replace the Vienna-Berlin alliance with an Austro-French alignment. One of the ties that bound him to Szeps was the fact that a Szeps daughter was married to the brother of Georges Clemenceau, the powerful French politician destined to become famous as premier during the Great War. As a matter of fact, in 1886 Szeps had smuggled Clemenceau into Rudolf's apartments in the Palace for a talk. The rapport thus established might have changed world history — had Rudolf been alive in 1914.

But now it was 1888, and arrows came hurling at the Crown Prince from across the Rhine. "Frischauer was with me," Rudolf wrote Szeps. (Frischauer was one of the *Tagblatt*'s chief correspondents). "He is almost scandalized by my philosophic calm. I can no longer manage to get very angry over anything, least of all over things that concern me. I am a Francophile, intimate with the journalists and newspapers there, and for those very circles to attack me means they are shitting in their own nest."

The French attack infuriated Rudolf not only because it was French but because it hinted at debaucheries. Rudolf felt that if a profligate must be named, Wilhelm should be the one. Actually he didn't just feel. He *knew*. The guerrilla war between the royals ranged from skirmishes in the public prints to very, very private reconnoitering.

Rudolf, for example, kept in steady communication with a certain Frau Wolf. A multinational madam of the first order, Frau Wolf operated from Vienna a network of girls reaching across the border into the innermost weaknesses of the highest personages. Frau Wolf was the unofficial wing of a system that monitored Wilhelm. Lieutenant Karl von Steininger, military attaché of the Austrian Embassy in Berlin, constituted the more official contact. Rudolf himself provided liaison between the two.

Frau Wolf "would like certain events in Berlin to be known here in Vienna," Rudolf had written in a letter as remarkable as it was confidential. He had addressed it to von Steininger in 1887, not long before Wilhelm's accession. "These are [Frau Wolf's] statements: In the course of the winter, Wilhelm has had frequent trysts with an Austrian girl named Ella Somics, resident at Linkstrasse 39, who was once the lover of our Ambassador. In front of this Ella, and in the presence of Frau Wolf herself, who recently came to Berlin for business reasons, Wilhelm made some inebriated and tactless revelations about his most intimate thoughts. He spoke less than respectfully about our Emperor, slanderously about me, put me in the same category as his father — that is as a Judaized, vain, arty, scribbling popularity-seeker without ability or character. He said that only Prussia was sound . . . that our Monarchy was in decay and close to dissolution, and that our German-speaking regions would drop like a ripe fruit into Germany's lap; that they would end up as an insignificant duchy, more subordinate [to Prussia] than even Bavaria. . . . He said furthermore that he didn't mind hunting with us [Habsburgs], we are a not unpleasant lot, but that we are also useless and sissified sybarites incapable of survival; that there was no such thing as sentiment in politics; it would be his task to raise Germany to greatness at our cost. . . . After praising himself . . . as generously as he derided me as well as his wife and his parents, he closed this edifying conversation . . ."

Rudolf continued: "I must also mention that I've had in my possession for five years a letter which Wilhelm sent officially, in his own undisguised hand, to Frau Wolf in Vienna and which is . . . a collector's item of imprudence and incivility . . . Nobody knows anything on this subject except Szögyény [Rudolf's confidant in the Foreign Ministry]. I did not inform Count Kálnoky [the Foreign Minister] because he would take it too seriously. It must never be known to the Emperor. It would shake our nobleminded sovereign too deeply and perhaps lead to a chill in our relations with Wilhelm and with Berlin in general, which would not be opportune right now. . . . Please burn this letter instantly. . . .* Through it I wanted to alert you about the abovementioned Ella Somics. Perhaps one can gain further information through this channel . . ."

* Obviously, this instruction was not obeyed.

It was through a similar channel, however, that information also flowed the other way, toward Wilhelm, about Rudolf. Rudolf's Sweet Girl, Mitzi Caspar, knew through her family a lawyer named Florian Meissner. She had no idea that Meissner handled some discreet legal business for the German Embassy in Vienna and operated even beyond legal perimeters for the same client. Through him Rudolf's affair with Fräulein Caspar was no secret to Wilhelm.

But just then, in the fall of 1888, Mitzi had become less important to the Crown Prince. They still shared dear episodes. With Bratfisch whistling as he drove the fiacre, they rode fast, too fast, into the Vienna Woods and looked at the leaves whose death made the slopes so beautiful. When they returned to the city, Rudolf's cheeks were still gray with anticlimax and frustration.

He'd given the Prussian as good as he'd gotten; yet when all was said and done and thrust and parried — why, then Wilhelm was still the new Kaiser about to supersede a Bismarck, while Rudolf was cut off even from business directly under his jurisdiction as the Army's Inspector General. No Mitzi Caspar could cure that. Mitzi Caspar could not undo the latest insult from the War Minister. Undoubtedly at All Highest behest, that gentleman had again failed to invite Rudolf to an Imperial Command Conference, this one to take place from the twenty-first to the thirty-first of October. Wilhelm ruled, Rudolf rusted. Rudolf was a chained Prince Charming, good for dressing up a diplomatic maneuver perhaps, but waiting forever, waiting for fulfillment, legendary but incomplete, waiting as the rest of the world sped on toward things grand and new, waiting while the Empire fissured along the Danube.

Meanwhile Mitzi Caspar was sweet. Only sweetness was no longer enough. Rudolf needed stronger stuff. On October 8, he joined the Prince of Wales in Görgény Szt. Imre, Hungary, for some arduous hunting. He bagged three bears and enjoyed Wales's jests. Then he had to return to Vienna.

"I could not fail to notice an alarming change in him," his wife would say in her memoirs. "It was not only that he was more

Mitzi Caspar, Rudolf's "Sweet Girl," with whom he spent his last night before killing himself with Mary Vetsera at Mayerling

restless and distraught than ever before. In addition he had become prone to outbursts of fierce anger on the most trifling occasions . . . he was often quite unrecognizable."

The register of the Court Apothecary shows, toward the end of 1888, renewed morphium prescriptions for the Crown Prince, supposedly to cure a chronic cough. But neither this drug nor the champagne he liked to lace with cognac could soothe much else in Rudolf that October. He was not a drunkard, but he was not a happy man either. The concentration he needed for his secret journalism came harder and harder. In his letters to Moritz Szeps he harped increasingly on the hope that "war must come soon, a great time when we shall be happy because after its glorious end we could build the foundation of a great and beautiful Austria."

He meant war with Russia, the realm of satanic reaction, doubly tainted because the Tsar was being wooed by Wilhelm in 1888. Fighting St. Petersburg was a holy cause to liberals, but to Rudolf it signified something more. Such a war would be a drastic denouement, a beautiful explosion, a convulsive redemption in which present staleness would find a brilliant end.

Other contemporaries — Herzl, Freud, Schnitzler — also longed for release. But Rudolf's need for greatness was more desperate still, exacerbated by the spotlight of universal expectancy forever trained on his face. Would a crusade against Muscovy deliver him?

It did not. The Russian war never came for Rudolf. But in October 1888, Mary Vetsera did.

Chapter 12

Her approach had to cover a considerable and difficult distance. Yet she moved inexorably.

"Dear Hermine, don't worry about me," Mary Vetsera wrote to her former governess that fall, replying to a cautionary letter. "Everything you say is true. Still, I cannot change the facts." The facts were "that I cannot live without having seen or spoken to him."

She was still seeing "him" the way an audience sees a star. After that initial encounter at the Freudenau races, she glimpsed Rudolf at the farewell performance of the old Court Theater on October 12. Goethe's *Iphigenie auf Tauris* was on the bill, but in the Vetsera box Mary paid little attention to the sacrifice of the Greek maiden on stage. In the Imperial Box Rudolf sat, slender in his blue uniform, rather quiet between the whisperings of his wife Stephanie and his sister Valerie. The Emperor came in late, and when the play was over a footman handed him a scissors with which to cut off small snips of satin drapery as mementoes for his family.

Baroness Vetsera was not a Habsburg and therefore could exercise no proprietary rights over the Court Theater. But she, too, had scissors ready, small and secret but also gleaming and sharp like her teeth that were so admired in the fashion columns. When she climbed into her coach, her reticule enclosed a few choice bits of Imperial substance from her own box curtain.

Now she turned toward more important booty. After this new sighting of the Crown Prince her tiny incisors would have bitten through steel doors if they had barred her way to her destiny. It happened that there was no need of that. She had a high-society acquaintance, a woman who was a specialist in making forced entries look natural.

That woman has gone down in the history of intrigue as Countess Marie Wallersee-Larisch* — the very lady who had been so impressed recently by Mary Vetsera's "nerve" in shrugging off a duke's courtship. Marie Wallersee's father, the Duke Ludwig in

---

* After her divorce in 1896, she used the hyphenated combination of her maiden and married names.

Bavaria,* was the Austrian Empress's brother. Therefore she had access to the Imperial family. Her mother was a Jewish actress named Henriette Mendel (raised, after Ludwig married her morganatically, to the rank of Baroness Wallersee). Therefore Marie Wallersee knew people like the Vetseras who wanted to know the Imperial Family. Marie herself was not quite accepted by the first world nor content with the second. Instead of the acceptance she had not inherited, she tried for usefulness she might earn. Merchandising her hybrid nature, she acted as a go-between. In 1887 she had married a Count Larisch, but it was a rather remote relationship and she conducted much of her life in a spirit not too different from Frau Wolf's.

To Countess Larisch Mary unburdened herself of her feelings for Rudolf. And two days later, in mid-October, Countess Larisch asked for an audience with her cousin, the Crown Prince. After some minutes of idle chatter about Nicky Esterházy's bad luck with horses, she mentioned, not quite so idly, her friend Baroness Mary Vetsera's great thrill at having been introduced to Rudolf by the Prince of Wales at the Freudenau races recently — and Mary's regret that the occasion had not allowed her to express the loyalty and admiration she felt for the Crown Prince.

When discussing trivialities Marie was often on carefree terms with Rudolf. Now her sudden formality of language conveyed the message underneath.

Wasn't this the young lady very much in the fashion news? Yes, Countess Larisch said, her friend was a most interesting and captivating person. Then wouldn't she be present at the new Court Theater opening? Of course, Countess Larisch said. The Vetseras would occupy a parterre box to the left. He would make a note of that, the Crown Prince said.

For sixteen years Vienna had waited and now the time was at hand. English journals had already called the new Court Theater the most beautiful temple to Thespis in history. From all parts of the Monarchy, from all over the world, the curious came to gape.

---

* The Dukes *in* Bavaria were a collateral line to the reigning Dukes *of* Bavaria — the family that provided Bavaria with its kings.

*Contemporary magazine illustration showing a gala
audience arriving at the new Court Theater in Vienna's
great fall season of 1888*

And on October 14, the theater opened at long last. By noon
hundreds jostled one another on the sidewalks for a good view of
something which would not happen for hours. In the afternoon
guards brought barricades. At 5 P.M. the crowd was estimated at
seven thousand. It grew by the minute. Mounted police were ready
to clear a path for the audience proper.

At 6 P.M. that audience began to arrive. Only a few humble ones
among these elect came by foot. They had their own Pedestrian
Gate. The coach-borne nobility used a different door. Archdukes
and duchesses alit by *their* portals. At last the Imperial Family itself
arrived in their great coaches. They vanished into an exclusive
entrance which led through a hidden passageway to a hidden
Imperial Lobby, which in turn led to the gala Imperial Box. Thus
the All Highest group could reach its chairs without passing
through corridors used by anyone else.

By then the sun had set — a signal for another sun to rise.

Suddenly four thousand electric light bulbs crystallized the edifice in the dusk. Its ultratheatrical facade flashed up; a statue-studded neo-Renaissance wedding cake, flanked by two huge wings containing nothing but grandiose staircases for entrances and exits.

That was the spectacle outside, and the one inside matched it. Naturally the true star of the evening was the landlord. The show began with the Emperor arriving in his box and accepting, with small hand waves, a series of standing ovations. At last the lights — *electric* lights again! — dimmed, and on stage a series of dramatic presentations contrasted the spirit of the old Court Theater with that of the new, flattering them both. Frau Charlotte Wolter — her delicate throat cured once more by Professor Schnitzler — scintillated. So did the ever-rosy Frau Schratt, whose image, copiously Rubensesque, shone also from the painted curtain as Thalia, the comedic muse.

In the street the people packed the sidewalks, waiting. They watched footmen seated on long red-plush benches in the lower lobby, immobile in their top hats and their long livery coats ribboned with the colors of the houses they served. On their knees rested, ready, the precious furs and great wraps of their lordships.

At 10:30 P.M. the performance ended. The streaming-out was as concerted a splendor as the streaming-in. On the street the crowd swelled still further, until finally it swept aside the barricades. An iron railing broke in the crush. Twenty people were hurt, over a dozen women fainted, and the tumult to see the Emperor made a policeman faint and fall off his horse.

It was much ado about very much indeed. Next morning the newspapers glittered with the event. They reported that His Majesty, creator of the Ringstrasse, had been most pleased with this, its luminous culmination. Strolling with the King of Serbia, with Rudolf (who wore the uniform of the 10th Infantry Regiment) and with the Prince of Wales, he had examined Gustav Klimt's ceiling murals during intermission, approved of them again but also noted some of their interesting elongations. Full of good humor, the sovereign had explained to his companions that apparently the pictures had come out too small and therefore "had to be added on to." A pride of archdukes had promenaded with the Rothschild clan. Professor Johann Schnitzler had chatted with Johann Strauss.

And the evening had produced a veritable flood tide of fashion. A lush, deep-colored tide, because the walls of the new theater were white; naturally the ladies chose tones which would let them stand out by contrast. In the absence of the Empress (she had left again for Greece) the papers paid dutiful attention to the Crown Princess's ensemble: her lace décolletage, her faille dress of brocade, dark-red roses patterned against blue, her fichu of white lace trimmed with diamonds, her diamond rivière, and the blue feathers with diamond needles in her pompadour.

Various archduchesses received their due of *haute-couture* homage, differing in intensity in different journals. But all reporters sang in the same high pitch about a party that was definitely sub-ducal.

"Many an admiring glance was cast," the *Wiener Tagblatt* wrote, "on the parterre box of the Baroness Helene Vetsera who sat with her daughters Hanna and Mary. The young Baronesses wore décolletages of white tulle with dark Atlas bands. Baroness Mary, who wore a half-moon of diamonds in her beautiful hair, provoked especially widespread admiration."

The half-moon of diamonds audaciously resembled the tiara seen as a rule only on princesses or the consorts of kings.

Mary Vetsera's intention, implied by the jewels in her hair, struck a resonance in Rudolf's mood. He had participated in the surface bombast of the premiere — but to what avail? In what way had it helped the city? What had it changed in his life? He needed to embrace something truly revivifying.

Vienna's sense of dissatisfaction matched his own, and the new Court Theater had contributed only an extra wrinkle to an old malaise. It was now pointed out how many of the higher aristocrats had stayed away from the theater's opening. Apparently they considered it just another Ringstrasse to-do, another nouveau-riche festival. The foreign press admired the brilliance of the debut, but noted that much of the showmanship had taken place among members of the audience: the theater's boxes were arranged so that they contemplated one another rather than the stage. No wonder a prince was apt to train his binoculars on a young baroness, not on the play. And the imperfect acoustics only encouraged such distractions. (Vienna's wicked tongues pronounced all this to be quite logical: In the new Court Opera you couldn't hear. In the new Parliament you couldn't see. In the new Court Theater you could neither see nor hear.) In general, critics felt that the emphasis on technology backstage and the insistent look-at-me! pomp of the auditorium would lead to a neglect of true theater values. Actors complained of a lack of intimacy in the new house — indeed, Frau Wolter dared voice this opinion to the Emperor himself.

Again a "hangover without a spree?" The spree, at any rate, was obliterated by the hangover. Once more a great promise had ended in a letdown. There was such beauty and such potential in Vienna, but somehow, lately, it always fell short of realization.

On the day after the great theater opening the city was shocked by a double suicide. A young man had poisoned himself and his lovely girlfriend because he had not lived up to his father's expectations in school.

Even the blue Danube itself, the heart of the Austrian myth, was tainted now. In Vienna the river constituted a menace. Some of its wild arms near the Prater had become pestilential swamps that badly needed cleaning up. They had already infected part of the city's water supply. Typhoid cases were reported here and there toward the end of October.

Many of the sick were sent to the Billroth Clinic, but a mishap in that very clinic cast a shadow on another Austrian byword: the supremacy of Vienna's medical school. Theodor Billroth was its most eminent surgeon; most popular, too, because though German-born he had become so Viennese in spirit: He made his home the city's foremost musical salon and enjoyed the *jus primae noctis* (as he phrased it) over all of Brahms's compositions. Just a few weeks ago, Brahms had played his newest *Lieder* in Billroth's apartment. And now the Billroth Clinic, maintained mostly for the poor at public expense, had degenerated into a scandal. Despite Billroth's appeal for funds, it was so badly kept up, its ventilation system had fallen into such disrepair, that a medical student watching an appendectomy fainted from the fumes and nearly fell on top of the patient.

Then there was the matter of Parliament — this Parthenonlike palace, one of the ornaments of the young Ringstrasse, a neoclassic jewel. On October 22 a deputy pulled a huge hunk of concrete out of his briefcase to display it to his colleagues. It was a piece from a cornice of the building. It had dropped as he passed, nearly killing him. Only nine years old, the neoclassic monument had already started to crumble.

Inside the monument, life was getting ever more abrasive and fragmented. Did those deputies have to be so rude? So dismal? Every ethnic group snarled at every other. The Grecian pavilion rang with a polylingual babel of curses. It concentrated all the conflicts caused by the multilevel nationality problems of the Empire. The situation disheartened Rudolf, since he had no power to improve it. His father's realm was not only a contending arena of component states; but each state was in turn wracked by its own ethnic friction. Leaders of the Czech delegation were threatened by a younger, more drastically nationalistic faction, thus straining the government coalition based in part on the older Czechs. Back in Bohemia itself, the German representatives stalked out of the local Diet. Slovenes in Celje, Styria, threatened to secede from the largely German-language province if the local grammar school refused to institute Slovene classes. In Galicia, the Ruthenians swore to stop oppression by the Poles. From Hungary the Croats could be heard yelling that they had had enough of the Magyar yoke. Resentment and revenge rose up everywhere, converged on the pillared hall on the Ringstrasse to clang and clash and clamor away.

The weather added to the sullenness. A chill wet fog licked the streets. A glum foretaste of winter. It was time to start lighting the stoves. In Ottakring and other workers' districts, meals must be skimped on to save up coal money. On Sunday, their one rest day, many workers trudged off to forage for kindling in the Vienna

Rudolf, "the elegant prince," in hunting costume

Woods. On street corners the public porters — the *Dienstmänner* — put on overcoats to keep from freezing while standing around. Few could afford to hire them during the colder months.

Their idleness was shared at the other end of the scale. The Crown Prince found himself less gainfully employed than ever. King Milan of Serbia was in town and had to be given a most tedious state dinner at Laxenburg, Rudolf's suburban castle. That on the one hand. On the other, Rudolf had once more been left uninformed about the proceedings of another Imperial military conference to which he, the Inspector General, had again not been invited. And meanwhile the Kaiser's hirelings in the German press kept hissing at him. He was being attacked for deficiencies in the Austrian Army — the very Army over which he had no real control.

How was he to console himself? With his smug lump of a wife who studied folk singing while not caring a whit about the folk? With yet another hunt at which the King Milans might tag along with their enervating blather? With still another dose of sweetness from Mitzi Caspar?

He needed something fresh and fierce. And he remembered now: that young face under the tiara at the Court Theater opening; the one who had raised her opera glasses at him with such directness from the parterre box. The Vetsera girl Marie Larisch had mentioned.

He had intended to go to Mayerling with his driver Bratfisch and compose an angry pseudonymous piece for the *Wiener Tagblatt*; a polemic against the outmoded and therefore dangerous influence of feudal ideas in both military affairs and social issues in Austria. But right now he was too tired for anger; too distracted for sustained brain work. It was much simpler to send his old valet Nehammer with a message to the Countess Larisch.

Chapter 13

"I have two friends," Mary Vetsera wrote her former governess that year. "You and Marie Larisch. You work for my soul's happiness. Marie works for my moral misfortune."

On a raw fall day late in October, not long after the Court Theater opening, Countess Larisch drove into the Prater park. Mary Vetsera sat by her side. Their coach stopped under a huge chestnut tree, next to a fiacre. Bratfisch already stood by to open the doors of both vehicles. He did this deftly; you could not see from the road who was passing between them.

Within seconds Mary Vetsera had left the Larisch carriage and entered the fiacre. Then, preceded by Bratfisch's soft whistle, Rudolf and Mary floated together through the cool mist of the afternoon, beyond the formal view of the park into the wild heather by the Danube's banks, and back again to where Marie Larisch's coach was still waiting.

A few days later Countess Larisch told the elder Baroness Vetsera that she needed her daughter Mary's advice on buying a shirtwaist. It sounded reasonable. Mary, after all, was a fashion leader.

"Today you will get a happy letter because I have been with *him*," Mary Vetsera wrote her old governess, her chief confidante. "Marie Larisch took me shopping with her and then to be photographed at the Adele Studio — for *him*, of course. After that we went to the rear entrance of the Grand Hotel where the fiacre driver Bratfisch waited for us. We climbed in, hid our faces in our boas, and off we zoomed in a gallop to the Imperial Palace. An old servant [Nehammer] was waiting for us by a small iron door. He led us through a number of dark stairs and rooms, until he asked us to enter a certain door.

"As I crossed the threshold a black bird, some kind of raven, flew at my head. A voice called from the next room, 'Please come in.' Marie ushered me in. We talked awhile about Vienna, then he said to me, 'Pardon me, but I would like to talk to the Countess privately for a few minutes.' Then he went with Marie to another room. I looked around me. On his desk was a revolver and a skull. I picked up the skull, took it between my hands and looked at it from all sides. Suddenly Rudolf came in and took it from me with deep apprehension. When I said that I wasn't afraid, he smiled . . .

"You must swear never to tell anyone about this letter, neither

Hanna [her sister] nor Mama, because if either one heard about it, I would have to kill myself."

All this took place on November 5 in Rudolf's old bachelor apartments on the third floor of the Palace; quarters he had kept even after moving with the Crown Princess into still more spacious quarters nearby.

His early meetings with Mary Vetsera produced enormous intensity but — by every reliable account — no consummation. From the very first the affair took a course extraordinary for both members of the pair. Most of Rudolf's amours — before and after his marriage — were marked by his flair for combining gallantry with expeditiousness. Mary Vetsera, on her part, was not the kind to spin out preliminaries for preliminaries' sake. She was discreet, but not prissy. Fashion was not her only precocity.

Better than most women she knew what one did with clothes. But she was just as clever about what one did without them. She had learned the art of consent though she never lived to reach the age for it. In 1886, not yet sixteen, she had taken a trip to Egypt with her mother and there had already been an English brigadier. There was the Duke of Braganza. There were other admirers — always select ones and chosen on an ascending scale — whose admirations she had not let languish too long.

Suddenly everything changed. With Mary, Rudolf was not Rudolf. With Rudolf, Mary was not herself. Why? For one thing, she kindled in the Crown Prince a necessity unknown to him until then. He had begun to need a woman who could offer him more than surrender. He needed to be embraced by a mystery. He must be saved by some midnight beyond reason: the logic of daytime was sinking so fast. The very shimmer and vastness of his inheritance had become frustration — frustration, taunts, and despair. All his faith in liberalism, in science, in reason and technology and progress — where had it left him? In a dead-end alley with golden walls. Now he must place his trust in something more transcendent.

He had been brushed by that something once before. Soon after the Crown Prince had met Baroness Vetsera he had ordered that three dozen red roses be placed on a certain grave in Prague. The executor of this instruction was Victor von Fritsche, one of his aides-de-camp. From Fritsche's sworn testimony emerges a story that began long before Mary Vetsera. Despite its fairytale gothic it is an all too believeable augury of Mary's advent.

A decade earlier, during his tour of duty as Colonel of the 36th Infantry Regiment in Prague, the Crown Prince had been visiting the ghetto cemetery just as a cantor was singing a body to its grave. Rudolf had been struck by the ceremony — and by a dark-haired girl who turned out to be the cantor's daughter.

No words were exchanged. No words were necessary. The girl became possessed by the vision of the pale, comely, silent Prince, surrounded by his officers. Her father, to stop the infatuation, sent her off to relatives in the provincial town of Kolin. But she returned and stood under the Prince's window in the Hradz Castle, night after night in the shadow of the battlement, in the moonlit winds of winter. Rudolf learned too late of her vigils. By then, in January 1879, she had died of pneumonia. All he could do was to complete the opera, as it were, by laying roses on her tombstone.

In the fall of 1888 he now saw her resurrected in the dark hair and sinuous fire of Mary Vetsera, who also had Jewish blood on her mother's side. Sometime in mid-November he gave Mary an iron wedding ring with the inscription: ILVBIDT. The letters, he explained, stood for the phrase *In Liebe Vereint Bis In Den Tod.* (By love united unto death.)

She wore it on a thin chain around her neck, under a bodice that was the latest cry of the fall vogue. A demon had driven this seventeen-year-old to the peak of fashion, ahead of much more fully blossomed sophisticates. The same demon now drove her past the Crown Princess, past Sweet Girls and demimondaines, past Mitzi Caspar and all other competitors, into an exclusive niche of the Crown Prince's life. If that niche was redolent of something no longer quite of this world . . . why, then she would perfume herself with otherworldliness.

"If I could give my life to make him happy," she wrote her governess, "I would gladly do it, because I do not value my own life." And talking of her and Rudolf's fear that their meetings might become known, she wrote, "We have made a pact covering such an eventuality. After a few happy hours at a place nobody knows, we will enter death together."

For a while the concealment of their relationship was so intoxicating, it took the place of carnal fulfillment. Their meetings were less than trysts, and just because of that, so much more. To the physically routinized lovers they both were, this half-chastity was like a sacred mist they had created only for each other. Again and again they luxuriated in it: above disused Palace stairs guarded by old Nehammer; or on a coach ride through parks whose twilight heard nothing but the sound of hooves and Bratfisch's low whistle.

Their secret had no coarse practical purpose. Mary's mother was herself an ambitious conspirator, an expert in the practice and detection of liaisons; her later protestations to the contrary, she would not have been shocked by her daughter's high intrigue as long as it was nicely dressed in discretion. As for the detectives forever at Rudolf's heels, they would have made just another smirking little entry in their little books. Yet for many weeks that fall nobody knew of Rudolf and Mary except their accomplices. They defeated the curiosities of the entire Empire with a cunning, with an agility that was as thrilling as coitus. Every day the Imperial machinery ground up Rudolf's will anew; through this secret he asserted a superb willfulness — and Mary vibrated to her Prince's wish. Together they became voluptuaries in deception.

On November 1, Laurent Flönt, a tightrope walker in Vienna, knotted one end of a rope around a window handle, and the other around his neck. Then he jumped from the window of his tenement. A note taped to the wall said: "The rope was my life and the rope is my death." He left a diary which consisted of paper scraps artfully tied together by a miniature rope. On the first little scrap was written: "My diary, several scraps of my now extinguished life, torn out and glued together by Laurenz Flönt, gallows humorist."

Just a few days later a famous colleague of Flönt's elected a still more professional way of doing away with himself. This suicide event consisted quite literally of a show, complete with spotlight and orchestra. It took place in Vienna's best variety theater, Ronacher, and starred the current program headliner, the renowned trapeze artist Don Juan de Caceido. Don Juan had an altercation with his wife a few minutes before his act. He went

Chapter 14

on just the same. But at the climax, poised high on the rope to the drums' roll, he dramatically threw away his balancing staff and dove head first into the arena. It was done with such verve that the audience applauded — until they saw attendants running toward the lifeless body.

Vienna's suicide rate, already Europe's highest, rose further as autumn progressed. Not everybody who contributed to it had the inventiveness of the two rope artists. Some just jumped into the Danube and let their bodies wash ashore without known motive or identification. Yet the city took care to decorate these deaths properly. The corpses received burial in a special resting place, the *Friedhof der Namenlosen*, the Cemetery of the Nameless. And now All Souls' Day was celebrated on November 2; citizens from hovels and palaces made pilgrimages to the Nameless Ones and leaned bouquets against unmarked crosses.

In fact, all the many cemeteries in Catholic Vienna came alive on November 2 with commemorations and supplications for the dead. The city still had not connected with the great future this fall, but death was an eternally great occasion and Vienna knew how to abandon itself to its ceremonials. Even on the day before All Souls', on All Saints' Day, endless throngs traveled to their family graves carrying wreaths and nosegays, wax candles, colored lanterns and holy images.

Often they were accompanied by a special breed of ancient women hired for the purpose. When the mourners departed, these others kept vigil throughout the night. Cemeteries stirred and murmured with multitudes of such crones, all hooded in black, their wrinkles twitching in the flicker of the candles they kept lit by each grave. By the thousands they mumbled liturgies from their prayer books and munched bacon from their baskets of food; mumbling and munching they stooped over the tombs until dawn made pale the candle flames, and the mourners themselves returned by daylight to implore the Holy Ghost for their dear ones in purgatory.

Most newspapers in town — the *Neue Freie Presse* first and foremost — ran critiques of the floral displays on celebrity tombs like

*Arthur Schnitzler at twenty-six, an unsuccessful
physician and would-be writer*

those of Beethoven and Schubert. Reviewers of graves trained on
their subject as much detail and discrimination as their colleagues
did on opera premieres. The town was given over to the dramaturgy of death.

This preoccupation affected Vienna's more sensitive spirits. All
Souls' Day — or at least its gloom — touched Arthur Schnitzler
during what was for him an at least spasmodically buoyant fall.
The new Court Theater opening had excited the young man, as
it had the rest of Vienna. He had not, like his powerful father, been
invited to the premiere, but his father's influence had gained him
access to a dress rehearsal. And with his father's money he rented
a small apartment of his own in his parents' building. In his diary
the sexual graph is encouraging.

October 6th. Saturday. Jean. (3)

And not long afterward:

October 19th. Friday. My new apartment. Jean. (2)

At the end of October the diary computed three hundred and fifty-five copulations with Jeanette so far.

The creative juices were flowing too. He polished "Wedding Morning" and completed another draft of "Episode," two of the seven short scenes making up the *Anatol* cycle that would bring him his first renown. In this play he displayed a ruthless grasp on the hypocrisies of civilized sex. Here he began to turn a new light on that subject as well as on other crevices in the human psyche — a light so revealing that years later Freud was moved to write him: "You know through intuition, or rather through self-observation, everything that I have discovered by laborious work on other people."

Schnitzler's self-observation was the key. It did far more than quantify sex into numbers. It was an instrument tuned to every half tone of his psyche. In our fall of 1888 his diary not only reflected his upswings but caught all beats in a despondency which kept recurring toward All Souls' Day.

Hypochondria, melancholia, make me more gloomy every day. My so-called artistic ability can't break through. Often I'm near desperation. Medicine is still alien to me. Nowhere am I taken seriously as a physician. For the other thing [literature] I don't have the necessary calm, clarity and real talent. My youth is over, I'm a mature man, but I've come to nothing. Nobody believes in me. The time of being a talented young man is finished and now I must really perform. . . . I can't take hold. . . . I can't concentrate even for an hour over any medical book. And now again this scribbling. I've again looked at my old things. Nothing that's really good. Nothing with which I can really stand out. The divine spark was just a lie. But I'm posing again, I really like myself in this wonderful

*agony as I'm describing it here, and through its description
excuse myself — miserable, miserable again . . .*

Theodor Herzl wrote similarly somber lines, not in his diary
but in the *Neue Freie Presse*. Their blackness was well-timed: they
were published just a few days before All Souls' Day. In a story
Herzl described the experience of a man who had suffered a very
deep cut on his arm. As the doctors worked on the wound he saw,
for one moment, his own bone. There was terror as well as a
certain harrowing beauty in that glimpse. It showed what he was
to be before eternity. The man — a dandy, a world traveler, a
sybarite — became obsessed with his own skeleton which he came
to call "The Beautiful Rosalinda." And that, in fact, was the title
of Herzl's piece.

His pensive brilliance here contrasted with his main project that
fall: the play he was co-carpentering with his colleague Hugo
Wittmann of the *Neue Freie Presse*. It was called *Wilddiebe*, which
could be freely translated as *Love Poachers*. Tailored for the Court
Theater, it toyed coyly with flirtation, deception, jealousy. Its char-
acters had neither skeleton nor flesh nor blood nor true lust. The
idea of the comedy was not to squeeze a maximum of innuendo
from the plot, but to make a pseudoerotic situation yield a wealth
of elegant epigrams and gestures.

The same was true of Herzl's real-life romance. He'd fallen into
a facsimile of love with a girl who seemed precisely the right
drawing-room heroine for the hero he hoped he would one day
become. At twenty-eight he had reached the best of his extraordinary good looks: tall, with eyes as mesmerically dark as his
imperious beard, fiercely handsome, absolutely elegant, deucedly
clever, devastatingly articulate. He was also deeply, if secretly,
skeptical of his talent and much struck by his life's puzzlements
and by his death's certainty. Last but not least he was quite unsure
about his Jewishness.

His bride-to-be, Julie Naschauer, was Jewish too, but blonde and
blue-eyed like most heroines in his plays. She came from a family
much richer, still more assimilated, more *haute-bourgeoise* than the

Herzls. In her own restricted group, her fashionability almost matched Mary Vetsera's higher up. In Julie, Theodor worshipped the first woman in Vienna to paint her fingernails.

A number of people considered the Naschauer girl willful, vapid and neurasthenic. And Herzl was much too intelligent not to suspect, now and then, that marriage between two inveterate narcissists must mean catastrophe. No matter. The courtship was such good show. In his letters to his parents he called Julie "the little one." In his diary she is "the little princess for whose sake I shall slay dragons. . . . She is sweet, sweet, sweet."

She was hardly sweet and he hardly honest with himself. But they looked wonderful together, promenading on the Ringstrasse's smartest stretch between the Court Opera and the Schwarzenberg Platz. The skeleton "Rosalindas" inside the couple participated in the walk, waiting. Waiting, especially on All Souls' Day.

Herzl preferred to frequent only the chic part of the Ring. But one of his contemporaries had a habit of rounding the entire four-kilometer circle of the boulevard each afternoon. He walked very fast with long athletic strides rather surprising in a short man; on brisk fall days like these he came close to the tempo of a run. On All Souls' Day a flower woman would try to stop him here or there, holding out a fifty-kreuzer bouquet, thinking that he was hurrying to some cemetery before it closed.

He would brush her aside. He paced impetuously; stopped of a sudden before a bookstore window near the University part of the Ring; glared; stormed on. He hoped to have stomped away his daily bad temper by the time he reached his apartment on the Maria Theresienstrasse. All kinds of cares awaited him there, mostly financial. But what worried Sigmund Freud the most was his own irritability with his beloved Martha. Again and again, by letter and face to face, he had apologized, he had tried to explain: "Since I am violent and passionate with all sorts of devils pent up that cannot emerge, they rumble about me inside or else are released against you, you dear one. Had I only some daring activity where I could venture and win, I should be gentle at home, but I am forced to exercise moderation and [professional] self-control, and I even enjoy a reputation for doing so."

"Moderation and self-control." He was wrong. Just as he was wrong in a self-appraisal somewhat later that "I am not a genius . . . not even very talented." The facts were that he stomped without moderation along the Ringstrasse and that he could not control those essentials in his behavior that prevented fashionable success in his field or for that matter in any other field in Vienna. He never could summon the surface charm which Professor Schnitzler could produce so easily and which even his son Arthur could manage when he tried. He did not possess Herzl's electric suavity or Mahler's instinctive flamboyance, nor Bruckner's child-like appeal. He was no heartbreaker like Rudolf and anything but a fascinating cherub like Hugo Wolf. The stage instinct of the Viennese, the flair that commanded attention by seducing it, escaped Freud entirely. He could not even affect a popular consultation-room manner. That was another reason why his waiting room, despite its modish address, was so often empty. Other nerve doctors circled charmingly around their patients' problems. He strode and stomped toward the center of things, governed by intuition rather than tact.

He also found it hard to be diplomatic with colleagues in the echelon above. The article on hysteria into which he poured what energy he could spare from money-grubbing chores — the danger in that article was becoming apparent; the longer he worked at it, the less respect it showed to psychiatric postulates sacred in Vienna. But then it would no doubt be ignored like all his other endeavors. Neither his life nor his thoughts attracted much interest. He was just a family-minded sobersides, stubborn and industrious, often full of a cold, apt, inconvenient wit, too often heedless of established truths, but otherwise unspectacular to himself and to others.

Except when he was storming around the Ringstrasse. Strollers parted before the speed of his orbit. Heads turned toward this waistcoated academic-looking strider. He stopped abruptly before yet another medical bookstore. And shook his head. And stormed on once more. He shouldn't look at other people's publications. They only stoked his temper.

These works were by people he admired — books by Jean Martin Charcot, monographs by Rudolf Chrobak and Gustav Breuer. Charcot, of course, had initiated his research into hypnosis. Chrobak, Vienna's leading gynecologist, had generously shared cases with psychiatric overtones. And Breuer had not only made him partner to his studies and discoveries in hypnotic suggestion. Breuer had also loaned Freud huge sums. They had totaled no less than twenty-three hundred gulden before the young man's engagement and were far from paid off on All Souls' Day of 1888. But Breuer, like the other two, exacerbated Freud's bafflement.

He could not understand it.

Why did all three of these admirable minds stop short before a subject to which their own keenness had led them? Years earlier Breuer had explained the aberrations of a woman patient with, "Such cases are always secrets of the marriage bed," and shrugged off Freud's further questions. Charcot, discussing the bizarre symptoms of a young bride, had said, "In this sort of situation it's always a question of the genitals — always, always, always . . ." And much more recently Chrobak had said to him that the ideal prescription for a certain patient — a severely disturbed wife with a feeble husband — would be: "Rx: One dose of normal penis, to be applied repeatedly."

But none of the three great doctors had in any way pursued this insight conceptually or clinically; their inertness before their own diagnoses baffled Freud more and more in 1888. The theme remained untouched in any of these men's publications he saw in any bookstore window.

Here was an invisible resistance. It reminded the young doctor of the barrier that kept him from solvency, from success, from pushing his own ideas into crystallized conclusion. He was storming past the new Court Theater, which had no bookstores, mercifully, but whose fustian portals vexed him. Did everything have to be histrionics in Vienna? All this overblown manneredness concealing sex! All this embroidery of death with petals and ikons!

He brushed past more vendors of All Souls' Day flowers. Once more he would not come home tranquil to his Martha.

Johann Strauss fled Vienna on All Souls' Day. He had never liked funerals or things funereal. Now he was sixty-three and the dislike had become phobia. He made wide detours around cemeteries, boycotted death. His inspiration, in turn, boycotted him. He could not get on with the project that would place his name in the first rank of serious art: with his opera *Ritter Pazman*. All these unpleasantnesses he now evaded by leaving his composing chores in Vienna for some conducting enagagements in Prague. Here he gave a series of benefit concerts early in November.

Prague, like any other city in the West, lived under the Waltz God's spell. The lectern awaiting him was wreathed with his votaries' laurels and roses. Applause began long before his appearance. Finally he materialized in a swallowtail coat, slim and gallant and discreetly corseted. Slim and gallant, hand pressed against his heart, he accepted gales of homage. He bowed and smiled under his dyed mustache, smiled and bowed until the clapping melted into devout silence.

His hand, gloved in white glacé, picked up the filigreed baton. (The violin bow of his youth was now far beneath him.) The many bracelets on his wrist dangled and shone. The baton swung, the orchestra surged, the universe swirled into three-quarter time.

When it was over, he bowed to endless ovations, hand pressed against his heart. He picked a flower from the many on the lectern, kissed it, put it into his buttonhole, bowed again, and walked out only to be called back for yet more bows. If his gratitude was studied, it was also real. Such enthusiasm defied aging, death and All Souls' Day. What he craved to be forever — what he had to prove anxiously anew — had come true once more: he was still the world's immortal young darling.

After Prague he did not return directly to Vienna. He and his Adele went to nearby Franzensbad for the cure that preserves youth. The season there had already run its course, but the best hotel remained open for the maestro and offered its best suite.

Johann Strauss. At sixty-three in 1888 he was a figure of consummate public glamour and recurrent private misery

The spa orchestra stayed on to play just for him. He smiled and clapped, enacted his public charm. In truth he hated the music, was appalled at the prices, feared that the extravagance would be ruinous. By day he bravely took the turbid baths and sipped the acrid waters. By night he worked grimly on his opera. He could not get on with it. Not so well nor so fast as he liked. Soon he wanted to leave again. But leaving meant going to the train depot and, like young Freud, he feared trains. (The moment motion started, all shades had to be pulled in his compartment; passing through tunnels, he lay on the floor, face down.) Furthermore, boarding the train meant going home, and home was Vienna. And Vienna? . . . He, whose name was already what it would be forever — a synonym for Vienna — was ambivalent about the city. A dour letter he wrote from Franzensbad wound up suddenly, without transition or explanation: "Austria will get her lumps."

He did go home after a week. He must. Rehearsals were about to begin for his Emperor Waltz, which would premiere in Vienna's Musikvereinssaal on December 2, the fortieth anniversary of the Emperor's reign. Despite the waltz's title, the Emperor's First Lord Chamberlain had already indicated that His Majesty would not be present. It was a bitter tradition. Franz Joseph had never yet attended a Johann Strauss premiere. Why? A long time ago, in 1848 when Strauss had been very young and foolish, and as unpolitical as he was now, he had played the republican "Marseillaise," at some inn; for which crime he'd had to undergo police interrogation. Was that the problem? Did His Apostolic Majesty nurse so long a grudge? Whatever the reason, the Emperor had declined the invitation to the waltz named for him. Strauss nearly took up the suggestion of his Berlin publisher Simrock — to dedicate the Emperor Waltz to Kaiser Wilhelm.

In the end Strauss refrained. The waltz remained undedicated, which was eloquent enough in Franz Joseph's jubilee year. Strauss went to work again on *Ritter Pazman*. The opera was very, very hard going. Good ideas turned treacherous. He discovered that a symphonic czardas he'd composed during the summer was an unconscious plagiarism of someone else's tune.

Once more it was all a bit too much for his nerves. He went into a "phase." The Waltz Palais on the Igelgasse became a tomb. For days he spoke with no one, not even with Adele. He never lifted his glance from the tips of his polished patent-leather boots, just paced from his study to the stable in the yard, and back to the cage of his parrot Jacquot who whistled piercingly the opening bars of "The Blue Danube." It did not amuse him. The drawing instructor who coached him in the art of caricature was told to stay away; so was the private billiard teacher retained for Adele. The billiard table remained hooded in canvas. The tarok cards in the "Coffeehouse Room" remained untouched. His cronies knew better than to come. He couldn't have stood their chatter. But he also hated the silence and the emptiness.

During his "phase" he felt not the elevation of great fame, but its isolation. The awe generated by his name walled him in. He loved so much to be loved. The worship he received from the Viennese — there was not . . . well, there was not necessarily much fondness in it. They were so proud of him; the question was whether that pride contained warmth. He went out to buy his special blend of pipe tobacco; only that errand would make him leave the house during a "phase." To the tobacconist he would say, not without tartness: "Send it to Igelgasse 4. My name is Strauss, Johann. I am the brother of Edi."

His brother Eduard, the handsome, exuberant fiddler-conductor — *him* they loved. He, Johann, had become a kind of ikon, something like an extraterritorial deity. Literally extraterritorial. Four years ago, in 1884, he had been made Honored Citizen of Vienna. Now in 1888 he was no longer even a legal resident in his native city. He was no longer even an Austrian citizen.

Few people knew that. It was a heavy thing for him to accept. It had come about because an Austrian subject of the Catholic faith could not divorce or remarry. That is, no ordinary subject could. And he, apparently, was ordinary. When he'd wanted to wed his Adele in 1887, the powers-that-be had not arranged annulment of his previous marriage through the Vatican, an accommodation finessed often for lesser luminaries. Not for Johann Strauss.

No, Johann Strauss had had to apply for citizenship in the

German Duchy of Sachsen-Coburg-Gotha. He'd had to change his religion from Catholic to Protestant. He'd had to rent an apartment in the distant principality to establish residence. Only after that could he put a ring on the finger of his beloved, and return to the Blue Danube without fear of clerical or secular reprisal.

During his "phase" he would brood about that. Everything taxed his nerves, even the limited Court Mourning caused by the death of the Emperor's father-in-law; it was like a prolongation of All Souls' Day. And the weather, which had turned unexpectedly balmy in November, grated on him. The lack of rain was an exasperation. He needed the dark, the wild, the wet, in order to work. He decided to get away again for a few days, to his country seat in Schönau, to enjoy the rougher sub-Alpine climate. But would it be safe in the country at this time? It was deserted out there in late November. He had come to distrust people. On the other hand he feared their absence.

"I've read about the dog exhibit that will open soon," he wrote in a note to his friend Priester. "Please buy a big and very alert dog. Beauty is much less important than alertness and size. Our villa in Schönau is so hidden that cutthroats could easily be attracted there. If you find a beast that can do more than just bark, and really go for the jugular, take that one . . ."

He did not want to lie in an overornamented honor grave, come next All Souls' Day.

It was on All Souls' Day of that year that Countess Festetics, a lady-in-waiting, met Rudolf in a rococo corridor of the Imperial Palace. He nodded at her curtsy and placed a finger on her arm.

"Off to the cemetery, Countess?"

"Yes, Your Imperial Highness. To pray for my dead."

"When I'm gone, will you pray for me?"

"Your Imperial Highness!"

"Will you include me among your dead?"

"Your Imperial Highness is smiling. It is a joke."

"A smile doesn't always mean a joke."

"Your Imperial Highness — I am much older than you. I pray God, I shall never have a chance to — to do what you ask."

"But if I should be gone, will you pray for me on All Souls' Day?"

"I hope never to see such an All Souls' Day — "

"If you do, will you pray for me?"

"Yes — yes, of course, Your Imperial Highness."

"Thank you."

For many years the Countess remembered this conversation verbatim. It was a strange scene for the unchurchly Crown Prince.

All Souls' Day on November 2 was appropriately marked by Hugo Wolf. In the final October days of 1888 he composed the melancholy song "He Who on Solitude Is Bent." Based on the Goethe poem, its final phrase read, "Oh come at last relief: lone in the grave at peace. Then I shall find release." On November 4, Wolf set to music Goethe's no less sepulchral "Anacreon's Grave."

At the same time autumn brought an intensification of his very private life which was lively but hardly gay. The circumvention of sexual reality, which so piqued Sigmund Freud, was practiced in November as an increasingly difficult art form not only by the Crown Prince and Baroness Vetsera, but by Hugo Wolf and Melanie Köchert as well.

The Köcherts had moved back from their country seat to their townhouse in Vienna's core. Wolf, restless, commuted between the empty summer places of friends and the equally empty suburban apartment the Köcherts had put at his disposal. Frau Melanie Köchert remained an exquisite woman of high repute, managing an elaborate household for her husband and children. Wolf was very Austrian like Rudolf. When he chose to, he could be a master of the outward form. Arriving at the Köcherts' house, he bowed to the Court jeweler; he kissed Frau Köchert's hand; observed all urbanities and courtesies due to the wife of the man who kept him financially afloat and who, in turn, was kept solicitously innocent of the truth. None of Melanie's three children, always about, entertained any suspicions. None of the friends Wolf and the Köcherts had in common ever noticed a single nuance exceeding the socially permissible. Frau Köchert, attractive and accomplished as a hostess despite her retiring nature, was thirty-five and

Hugo Wolf at twenty-eight, already becoming the modern master of the Lied. *This photograph was taken in February 1889. Wolf's short beard is so sparse because of his edgy habit of plucking out the hairs.*

147

showed nothing but the most ladylike kindness to the composer who was so young — only twenty-seven — so poor, so diminutive, he looked like a child who had glued on a blond mustache.

But they kept touching in secret ways. Throughout the fall their code-name messages throbbed in the classified columns of the *Neue Freie Presse*.

> *R: Received your letters — full of desire for a reunion soon. I give a thousand thanks. Take care. Wholly yours . . .*

R. still meant Rinnbach, the hamlet close to the Köchert villa in the Salzburg Alps. At the Rinnbach post office in the summer, and now at the Vienna office of Wolf's music publisher in fall and winter, they left each other notes arranging assignations. They stole hours from their official lives and intertwined furiously in little inns in the Vienna Woods. Outside those rooms, outside the closed window shutters on which hearts had been carved, the leaves turned color as gently as the leaves in the Palace gardens outside the room where Rudolf was meeting Mary.

The letters Melanie wrote her lover that fall breathe the vehemence and the difficulty of the torrent that *must* run underground. Her lines seem to buckle under the stress: "Save me! Save me! . . . You don't know what I've suffered. . . . I have only one wish more — once more again to possess you wholly, then to die . . ." One of her letters described how she waited for him on a bridge over a brook. But something kept him from the rendezvous. His small figure never appeared. She returned home and suddenly found herself opening all the windows wide in the hope he would *fly* in.

If all this furtive incandescence burned Melanie's senses, it goaded Hugo Wolf back into his music. The summer interlude at Bayreuth had been a brief sabbatical. But now Melanie had re-entered and quickened his life. From each meeting with her he rushed to the verse of Mörike and Goethe, turning their poems into *Lieder* with an élan, a confidence and an impatience he would never quite reach again in later years. He scribbled on note paper indoors and outdoors, on restaurant tables, tree stumps, in mail coaches and train compartments.

"I am working day and night," he wrote his friend Friedrich Eckstein just before All Souls' Day, ". . . I no longer know what rest is. . . . All the songs are truly shatteringly composed. Often the tears rolled down my cheeks as I wrote. They surpass in depth and conceptions all the other settings of Mörike. . . . Have you taken steps in the matter of separate printings of the poems? Do have them copied so that the matter can be finished. But hurry! hurry! hurry!"

Chapter 15

Hugo Wolf's art throve on the dissembling he had to do for propriety's sake. In Vienna, however, propriety was not bleak compulsion but velvet stagecraft. Propriety acted less to inhibit sex than to stimulate erotic games. Since the middle class felt here sooner than elsewhere that it would never arrive at an organically satisfying style of its own, it also held on here, longer than elsewhere, to the old protocols borrowed from nobility: the pageantries of death and the courtly plays of love. Electric bulbs had begun to flash by the Danube, but when men and women coveted one another in Vienna they moved like candlelit actors and actresses, distilling carnality into vintage charades. The classified-advertisements page in any newspaper showed that day by day:

> To the blonde exquisite lady sitting in the Café Griensteidl with a male escort yesterday: she had the kindness to hand a copy of the magazine *Kikeriki* in a most sympathetic manner

to a gentleman at a neighboring table, and would do said gentleman an even more incalculable kindness by indicating to Box 672, this newspaper, when and at what café he would be allowed to hand a *Kikeriki* to *her*.

The gentleman who stumbled by mistake into the funeral feast at the Hannes Saal yesterday and who read such wonderful forgiveness in the eyes of the lovely lady in the feathered black hat with the veil on the side . . . said gentleman would be plunged into mourning as well, if the lady would not grant him the chance to make restitution for his blunder at a meeting he prays might be arranged through Box 871, this newspaper.

The lady in company of what must be presumed to be her father, whose dog had the inspiration to break loose on the Kärntnerstrasse yesterday afternoon, is hereby begged a great favor by the retriever of the dog: he has presumed to procure a small gift for the pet in gratitude for causing the encounter and would like to present it in the presence of its gracious mistress at whatever place or time she might have the goodness to stipulate to Box 254, this newspaper.

November, which saw all these smaller byplays in Vienna, also brought to town the grand empress of thespian passion. This was the world's most famous star, Sarah Bernhardt. She could not only lose her heart and her virtue to surpassing effect. She could also — she opened the week of All Souls' Day — perish more beautifully before the footlights than anyone else. Her engagement at the Theater an der Wien evoked greater curiosity than the Kaiser's guest appearance at the Imperial Palace. Certainly La Bernhardt, now in her mid-forties, had more interesting fans than did Wilhelm.

During her summer run in London she had flabbergasted Theodor Herzl, who was passing through as the *Neue Freie Presse*'s blasé man in England. As such he had maintained an iron sophistication; he described how incomparably she died "once a day and twice on Saturday," and only then allowed himself to be amazed by "this slim red-haired phenomenon." In Paris some years earlier he'd been able to admire her more frankly. Freud, studying under Charcot there at about the same time, lost his usual coolness to theatrics: "How that Sarah plays! After the first words of her vibrantly lovely voice I felt I had known her for years. Nothing she could have said would have surprised me. I believe at once everything she says . . . every inch of that little figure lives and bewitches. Then her flattering and imploring and embracing . . . it is incredible what postures she can assume and how every limb and joint acts with her. . . ." In Paris in 1885 Freud had been a poor bachelor physician, barely able to afford a ticket to the Porte St. Martin theater. In Vienna in 1888 he was a poor married doctor and such dear luxuries must be ruled out altogether.

Franz Joseph, away on an official hunt in Hungary, also found himself unable to see the one and only Bernhardt. Very much to his regret. "If you go to see Sarah Bernhardt," he wrote Frau Schratt, "please give me your impressions . . . you'll do me a favor if you write me theater gossip. Perhaps it's not very nice of me to ask for that but, alas, it's true."

It was on the level of gossip that the Vienna press pounced on Bernhardt. To a degree she herself provoked such a reception. Hadn't this French nonpareil once mused aloud that no, she wasn't quite sure who was the father of her child, Victor Hugo, or General Boulanger, or Prime Minister Gambetta?

Notoriety is naturally more famous than fame. But initially Vienna received Sarah Bernhardt as a curio without equal — and as nothing else. This bitchiness was inevitable. Vienna and Madame Bernhardt met not the way a fresh new audience meets a star, but the way one knowing prima donna meets another. Both Bernhardt and the city were practitioners of the same superb tricks. But Bernhardt played at the center of the world's attention whereas Vienna suspected herself of being on the passé fringe. Bernhardt enjoyed a very contemporary prominence. And Vienna? . . .

Vienna gave her colleague a not particularly merciful once-over. Bernhardt's press notices consisted of ironic glosses: on her fabled slenderness (it had become "rather, uh, rounded" as one critic put it); on her temper (the *Wiener Tagblatt* reported how enchantingly she had smiled at the applause ending the first act of

Camille — only to scream like a fishwife, as soon as the curtain was down, about the lousy lighting and the absence of rugs in her rotten dressing room); on the *haute couture* of her death scenes.

Of course, dying was her specialty. She had been known to die standing. No one doubted that if she chose, she could die at great length, dancing. No stage personality commanded such a masterful repertoire of death agonies or a more ravishing gamut of ensembles in which to suffer them. The orange-and-black lace bodice of her Camille's last heavings stimulated more descriptive prose in newspapers than did the heavings themselves.

Further lengthy commentary concerned the clothes worn by the audience on opening night. Rudolf appeared in the Imperial Box in his sky-blue Hussar's uniform. The Vetseras sat in a proscenium box, with Baroness Mary unmistakable in her sable cape. Between these two poles passed many private glances. Around them sat an array of notables equal to the recent Court Theater opening. Habsburgs, Rothschilds, Frau Schratt, Princess Metternich, Professor Schnitzler, etc., etc.; a mighty panorama of fashion.

But how was La Bernhardt in person?

The day after her first night a reporter from the *Wiener Tagblatt* visited the Divine One at the Hotel Imperial. She resided here in the very suite just occupied by King Milan of Serbia. This, of course, gratified all preconceptions; as did the fabulously brocaded robe Madame was wearing; as did the lunch on which she nibbled — oysters, truffled paté, fruit omelet, Bordeaux of select vintage.

Madame began the conversation amiably enough, with the regret that she would have insufficient time to really see and absorb the Ringstrasse and the rest of the beautiful new Vienna, though she intended to devote three full days of the twelve of her engagement here to inspecting the Court Theater, which she understood to be the finest such house ever built.

So far so good. But soon the interview veered into a peculiar direction. Madame Bernhardt mentioned that after each performance she liked to read a very difficult book in order to fall asleep more easily. But just the night before she had read, by accident, a book which would not let her sleep at all because it was so vicious. It was called *La France Juive (Jewish France)* and it had infuriated her because of the perversions and fabrications of the author who was obviously a paid henchman of the lowest reaction.

Now, the author of *La France Juive* happened to be the same Eduard Adolphe Drumont who in a tract just published had attacked Rudolf for his Jewish friends. The very week of Bernhardt's opening, Rudolf had reacted to the tract in his bitter letter to Szeps. Szeps would have sympathized with the star's feelings about Drumont, but his own *Tagblatt* reporter was puzzled to find such political preoccupations in an actress. He became a bit impatient.

"We came here to chat with the lady about her profession and perhaps her gowns," he wrote,

> and suddenly found ourselves in a discussion of social themes. She, the incarnation of chic, elegance and perhaps frivolity, talked like an intellectual socialist. That was too much for us, and we attempted to get back to her own territory which admittedly includes many provinces. This most prominent actress of our time is also a sculptress of some critical as well as commercial repute. She writes, too. Her one-acter, *L'aveu*, is supposed to be a gripping play. She says she will play drama only for another three years. Then she will have sufficient means to do nothing but sculpting and writing and, one supposes, preaching. . . .

That was the tone, silky-nasty. Vienna placed the star on a pedestal made of high ambivalence. Madame Bernhardt was "unique," to be sure, but in a slightly inexcusable way. After *Camille* she'd chosen as her next vehicle Sardou's *La Tosca*, drawing reviews that couldn't be more wildly mixed. "A terrible play," one reviewer wrote typically, "a dramatic crime. The actress, by forcing us to become interested in it through her virtuosity, compounds the crime."

Never mind. Bernhardt acted her way past scribblers' gibes and clear across the language barrier. Performing in French for a German-speaking audience, she sold out the house night after night. Night after night fans mobbed her on her way from the stage door to the Hotel Imperial. A widower, whose advertisement for a wife was answered by a supposed letter from her, went crazy when he discovered it was a hoax. And Josefine Gallmeyer, Vienna's foremost impersonator, who'd studied Bernhardt's performance in order to mimic it, was confirmed in her verdict: "Her art is too great for parody. She is a genius. We can all clean her boots."

In the end Vienna seemed to surrender to Sarah Bernhardt even though she had the gall to conduct a "serious" private life. After all, the lady did spend one hundred thousand francs on costumes, and anyone investing so much on disguises warranted forgiveness from the city.

Bernhardt crowned her local engagement with *Frou-Frou*, closing November 13 on what seemed at first to be a triumphant note. True, Rudolf was not present because, according to the Court calendar, the Crown Prince was hunting at Orth on the Danube. Baroness Vetsera did not come for reasons unstated. But these excepted, every great light in Vienna assembled in the Theater an der Wien, including an unusually large complement of archdukes, Katharina Schratt, the inevitable Professor Schnitzler, and most ambassadors of the diplomatic corps. The curtain dropped to a typhoon of applause. Within minutes Madame Bernhardt's dressing room, already vernal with bouquets and laurel wreaths, coruscated with highnesses and excellencies. Presently these were joined by another interesting presence.

A bailiff.

In the name of the Municipality of Vienna this gentleman put a tax lien of three thousand gulden on box-office receipts.

Gasps all around. The bailiff quoted a municipal ordinance subjecting a foreign theatrical company to a levy based minimally on a six-months run, whereas Madame Bernhardt's manager had only paid a tax for the actual two weeks of the engagement.

More gasps. A flurry among the journalists present, dismay among the *illuminati*. Madame Bernhardt's general manager protested that the Theater an der Wien received forty percent of the profits and therefore should pay forty percent of the tax, which they had so far refused to do. The theater manager only cleared his throat. Madame Bernhardt's husband, a hitherto rather inconspicuous supporting actor, sighed and said it would all be straightened out by lawyers. Madame Bernhardt's secretary kept saying it was getting late, the private train was waiting to take the company to its next engagement in Prague.

And Madame Bernhardt herself gathered up her magnificent skirt. She cradled the biggest bouquet of roses in her elbow and smiled her singular smile: it had all been most memorable. She was taking with her the most interesting memories of Vienna.

Next morning the Viennese gobbled it all up over their coffee. For a change, they grinned instead of griped about the tax people. And for the first time they loved the great Sarah truly, without reservation, the kind of love we lavish only on superiors in trouble.

Chapter 16

Madame Bernhardt's misadventure encouraged Vienna. Madame's great reputation had fallen a little short. So had Vienna's so far this season. Yet Bernhardt continued to shine. Perhaps so would Vienna. And another nice parallel: Both the lady and the city had gone a nuance past their prime. But that nuance could be delicious and did not preclude marvelous moments ahead. In fact, the winter still promised highlights in the city: the benison of Christmas, New Year's Eve excitement, and then the Viennese carnival with its unique swirl of myriad balls. Nobody could say *vale* to *carne* — nobody could bid farewell to the flesh — with more dash and glamour than Vienna before Lent. The season would bring dazzle yet.

Politically there was another hopeful indication. By November it became clear that Prime Minister Taaffe had scored a great coup.

At least for the time being he had defused that imbroglio between Germans and Slovenes which had started in the small Styrian town of Celje but quickly spread beyond. The Prime Minister had found — or rather prestidigitated — a solution. He had pacified the Slovenes by decreeing that their children were indeed entitled to Slovene instruction in Celje's schools. He placated the Germans by postponing, indefinitely, execution of the decree.

His ambidexterity produced a prospect of peace in Parliament. Confounded were forecasts that warring nationalisms would be the end of Habsburg's empire. Perhaps the end would never happen. His Excellency, the Prime Minister, had once more pulled out of his sleeve a miracle sustaining that "perhaps." Count Taaffe excelled in endless improvisation. He would not be indentured to any finality, nor even to a principle. Indeed he did not ever burden himself with even half a principle; but possessed instead ten thousand expedients, like the cigar box which he offered with irresistible joviality to any opponent he wanted to turn into an accomplice.

Count Taaffe made good use of his ancestry. A descendant of Irish peers who had settled in Austria after the Thirty Years' War, His Excellency was Cork County handsome, with a dark, softly curling mustache. He parlayed blarney, *Gemütlichkeit* and elegance into a political infallibility which kept him at the right hand of the throne longer than any other Prime Minister during Franz Joseph's long reign. Armed with adroit ideas, unencumbered by ideals, he cheated the inevitable, crisis in, crisis out, for fourteen years. Clericals liked him for his industrious churchgoing. Anticlericals were disarmed by his statements against the Vatican concordat. His federalist leanings appeased Czechs and Poles, while German liberals liked his asides that personally and emotionally he was really one of them. Anti-Semites sometimes detected a sympathizer in him when he spoke out against "foreign capitalists." But Jews did not worry: Wasn't His Excellency's chief counselor named Blumenstock?

Nobody could worry effectively in Count Taaffe's presence. With a bit of lighthearted manipulation here, a touch of jovial chicanery there, he not only reconciled irreconcilables but spun out of them a parliamentary majority: Catholic politicians, Slav nation-

alists, aristocrats, and even a smattering of Liberals. His fine-tuned
ambiguities, his opaque showmanship enabled the Emperor to remain sober, straight and immaculate. Bravo, Count Taaffe! He
rode the steeplechase, jumped the moats, leaped barriers while blow-
ing smoke rings and lifting his derby to the ladies.

Vienna loved him for that. It loved him particularly that fall
because he made an old Viennese slang word officially immortal.
"Our government's policy," he said in a speech before Parliament,
"can be best defined as '*fortwursteln.*'"

Henceforward *fortwursteln* stood legitimized not only as a
statesman's philosophy but as the eternal Austrian way of life. The
genus loci so saturates the word that *fortwursteln* cannot be transported intact into other languages. Maybe its English sense could
be rendered best (but still inadequately) by a mixture of three
phrases: *Keep improvising . . . keep slogging on . . . keep clown-
ing . . .*

Fortwursteln constituted not merely Taaffe's Five Year Plan,
the long-range program of his administration. It also described the
weather by the Danube in November 1888. Like a sleight-of-hand
trick, spring warmed the streets on the brink of winter. After the
bitter cold of October — there had even been some premature snow
— the mercury climbed to an unbelievable nineteen degrees Celsius.
A summer sun beamed in a sirocco-blue sky. In the Vienna Woods
the bare branches of some chestnut trees revealed a bizarre swelling
of buds.

Suddenly Vienna was not just incomparable (it had always
remained that); but, in addition, it was now also bearable. The
Vienna-loving Viennese could tolerate their city again. For the
first time in many months the price of meat went down instead of
up. Sugar held at least steady. A new rent-control law passed,
spreading some overdue cheer among the poor.

The posh side of town, too, showed signs of buoyancy. The nice
strolling weather populated the Ringstrasse. Unseasonably many
passers-by (and coins) came Johann Pfeiffer's way as he, the King
of the Birds, performed with his parrots near the new Court
Theater. Other landmarks prospered as well. Eduard Sacher, the
hotelier and restaurateur, announced that "in appreciation of the

excellent execution of His Imperial Highness's orders," Rudolf had appointed him patissier to the Crown Prince. Demel's, torte-baker to the Emperor, opened its new quarters on the Kohlmarkt. At the stock market, prices were sweetening — a bit too much, in fact, for insiders.

Item: The shares of a certain metal company shot up madly at the news that controlling interest had been purchased by Karl Wittgenstein,* not only sire of the prodigious family, but head of the Empire's leading industrial enterprise, the giant Prag-Eisen consortium. Karl, of course, would survive in the history books as the father of Ludwig Wittgenstein, who would be born the next spring and grow up to turn modern philosophy upside down with his linguistic skepticism. But in November 1888 Karl's fame was his own, and his business leverage awesome. Any enterprise blazoning the name Wittgenstein attracted investors all over the Monarchy. So much so that this month he had to cool down the plungers, even though it cost him a nice fast piece of profit-taking.

"Two weeks ago," said his Letter to the Editor in the *Neue Freie Presse*, "I and some friends bought a majority interest in the Egydy Iron and Steel Company. This was done not so much to score a bigger profit but mainly because it seemed advantageous to become owner of said company, in view of the other companies my friends and I already hold. Since then there has been a great rise in the price of Egydy securities which, in my opinion, is unjustified. . . . I don't want to confirm, indirectly, through my silence, any unreasonable hopes and expectations that have recently arisen in connection with said company."

Wittgenstein stopped this particular speculative geyser. Still the general excitability remained high. Some people did fall victim to "unreasonable hopes."

One of them was Professor Anton Bruckner. Whenever he could, he took advantage of the warmth so uncommon in November. He missed the hay-scented fields of his Upper Austria but at least he could stroll the meadows by the Danube. Nearby, in the Prater,

* See pp. 69–71.

the Trade Fair (sponsored by Rudolf) still continued; and, being Bruckner, he was asked again to play the organ of the big Rotunde building. Here he underwent a sweet autumnal affliction.

A lovely young girl giggled for his autograph, bounced with rosy-cheeked, braid-tossing admiration, promised to chat with him again at a bench outside the Rotunde on the following day. The next day he sat there alone on the bench. For her he had bought a brand-new blue handkerchief to brighten the breast pocket of his loden suit. She never came. The handkerchief brightened him in vain. It lit up the humiliation.

That was only one of his troubles. His teaching at the Conservatory and his organ duties at the Palace Chapel didn't leave enough time for composing in the fall. The pressure made him yet more disorganized; and that, in turn, doubled the impatience of his housekeeper, Frau Kachelmayer. Once his left stocking simply vanished. Frau Kachelmayer finally found it in the piano. She was furious. He was baffled. But he was baffled by so many things. Some people told him that he was a great artist. So many others turned their backs. After the disillusionment with the braid-bouncing minx, he went against the city's mood: he sensed darkness ahead, and frustration. Toward the end of 1888 life seemed to grow worse instead of better, at least for him. He couldn't get his Romantic Symphony performed or even published without a subsidy.

"Herr Gutmann [a publisher] wants it," Bruckner wrote a friend, "and says I should ask the Court for 1,000 gulden for Herr Gutmann, which I cannot possibly do. I would prefer that he would just take it without paying me; after all, I have never ever gotten anything, whereas Brahms has gotten so much . . ."

There was the torment. The contrast between that other one in Vienna, Brahms, and himself. He, Bruckner, remained neglected by many important critics. Neglected or worse. Often jeers rained down on him over "his windy mysticism, his pseudo-Wagnerian noisings." Brahms himself had brutalized him; Brahms had publicly said that "in dealing with Bruckner one deals not with a body of compositions but a series of frauds."

The great Johannes Brahms, of course, received nothing but

overheated tribute. To a Brahms concert, Hanslick and all other high arbiters came as to a divine service.

In the *Neue Freie Presse*, as well as elsewhere, they published their adorations. They swooned before their deity's "classic limpidity"; they went on about Brahms's "great sense of line and sequence" and his "mastery of form." To Bruckner these words were a fancy way of covering up a plain old lack of invention.

But talent was the only thing Brahms lacked. Otherwise the man had everything. Brahms had all the decorations he wanted, whereas Bruckner scrounged for them in vain. Brahms had declined an honorary doctorate from Cambridge. Bruckner's application there had gone unheard. Brahms was published and performed everywhere. Of Bruckner's seven symphonies so far, four still went begging. At great occasions in the Musikvereinssaal, Brahms sat enthroned in the director's box. Bruckner had to buy his ticket for standing room in the gallery.

Bruckner was permitted to teach at the Conservatory and to sound the pipes in the Palace Chapel. Brahms permitted the world to adulate him. And the world, thrilled, made Brahms an honored member of the Musikverein as well as Honorary President of the Tonkünstlerverband (the composers' and musicians' association). They all treated him as *the* composer laureate. Bruckner might console himself with the thought of the pince-nez he shared with Beethoven. Brahms bestrode the scene as Beethoven reborn. It was a chilling inequity, no matter how warm the autumn sun. Bruckner was no anti-Semite, he had Jewish friends, yet sometimes in the past he had thought of applying for redress to his Upper Austrian parliamentary representative, Georg von Schönerer.

Schönerer, though, sat in jail. Of Bruckner's partisans, Mahler struggled in Budapest, and Hugo Wolf was too immersed in his Goethe *Lieder* and in his clandestine love life to offer anything more than sympathy. The injustice continued. It expressed itself even in the private lives of the two adversary composers. Both Bruckner and Brahms were old bachelors who drank lager beer and liked smoked pork with sauerkraut. But at Hessgasse 7, Bruckner was, at best, tempestuously served by Frau Kachelmayer.

It was lucky she didn't spank him. He was her unending vexation and she didn't mind saying so, loudly. She couldn't bear the chaos in his bedroom. She was tired of the snuff-stained inkblotted litter in the other chambers. Every two weeks she had to threaten to quit if the Herr Professor didn't stop throwing stacks of note sheets on top of his slippers.

At Karlsgasse 4, by contrast, Johannes Brahms's life moved in a dream of neatness. He controlled — and enchanted — his Frau Truxa with dainty hints. If a glove needed mending, Frau Truxa would find it lying on top in a drawer left "accidentally" open. If a pair of boots could use polishing, they would be placed a shade away from the wall, toward the middle of the room. Yes, Johannes Brahms was a giant and a dear. Even his terseness impressed and ingratiated. Friends treasured his aphoristic postcards. Bruckner, on the other hand, spent much more postage on long letters which began "Most Honored, Most Kind and Geniuslike Protector!" but which brought no remedy. The injustice continued.

Bruckner was a pathetic joke to many Viennese in 1888. Brahms was their marvel. They admired his very quirks. Brahms was the only notable in town to rise almost as early as Franz Joseph. He left bed at 5 A.M. After that he marched through his day's program with a self-assurance as solid and axiomatic as the Emperor's.

First he made his own special coffee, with beans sent him by an admirer in Marseilles. Next he took his early-morning walk and then settled down to work. In the fall of '88 his desk work followed a seasonal routine. All his actual composing was done during the hot months. From September to December he redrafted, modified, prepared for publication the music born during his Swiss summers. This autumn the *Zigeuner Lieder* had to be corrected and the Third Sonata for Violin and Piano in D-minor must be seen through the printer.

He worked till noon. Then he allowd Frau Truxa, who had arrived meanwhile, to help him into his overcoat. Fingers intertwined authoritatively behind his back, he started to walk north, toward the Inner City. He crossed the Ringstrasse with his massive figure, his powerful profile, his dynast's beard, his stunning gray mane. Children followed him as he moved down the Kärntnerstrasse. There was always candy in the great man's pocket. It didn't matter that he talked with a harsh North German accent in a surprisingly thin high voice. He was so kind, handing out sweets. He knew how to lace distinction with affability.

When he reached his inn, Zum Rothen Igel in the Wildpretmarkt, he passed by the main dining room frequented by higher government officials. A *Stube* farther back was his favorite; coachmen cut into their goulash here, and here a corner table was famous for being the Brahms lunching place.

He ordered his roast pork, kraut and pilsner, received friends and admirers. Then he walked back to the Ringstrasse, toward another table reserved for him at the Café Heinrichshof, opposite the Opera. There he reclined in a chair by the window and often would doze off after his mocha. Passers-by would pause to admire the Brahms monument which sat there behind the glass pane with closed eyes. It was a thrill to watch the statue come alive and tip the waiter.

His afternoons were spent at home, on musical politics played with wonderfully deft fingers. That November a delicate and rather strategic kindness occupied him. He helped arrange a celebration of Joseph Joachim's fiftieth year in music and donated one hundred gulden toward a Joachim bust. This was important because the violin virtuoso was one of Brahms' principal interpreters and a Brahms champion of international caliber. Yet in 1888 an estrangement had developed because the violinist thought the composer had taken his wife's side in a matrimonial dispute. By his contribution Brahms now turned the anniversary into a fine occasion for fence-mending. It was the sort of thing he liked to do after lunch: meting out, to enemies or allies, just deserts or sweet rewards.

Charity was another skill exercised during Brahms's afternoons. Huge royalty sums flowed toward him from all directions. Since his habits were frugal and his investments shrewd, he could afford to be truly generous, particularly to truly important people. In the fall of 1888 he sent fifteen thousand gulden, a princely sum, a munificence, to Clara Schumann, his aged and by now arthritic

Johannes Brahms on the terrace of Johann Strauss's summer house. The perfect manager of his own success, Brahms cultivated friendships with the rich, the titled, the famous.

friend. Not long afterward she arranged a recital against which he protested, but not too vehemently or effectively, because Clara insisted on making it all-Brahms.

It was all in a day's work. At night his touch was no less sure when he dined with Eduard Hanslick, Chief Justice of the Supreme Court of Music. Brahms' life was one steady craftsmanlike masterpiece; Bruckner's, an inspired shambles.

In the course of the fall the two would pass one another, face to face, in the building of the Musikverein. Bruckner might be on his way to one of his Conservatory classes, Brahms coming from a session of the high council of the organization. Along the corridors people would slow down to watch. They'd see Brahms nod with clipped courtesy. Bruckner would bow elaborately: "Most obedient servant, Herr President!"

A fraught encounter, a loaded greeting. By "Herr President" Bruckner let drop the implication that he recognized Brahms as president of the Composers' Association; that it was the bureaucratic title which warranted his salute, not necessarily the talent.

But that was just funny old Bruckner's view. Practically everyone else that mattered made obeisances to Brahms without reservations. Johannes Brahms was the only serious resident artist whom Vienna admired wholeheartedly in his own lifetime.

Why just Brahms? Perhaps because he produced beauty without creating anything really new and therefore frightening. Furthermore this German brought off something incomprehensible to the Viennese: he could actually cope with his own gifts. He was a genius, to be sure, but geniuses often made only a pale impression on the town. Brahms was a *middle-class* genius — that was the astounding, the mesmerizing difference about him. He was such a blunt, factual, coolly functioning genius. When invited to the Riviera, as he was that fall, he declined "because of the awful elegance of it all." Unlike Johann Strauss, who once tried to become a baron by having himself adopted by a baroness, it never even occurred to Brahms to covet a title.

He operated as the dry bourgeois administrator of his gifts. He was sufficient unto himself. And this simply thrilled Vienna's most dynamic yet uncertain class, all those burghers with hopelessly feudal souls. Inside their newly-escutcheoned Ringstrasse palazzi they proclaimed liberalism, progress and post-Baroque modernism. They liked to protest their vitality — even their superiority — vis-à-vis the hauteur of the nobles; and then gave themselves away by protesting too much in a lead article of their own foremost newspaper.

"The present generation of the upper aristocracy still wants to dominate the middle class," the *Neue Freie Presse* wrote in December.

> But they want to dominate the middle class without becoming acquainted with it. To them "the people" consist of a speeding fiacre and the laundresses they tease. In contrast to London where (even before our time) the Iron Duke bowed before Peel who was a weaver's son, the aristocracy here is sterile and sequestered. Forty years ago Mrs. Trollope spent a winter in Vienna and was quite astonished by the castelike separations of the various social levels. She had never met more graceful ladies than those in bankers' houses, yet these were not admitted to aristocratic circles. . . . Nowadays the bourgeoisie regards the social isolation of the nobility with complete equanimity. Yes, there are some Sons of the Factory who are ashamed of chimneys, who desire the Castle: who do not know that true nobility springs from work and who forget that only contempt awaits them if they try to uproot themselves. These young people would like to imitate the nonchalance of a count, the gambling and frivolity of a cavalier. They try to deny their origins. They are indolent in all questions of bourgeois freedom. We are not. The bourgeoisie must contend with the aristocrats, but it is sure of victory.

Very firm; very cocky; quite hollow. A few weeks before the *Neue Freie Presse* published such defiance, Duke Maximilian, the Empress's father, had died in Bavaria. To most Viennese he was just a remote name. Yet the very same *Neue Freie Presse*, along with the *Tagblatt* and other voices of the middle class, soon brought word of a change in the fashion note. Court was in mourning. The new *leitmotif* was black, with variations and mitigations — sable furs, pearl-toned sleeves, skirts and bodices in dark chinchilla shadings.

Only families of the loftiest quarterings, namely those admitted to Court, were expected to show public sorrow. But the Wives of the Factory read their *Neue Freie Presse* and off they went, shopping for blueblood grief at their furriers and dressmakers. They bought it, and had it fitted, and pulled it this way and that, and twisted it into an anxious burghers' elegance that spoke the opposite of pride in origin.

It was a queasy business, this need to *fortwurstel* upward.

Only few were immune to it. On November 1, a missive with an imposing seal had arrived by liveried messenger at Gustav Klimt's ramshackle studio on the Sandwirthgasse. It came from His Excellency, the Minister of Culture: "His Imperial and Royal Apostolic Majesty has deigned, in accordance with his All Highest decision on October 28, and in affable consideration of your outstanding artistic services in connection with the new Court Theater . . . to most graciously confer upon you the Golden Service Cross with Crown . . ."

At the age of twenty-six Gustav Klimt was rewarded for muraling the new theater's ceiling in splendid stereotype. And now he had the chance for other high favors, this time in connection with the *old* Court Theater. The City of Vienna had commissioned him and his partner Franz Matsch to do heroic portraits of the old house — Klimt's picture facing the audience from the stage, Matsch's the other way. Each view was to show some hundred-odd of the most prominent habitués of the house, and it was left to the artists to define prominence by painting it into the picture.

Two rather unknown young men had suddenly become the arbiters of fame. Power had been handed to them on a palette. It was a tremendous chance.

Matsch seized it and studded the old Court Theater boxes with Esterházys, Metternichs and others capable of advancing him. It was his first step toward eminence as Vienna's society painter.

For Klimt it was a step in the opposite direction. He neglected the chance assiduously — though even so it was hard to evade. Some choices were musts: The painting *had* to include Brahms, La Schratt, Prime Minister Taaffe and the new Court Theater's architect Hasenauer. Others Klimt may have put in because he liked their liberal politics, like Moritz Szeps and Eduard Bacher, publisher of the *Neue Freie Presse*. He painted in his brother Ernst Klimt and his sisters as well as a number of invented faces. But he ignored many offers to sit for him which came in letters engraved with crests. He ignored invitations to tea in the Ringstrasse salons of financial barons. At first he didn't even include Karl Lueger who was among the best-known Court Theater goers as well as a parliamentary star of great anti-Semitic brilliance. When the city fathers discovered the omission, Klimt had to rectify it. (After all, it was pointed out to him, Lueger's anti-Jewish figure would barely balance the Jewish ones already in the picture.) But the portrait he added belatedly is a bit less flattering than most others made of "handsome Karl."

For the most part Klimt didn't care very deeply. The picture was just more academic piecework done to support his parents, his brothers and sisters. He was still waiting for authentic inspiration to take control of his brush. Meanwhile he lifted barbells and used the warmer days to take long hikes near Mödling in the Vienna Woods. Thanks to the mild weather, the trees retained their foliage longer than usual. Red and gold, ocher and amber leaped to the eye. How beautifully the leaves aged on ten thousand twigs! No politics could produce such glory in a forest. Only so natural and simple a thing as death.

Chapter 17

A difficult duty of the Crown Prince is to keep silent, when the lowest subject of the state is free to talk. It is his duty to remain in the shadow even when he feels the necessity to step candidly and powerfully into the light of public opinion. This difficult duty had been a severe burden to the Crown Prince because so often he was convinced that what happened . . . was not beneficial to the fatherland.

On December 1, all Vienna could read these lines on the front page of the *Wiener Tagblatt*. Censorship had let them through for a simple reason. They referred to a foreign controversy. The words quoted were from a lawyer beyond the border, defending the publisher of the diaries of the German Crown Prince Friedrich; the Friedrich who had died in March after barely three months on the throne. Wilhelm, the new Kaiser, disliked his predecessor's liberalism and had interdicted publication of the diaries. His act had become an international *cause célèbre*. Moritz Szeps's *Wiener Tagblatt* was merely reporting on a hot issue abroad — good journalistic practice. It was a liberal paper and quite naturally quoted an argument stressing the historical importance of the diaries of a liberal prince. That was all.

Yet many readers sensed that wasn't all, at all. Moritz Szeps was too good a friend of the Austrian Crown Prince. Citing dead Friedrich's defender meant writing, between the lines, an eloquent essay on behalf of Rudolf.

Szeps still saw the Crown Prince regularly. He knew that Rudolf's life did not get easier as the year wore on to its end. When Rudolf traveled with Franz Joseph to his grandfather's funeral in Munich, his cough returned — an old complaint. But there was a complaint yet older and worse, which afflicted him whenever he had to accompany the monarch to a pomp of state. He felt he was being moved about like an overdressed archaic puppet. The Emperor pulled strings taut for the pettiest motions. "His Majesty has ordered," Rudolf wrote his First Court Chamberlain, Count Bombelles, "that neither you nor I should attend the Bavarian regimental anniversary [because of mourning], but that a courteous regret note should be sent now, and that later, on the anniversary day itself, a congratulatory cable should be dispatched."

On his return to Vienna, Rudolf had to playact his way through the usual ceremonial chores. Sometimes, rarely, he disconcerted courtiers with a flash of his real face, as he had with Countess Festetics on All Souls' Day. Mostly he concealed himself and his resentment beneath his official graciousness. He had to go on miming a role he loathed, and the court calendar scheduled him for many performances that fall.

He had to inspect the model for City Hall Park together with a host of newspaper reporters. He had to smile the Crown Princely smile though he hated the very idea of the park. Its execution would cost over a million gulden. It would dress up still more an already overembellished Ringstrasse neighborhood. The rich would promenade around its monumental fountain, their poodles would mince across those million-gulden lawns, whereas the poor would go on crowding into the dilapidated public clinic for which his friend Dr. Billroth could not even get an appropriation of a hundred thousand.

But he had to keep on smiling. He had to smile while sitting for a portrait commissioned by the City Council. One hundred and sixty copies of it would go as Christmas gifts to one hundred and sixty schools throughout the municipality. He was wonderfully popular. But most Viennese did not recognize him as a modern leader who wanted to raise the proletarian to bourgeois; who wanted to encourage the middle class so that its fruits — science, efficiency, progresss — might cure the Empire's languid rot. Too many Austrians saw him with an entirely unenlightened adulation as a high gallant, the hero of a living fairytale.

A fairytale? A bitter paradox. Rudolf Habsburg, who wished to pull the Viennese out of their baroque trance, was yoked to a plumed image that would draw them more deeply into it.

His image constantly undermined his politics. But it wasn't only the Viennese who bedeviled him with the wrong kind of fame. The Hungarians also misunderstood, or worse, misused him. In an official memorandum two years earlier Rudolf had attacked the oppression of non-Hungarians within Hungary's borders: Magyar bureaucrats, administering their autonomous part of the Empire, handled Slovaks "almost as if they were animals." Other Slavic minorities were treated — again in the words of Rudolf's memo-randum — with "contempt and brute measures which in the end must prove futile."

No, Rudolf had few illusions about Hungary. Its gentry, which ran the government, practiced gross chauvinism. Above them were the magnates, who lived exquisitely on the peasantry's back. They were a blend of high polish and tough reaction. In the sixteenth century they had put the leader of a peasant revolt on a red-hot iron throne; had placed a red-hot crown on his head and pressed into his hands a red-hot scepter. Then they had forced his retinue to eat his sizzling flesh. In the 1880s their regime had grown less savage and more dashing. No other system built on inequity man-aged quite so dapper a veneer.

At his writing desk Rudolf saw clearly through the bluebloods of the *puszta*. But on the hunting trail or over a bottle of tokay they knew how to beguile him. They knew how to play on the fact that he was the heir of the *dual* monarch; that he had a thorough Hungarian education; that he corresponded with his mother in Hungarian and that he himself possessed a downright Hungarian charm; and, last but not least, that among the dull aristocracies of the polyglot Empire, they, the Hungarian bloods, were a keen exception. The Telekis and the Károlyis stood out as Rudolf's few stimulating friends. Politically he disapproved of them. Emotionally they disarmed him. He was stymied.

The Czechs stymied him in a different way, and they constituted the realm's most critical nationality issue. "The conflict between slavery and anti-slavery parties in the U.S.A.," reported the Amer-ican Consul from Prague in 1886, "was not waged with more acri-mony and determination than the political strife now in progress between the German and the Czech subjects of the Empire."

Rudolf felt an instinctive sympathy for the Czechs. His happiest years had been his early twenties in Prague, commanding a Czech regiment. Shortly afterward he'd written a study that character-ized any policy which denied Slav rights as "a great danger to the ship of state."

But in Bohemia, Rudolf faced a problem whose emergence he

had himself foreseen. The struggle for Czech rights became increasingly split into two wings — young and old. The Old Czechs were led by great landed names like the Princes Schwarzenberg and by high clerics, and naturally Rudolf couldn't stomach them. "These feudal and nationless gentlemen," Rudolf once said in a letter, "just exploit the Slavic people for their own ends. The Slavs are liberal. The day will come when they will disown these gentlemen thoroughly."

Written in 1881, this was another of his eagle-eyed forecasts. Seven years later, political sentiment in Bohemia turned away from the Old Czechs toward the Young. The Young ones were middle-class firebrands of liberal persuasion, just exactly Rudolf's sort. Yet for reasons of foreign policy he could not be their protector nor they his supporters. The Young Czechs looked to an alliance with St. Petersburg, the world's most retrograde absolutism. But to Bohemian militants the Tsarist ideology mattered little. "The enemies of our enemies are our friends," one of their spokesmen had declared long ago, and dear Russia was Habsburg's antagonist on the international chessboard. The Russian press often served as mouthpiece for Young Czech diatribes. Rudolf feared that this faction, once given free rein in Prague, might create a Muscovite outpost within the Empire. In addition, many Young Czechs nursed a personal hatred against the Habsburg dynasty, and Rudolf — his progressive intentions notwithstanding — could not help being the Crown Prince. Among Czechs, therefore, the Old ones were abhorrent and the Young ones impossible. Rudolf had a constituency in neither.

In all the tangled ethnic politics of the Empire, Rudolf did possess one impassioned follower: King Milan of Serbia. Milan adored Rudolf's light royal touch and wrote him lines that often seem less from king to prince than from fan to star. Rudolf, however, despised Milan as a weakling; as an all-too-obvious Austrian vassal disliked by his own people. To be friends with Milan was to attract bitterness from the South Slavs. There was no firm support looming from that direction either.

Politics had become futility, a dead end, a quagmire. Rudolf's hopes for nourishment receded from his public to his private life. By the end of 1888 he saw in the gilded labyrinth around him only one figure worth clinging to: Mary Vetsera.

By December his meetings with her became more intense, but also more difficult to arrange. Countess Larisch, who had engineered them till now, was summoned to her husband's estate in Bohemia. The pair must find some other go-between. And found it in, of all people, Richard Wagner.

On December 11, the Court Opera began the Ring Cycle with *Das Rheingold*. Dowager Baroness Vetsera prepared to man the family box in full and triple finery. The fashion championship must be defended to the cries of the Valkyries. But suddenly Mary, the champion, did not want to go. She had a pretext: not liking Wagner. She had voiced her aversion before. Could she please be excused from the odious Ring? When that didn't work with her mother, she made sure to develop a bad headache, or washed her hair so late it couldn't dry in time for the performance.

One trick or the other always took. The evenings were clear. As soon as her mother and sister had driven off to the opera, she slipped out of the house. With her wet hair she ran to the corner where Salesianergasse met Marokkanergasse. Bratfisch was waiting in a spot beyond the range of lanterns. The fiacre would pick up Rudolf a few blocks farther and drive out to Schönbrunn Castle. Here the two walked the enormous park together in darkness, in silence, in continence. It was cold. The weather had turned raw. They whispered. Their breath came in clouds that merged and vanished. That was all. By 10 P.M. she was home again.

He still did not move toward consummation. Climax meant end. He was not ready for that. He shied away now from anything climactic. He was not ready to submit to the Empire's pervasive, graceful drift toward doom; yet he was not ready either to move against it. For he knew that any decisive act by him would trigger convulsion. He was not ready to act on overtures made to him during his hunts in Hungary — they spoke of crowning him king in Budapest, usurping half his father's realm. Was that the way to ride his liberalism to royal power? Through a conspiracy with Magyar nobles? Should he make revelers and shooting companions his partners in statesmanship?

No, he wanted to wait a while longer. He hoped for a more modern way out. Or at least for some partial, provisional resolution which might release him from futility, smooth his nerves, ease his sleep. Something might happen.

And something did. It began to snow.

On December 8, whiteness came down on Vienna. Life changed. The countryside fluttered into the city. Even the dirty cobbles of the Ottakringerstrasse became as clean and natural as the slopes of the Kahlenberg. During the day, Rudolf drove through the transmutation. The streets had taken on a playfulness, and play is hope.

Edifice and statuary joined a general relaxation. White dollops sat on marble helmets; they turned heroes into toys. The Ringstrasse looked like a tumbling ground of giant children in ermine rags who were so happy that, for a while at least, they needn't act like monuments; under the butterfly whirl of white flakes, greatness ceased to be an obligation. At fiacre stands cabbies in muskrat coats built snowmen to keep the ex-statues company. Many of these snowmen were coal-buttoned, broomstick-sabered cartoons of the fiacres' enemy — the police. And the police laughed and swung their arms against the cold, and walked on.

At the Eislaufverein, the new Skaters' Palace rose up with many cross-timbered turrets like a Russian grand duke's villa. The sports crowd pirouetted before it in muffs and top hats. And as if that weren't gaiety enough, Christmas had broken out in the streets. A whole pinewoods of Christmas trees had sprung up overnight on the cobbles of Judenplatz square. On another square, Am Hof, the *Christkindlmarkt* (Little Christ Child's Market) was a Lilliputian mirage. A townlet of little huts stood here, inhabited by thousands of dolls, marionettes, jumping jacks, tin soldiers, and small grave personages made of gingerbread and candy. They lived among gilded nuts, snowballs, sparrows and children's laughter.

Soon boots and horses' hooves stamped away the snow. But a happy scurry continued on sidewalks and in roadways. Everyone noted that now Vienna pulsed like a genuine metropolis at last. The rush of Christmas shopping had begun.

Rudolf saw all that, but the Imperial treadmill must be trod. He must inspect a cadet school in Bratislava, attend a regimental winter drill in the Carpathians, escort Balkan royalty through the Tyrol, stalk bears with a Rumanian prince in Hungary. But he could always hurry back to Vienna's Christmas. At the *Christkindlmarkt* he bought, as always, a basketful of gifts for his retainers' children as well as for his own little daughter Elisabeth. Nights he walked with Mary Vetsera through Schönbrunn Park in whose immense gardens snow patches still perched like owls, immaculately white.

Religion was flummery to him. Yet these weeks were full of the enigma of redemption. Perhaps the city would not hopelessly squander its possibilities. Perhaps his position was not altogether feckless. He might be able to do something real after all.

So he roused himself once more to action. For the Foreign Minister he wrote a report on his recent experience with King Milan. He argued that Milan's servility vis-à-vis Austria was a potential hazard; it might provoke a drastic Serbian reaction against the Empire. This memo repeated similar earlier warnings, but it was even more forceful, more cogently reasoned, more prophetic of the catastrophe to come in 1914 . . . and was even more smoothly ignored.

He kept on. He did not relax his guard against Kaiser Wilhelm. At the end of November the attacks against Rudolf had flared up again in Prussian newspapers. But he was ready. He'd sent Moritz Szeps a deposition on a whore who had stolen Wilhelm's monogrammed cufflinks during "a hunting entertainment" in Styria. He was now prepared to instruct Szeps to make this information public, if Wilhelm did not leash his press.

He would go that far. He could be that hard. But in the last weeks of the year he also had preserved the strength to be tender, and not just with Mary Vetsera. He remembered his tutor of long ago, old General Latour, who had been one of his youth's better spirits. "Because of all these emperors, kings and princes I had so

*Rudolf's mother, the Empress Elisabeth. Fifty-one
years old in 1888, she was still Europe's reigning
beauty, a superb legend and a remote wife.*

little time," he wrote Latour. "But we should at least hunt together. You ought to get some exercise in the fresh air."

Childhood stirred in him. He felt new love for the woman who had once been his mother. Empress Elisabeth had become still more remote in 1888, having spent much of the year in her exotic hermitage in Corfu. She was still beautiful, and stranger than ever. She had missed her own father's funeral, since the news had reached her too late at the faraway island. Now she arrived in Vienna in December, with an anchor tattooed on her shoulder. It shocked the Emperor. But to Rudolf this made her more like him — a fellow mutant. She, too, disliked Court etiquette. Her sensibility, too, rebelled against exalted emptiness.

In the winter of 1888 he remembered the springs of long ago when they had strolled through the gardens of Laxenburg Castle, hand in hand, mother and child, playing word games in Hungarian. Her birthday fell on Christmas day, and suddenly he wanted to give her something very special. She adulated Heine. Therefore he procured a book of Heine letters edited by Hugo Wittmann, Herzl's play collaborator. Not content with that, Rudolf had asked his friend Moritz Szeps to track down, through French friends, a packet of eleven rare original letters Heine had written to a relative in Paris. "Do you have the Heine material?" was a refrain in Rudolf's notes to Szeps that December.

On Christmas Eve the Imperial Family gathered in the damask-hung reception room of the Empress's apartment. On a table before the blue-fir Christmas tree lay Rudolf's Heine offerings for his mother's birthday. Rudolf had also put on the table exquisitely wrapped, signed copies of his *Austro-Hungarian Monarchy in Word and Picture* as Christmas gifts for his parents and his sister. His wife Stephanie, ever the bumptious dilettante, surprised Their Majesties with a gift of her drawings of the Adriatic coast. And Their Majesties in turn surprised their granddaughter, Rudolf's and Stephanie's little Elisabeth. They gave the child a delicious set of miniature garden furniture crafted in Corfu.

There were embraces and kisses as in millions of other households that remembered Bethlehem together. Archduke Franz Salvator of Tuscany attended the intimate gathering because his engagement to

Valerie, the Crown Prince's sister, was about to be announced. Rudolf considered him too closely related, too much the vacuous *fait néant* princeling. But he said nothing. He kissed his sister and hugged his future brother-in-law. When he put his arms around his mother, there broke out of him a sudden sob.

It startled the whole family. But this was, after all, a moving milestone in Valerie's life, and by the time the group sat down in the Empress's dining salon, Rudolf had resolved his features into their customary charm. The moon rose above the great roofs of the Ringstrasse, "Silent Night" came choiring softly from the Burgplatz, and, finally, the huge bell in the cathedral tower of St. Stephen's began to toll for Mass.

Chapter 18

Hugo Wolf had intended to go home to Styria for the holidays. A delay in the publication of his Mörike *Lieder* detained him. So he spent Christmas with the Köcherts in Vienna. Under the mistletoe he could kiss Melanie for one single licit moment. Then their mouths parted, carols sounded, and the secret resumed.

At Gustav Klimt's studio on the Sandwirthgassse, dozens of prettily ribboned food baskets had been delivered, with compliments of the season. He had just about as many Santa Clauses as there were ambitious rich hoping to be included in his painting of old Court Theater celebrities. He kept only the baskets containing fruit, which he ate with passion. The others he gave to his brother Ernst or to Franz Matsch, partners in art with whom he shared the studio. The cards attached to the gifts he tore up without looking, shredding all chance of future favors.

Brahms's Christmas was bluntly careerist. Unlike Hugo Wolf, he had made sure that the *Zigeuner Lieder*, *his* song cycle, was published promptly on time, promptly praised by Hanslick in the *Neue Freie*

Presse ("For years now we have received a holiday gift from
Herr Brahms's talent, and it pleases me to say that this year, too,
his songs make excellent Christmas presents . . ."), and therefore
sold promptly and briskly in the gift-shopping trade. The Sunday before Christmas he collected wild applause at Joseph Joachim's
performance (with cellist Robert Hausmann) of his Double Concerto. Christmas Eve he dined with the Hanslicks. Christmas day
the master took his lunch at Zum Rothen Igel, accepted gifts and
good wishes from admirers, napped punctually at the Café Heinrichshof at 1:30 P.M. and spent the afternoon supervising Frau
Truxa's packing. He was about to depart for the Duchy of Saxe-
Meiningen where the Duke sponsored a music festival built efficiently around the genius of Johannes Brahms. The Brahms annual
cycle completed itself on clockwork schedule.

At Burgring 1, the seignorial apartment house Brahms glimpsed
daily on his way to the Heinrichshof, Arthur Schnitzler experienced
Christmas in his own way. "December 23, Sunday," his tight-lipped
diary notes. "Trimming the Christmas tree . . . December 24, Monday. Christmas at home. Jean. (2). Kfh. Poker." Which meant that
not only the famous, though unbaptized, Professor Schnitzler in
his sumptuous residence celebrated the birth of Christ, but so did
his unbaptized, unknown son in the smaller flat under the same
roof. And that, after Schnitzler Junior had committed the act of
love twice with Jeanette, our young man went to the coffeehouse
to play poker, and then used his journal to sum up the day in a few
cryptic words to despise himself by.

Across the Danube Canal, at Stefaniestrasse 1, Jakob and Jeanette
Herzl celebrated the season with their son Theodor. He shared the
spacious apartment with them; here they were the first to see
Theodor's feuilletons or the newest draft of his play that *must* make
the Court Theater. On December 24 all three were decorating
what Theodor would later call "our Chanukah tree."

At Maria Theresienstrasse 8 the Freuds never indulged either in
Christian rites or their own Jewish ones. The holidays meant
simply a lighter schedule at the Pediatric Institute and still fewer
patients in the doctor's private practice. There was a bit more time

for his weekly tarok game with pediatrician colleagues in their local coffeehouse; more time for his daily stomp around the Ringstrasse. Above all, he could devote extra hours to his paper in progress on hysteria, exploring his heresies on the subject. The holidays, in brief, gave him more leisure with which to jeopardize his so-called career.

Opposite the Freuds, on the top floor of Hessgasse 7, all was dark, all quiet at the Bruckner flat. Frau Kachelmayer needn't fret over her frowsy Herr Professor. He had left town for a while, to overcome his old-bachelor loneliness during Christmas. The Abbot of Kremsmünster in Styria had invited him. Around the monastery, snow hung on the rolling woods. Inside, the monks sat in awe as Bruckner played the organ at midnight Mass, improvising far beyond the printed note into great godly dreams of sound. Afterward they prayed and gave him a little roast pork and more pilsner and much love.

Even in the insane asylum on the Brünlfeld there was, if not peace, good will among inmates. They presented their annual show starring Alois Bank, a well-known comedian who considered himself cured without ever expressing the desire to leave. At the Christmas revue he sailed through a routine of ten-year-old gags (the last he had done "outside"), but fell into a sudden stutter at the end. His audience took it to be intentional, and the evening ended with shrill gusts of hilarity.

In Vienna's working-class districts Christmas was the art of make-do. For an Ottakring family it wasn't uncommon to buy a fifty-kreuzer branch lopped from a big upper-class tree in the Inner City. This "tree," propped against the wall, fit the narrowness of the tenement and the scantiness of the presents. Father might get a nice cravat from the secondhand store; mother, a darning kit; little Anna, a pair of coarse warm socks rolled around a candy ball. All these bounties lay under the "tree," swathed in red tissue paper which, wrinkled but still serviceable, was kept carefully from one year to the next, as the stores charged extra for gift wrapping.

But even in Ottakring the night was very special. It was the one night in the year when the *Bettgeher* — the subtenant who rented only a bed, nothing else — joined the family for dinner; it featured not horsemeat but genuine beef that night. This one night of the year the oven serving the apartment did not go hungry. Christmas Eve of 1888 was crisp rather than cold, and coal so awfully expensive. Yet the father made sure that the oven was fully stoked before he retired; so that flames remained high throughout the Savior's night and nobody needed to wake chilled into Christmas Day.

The weather, not harsh for December, relented even more after Christmas. New Year's Eve came upon Vienna in an unseasonably warm fog. On the far side of this mild nervous haze hulked 1889. Chimneysweeps received more generous tips than usual, because the very sight of their sooty faces brought luck in the twelve months ahead. Johann Pfeiffer, King of the Birds, performing on the Schottenring, had an act ready for the occasion. For ten kreuzer, a parrot would fly to a shelf of envelopes inside the cage, pick one, and deliver to King Pfeiffer his client's horoscope for 1889. At New Year's Eve parties all over town, the climax was the lead-casting: After the midnight bells pealed, after the good-luck punch had been drunk, you would toss melted bits of lead into cold water — and *your* piece would freeze into a delphic shape hinting your destiny in the new year.

The new year. In the Imperial capital the past was a magnificence, familiar and cozy. But the future? Even the near future? . . . Where was the promised, the necessary greatness? The Viennese were never on comfortable terms with the forward-turned face of time. A quaver crept even into the magisterial accents of the *Neue Freie Presse* as it assessed the local temper on the first day of 1889: "There is a general air of discontent . . . a breath of melancholy brushes through our society. The rich do not enjoy their surfeit. The poor can bear their misery less than ever. At our St. Stephen's Cathedral there is a strange and ancient tablet with the inscription, 'Here I lie, Simon Paur, ambushed and killed in treachery and in envy.' The story of his death is not known. Nobody can tell who the unfortunate Simon Paur was; but his grave may become the emblem of our city. The envy that acted as his assassin has grown into the dominant passion fermenting the populace and jeopardizing the peace of our citizens."

"Dear, good mother!" Hugo Wolf wrote on December 30. "Best wishes for the New Year. If my success gives you joy, please think as I do of the incredible miracle of the past year. It was the most fertile and therefore the happiest year of my life. In this year I composed no less than ninety-two songs and ballads, and not one is a failure. I think I may be satisfied with the year 1888. What will 1889 bring? In that year the opera whose execution I will start in a few days will be finished. . . .* If my success can color your life in a friendlier hue, then you should see everything in the rosiest glitter. My young fame is now powerfully ascendant and perhaps I will soon play the leading role in the musical world. True, it may take reviewers long to understand my thoughts because my art is too new. But I have already gained an unprejudiced public. . . . I have every right to call 1889 a year that augurs luck."

"Most Highborn and Most Noble Herr Baron Wohlzogen!" Bruckner wrote to one of his protectors in Bayreuth. "From the bottom of my soul I call out to my high sponsor on this special first day of the New Year: *Hail! Hail! Hail!* . . . The Brahms cult here is becoming something altogether incredible! Hans Richter [the conductor of the Vienna Philharmonic] is uppermost in this respect. He claims the new direction [taken by Bruckner's music] has no justification in the concert world and he does not dare — because of Hanslick — to put anything of mine on the program. . . . But I have been working since June on the Third Symphony (the "Wagner" symphony) which I have thoroughly improved. . . . Oh, if the High Immortal One [i.e., Wagner] could see it! What indescribable happiness for me!"

Arthur Schnitzler wrote only to his diary at year's end. But his entry, though short, also bore a climactic note: "December 31. New Year's Eve. Jean. (2)." Since the diary's last previous total with

---

* The opera — *Der Corregidor* — would not be written until 1895.

Jeanette had been (398), the additional (2) signified that at the start of 1889 he and the Sweet Girl had had exactly (400) ecstasies together.

His Imperial and Royal Apostolic Majesty produced what was for him a voluptuous letter. It was an outburst caused by the conjunction of Christmas and the measles. The disease had struck Frau Schratt's little son Toni, quarantining the mother along with the child. For weeks now, the Emperor would be cut off from his solace. At this point, after nearly three years of their relationship, Franz Joseph dropped the conventional *"gnädige Frau"* (gracious lady) with which he had hitherto begun all his letters.

"Meine liebe theuerste Freundin!" he wrote on December 27 —

> My dear, most precious friend! You will allow me to use this address at a moment when the awful news came at me like a thunderbolt, and when, at the thought of the long separation ahead of us, I feel so vividly how much I hold you dear. Forgive me for this perhaps unseemly emotional eruption, but I am very sad not to see you for so long and it is my only consolation to confide in you at least by letter. But of course these are all egotistic thoughts, it is above all anxiety about you and your sick Toni which grips me . . .

And a few days later, New Year's Eve, in the same tremulous vein:

> My most precious friend! . . . May all your wishes be fulfilled and may you receive only joy from your Toni. If I may speak of myself, then let me say that I wish, hope and beg of you that you will keep your friendship for me in the year 1889, that you will keep on being as infinitely good to me as you have in the past and that you will continue being lenient with me when I am contrary, but, above all, that you will have a little love for me. . . . Perhaps you will think tomorrow a little about me and pray a brief prayer for me. . . . It really is often quite hard to be a Megaliotis . . .

"Megaliotis," the Greek term for "majesty," was the Empress's nickname for him. Among the many unmajestic letters Franz

*Katharina Schratt, Court Theater comedy star, Franz
Joseph's cozy, comfortable beloved*

Joseph wrote to his precious friend, this was among the most throbbingly humble.

During the same week, in fact on the very date of his father's earlier letter, December 27, Rudolf wrote a year-end letter of his own to his very different confidant, Moritz Szeps.

> Dear Szeps . . . In international politics there is a temporary quiet. The dangers threatening us from Serbia are postponed for the moment, but this uncanny stillness gives me the impression of calm before the storm. It can't go on like that; that is my consolation. . . . My wife and I are off to Abbazia [a fashionable resort on the Adriatic Coast] today and on my return I hope to see you.

Compared with the effusions of others, this strikes a composed or at least braced and certainly perspicacious note. Yet Szeps, who knew his friend well, did not read it that way. The New Year greeting he sent back sounds like an indirect answer to an indirect cry for help. Szeps's words seem meant for someone who is both lofty and lost, so urgent is the undertone of consolation whispering beneath the louder rhetoric of obeisance.

> Your Imperial Highness!
> "Uncanny is the calm" — to quote from Your Imperial Highness's last letter — "the stillness before the storm." The past year will figure in history as The Undertakers' Year [an allusion to the death of two German Emperors, Wilhelm I and Friedrich III]. It was no more than that. But under certain circumstances that may be enough. For if all that is withered, rotten and old is removed in order to make room for the fresh and the young, then this removal is an act of renewal and rejuvenation which is necessary for the world. The undertakers of 1888 have, however, not rejuvenated or removed much, and uncanny indeed is the stillness which broods over Europe.
> What will come of all this? When will the thunderbolts of fate hammer out those decisions that will form the beginnings of a new era? The oppressiveness cannot last forever,

surely the year of change will arrive. To bear up against the oppressiveness, to keep spirit and flesh strong for the time of action, that is the task which Your Imperial Highness has set for yourself, and this task is being executed daily by you with unceasing endurance and dynamism. You never tire, as do so many others who yield to the apparently inevitable. And since the Crown Prince does not tire, we maintain our hopes in a great, glorious, free and prosperous Austria.

You, Imperial Highness, have had to experience much malice and treachery, but you have shaken it off with remarkable aplomb. It is well known that you desire great things, that you are capable of achieving them, and he who does not know it of you, certainly senses it. Therefore you are now being attacked in various ways and barriers are being thrown into your path to the future. You already have many adversaries and enemies. But you rely on yourself, on your own re-sources, on your genius, your strength and your endurance, and you may justly depend on these qualities. Add to this just a little luck — not even as much luck as your sincere admirers and friends wish you — just a bit of this luck and you will accomplish great things for the Monarchy, for our Fatherland, for your own glory and for the people attached to you . . .

Chapter 19

The year 1889 did not begin well — certainly not in a sweet-tempered vein. The weather was uneven, enervating, and the general vexatiousness closed in on the new Court Theater. There'd been those earlier complaints. Now, suddenly, three months after the theater's opening, sporadic discontent changed into concerted attack. Hugo Thimig, a pillar of the theater's ensemble, cried out against "this ornamentation-choked mausoleum which makes performing a misery for me as well as for my colleagues." And on January 9, the drama critic of the *Neue Freie Presse*, Ludwig Speidel, loosed a curse at the impersonal pomposity of the house which killed all sophisticated acting, all the more subtle modulations of speech. "The incredible fact must be faced," he wrote, "that the spoken word . . . the very soul of our dramatic art, cannot come into its own in this house. . . . Only the most drastic measures can save our Court Theater tradition. Either a new, simpler, more artistically responsive house must be built; or the theatrical space in the present house must be radically reconstructed, brick by brick."

No new New Court Theater was ever built. Not until eight years later were acoustics and sight lines improved. But even instant improvements would not have produced smiles in Vienna. Behind all that abrupt dismay was a more general apprehension: Would the capital of this old grand Empire never achieve anything that was both new and great? For how many New Year's Eves could this failure be repeated?

In the week following the New Year of 1889, the town seemed unable to manage even its most assured brilliancys: the carnival. *Fasching*, as carnival was called in Vienna, started the day of Epiphany on January 6. But this year it sputtered rather than glowed.

Of course an external reason acted as dampener. Though the death of Franz Joseph's father-in-law had taken place months ago, Limited Court Mourning was still in force. The Court balls were canceled. A blight also fell on the Industrialists' Ball. Usually blessed with the "All Highest Presence," it was the most splendid of all the nonaristocratic balls, with the most expensive yet most sought-after tickets. Millionaires and notables who were genealogically inadequate to come to the Emperor at Court balls had their day at this affair, when the Emperor came to *them*.

Everyone knew that Katharina Schratt's first informal and fateful conversation with His Majesty had taken place at the Industrialists' Ball of 1885. But in 1889 Court Mourning precluded Franz Joseph's attendance. Tickets proved unsalable. The Polish Ball suffered a similar fate. It was another evening whose glory was nothing without The Presence.

Disappointment rippled down through all the strata: from the sybarite *Salonblatt*, which complained of the lack of fiacres roistering through the streets after midnight, to the pawnbrokers in the poorer districts who didn't do the business they'd counted on. The carnival affected every street corner. In Vienna there was no station of life, no concierges' fraternity, no sanitation men's guild which did not have its own ball. And if the mood were right, no decent working man would hesitate to pawn his silver watch in order to buy his daughter a new fan or his wife a new fichu for their particular carnival celebration. *If* the mood were right. A lot of silver watches in a lot of pawnbroker windows would have indicated a *feschen Fasching* — a fun carnival.

After New Year's Day of 1889 the silver-watch index read very low in the pawnshops of Vienna. But soon a harbinger of *fesch* was heard in the land. The Hairdressers' League proclaimed far and wide that Archduke Ludwig Viktor would send the band of the Archduke-Ludwig-Viktor Regiment to the Coiffeurs' Dance. The gesture intimated that though the sovereign himself could not attend the carnival, some members of the Imperial Family might. And things started to look better fast.

The Vienna Skating Club, which at first had difficulty disposing of tickets for its costume party, noticed a strong rise in demand. Indeed, a week before the event, the club could afford to be choosy about would-be participants; it announced that hunting attire would not be acceptable because it was too commonplace a costume.

On January 15, the club produced the carnival's first success. Electric lights and Bengal illuminations flickered over the ice where a real Siamese prince, furred-up as an Eskimo, glided about arm in arm with the real Countess Apponyi dressed as Yum-Yum of *The Mikado*. Rosa Papier, the great soprano (interpreter of new talents like Hugo Wolf), became a Biedermeier doll that did lovely figure eights, while a whole slew of chimneysweeps pursued polka-dotted red mushrooms. In actual life these skating fancies were for the most part money barons and real-estate comtesses. And what did that matter?

Soon it seemed as though the city, wanting to make up for its earlier dejection, rushed into abandonment. It took its pleasures freely at the Opera Redoute, once the classic bluebloods' revel. In 1889 as in other recent years, the aristocracy kept to itself in the opera boxes to watch the *haute bourgeoisie* below. But how unburgherlike the saturnalia down there! For this night — and for this one night only — a parquet floor had been laid across the top of the orchestra seats of the Court Opera so as to form one continuous level with the stage. Edi Strauss led his waltz orchestra in the middle. Hussar bands fluted and fifed in the promenade halls. Rainbow blizzards of confetti blew. Gentlemen cruised in tailcoats and top hats. Ladies must come masked, and that January dozens tripped about as Sarah Bernhardt, who had made such an exciting exit from town.

As usual, the disguised sex took a gamut of liberties with the naked-faced one. In the scented melee any decolleté domino was free to touch any gentleman with her fan; to wipe a drop of sweat from his cheek; to steal his top hat; to flirt or flee or both at once; to invite him to a waltz, tease him into a goblet of wine or a caviar canapé; to tantalize him over her identity, play scullion or princess, whore or nun; to bandy iridescent ambiguities as they strolled, arm-linked strangers, along candlelit and champagne-splashed marble; and then, if she wished, to stay with him and come face to face when midnight tolled and all masks fell.

The next highlight came on January 22 with the Hotelkeepers' Ball. Last year the Crown Prince's presence as its sponsor had provoked a sumptuous exorbitance in the ladies' costumes. This year it was feared that the expense necessary to breast the competition would discourage many from doing any breasting at all. Groundless pessimism. Rudolf was absent because of mourning, but he did send his First Lord Chamberlain Count Bombelles, and the sumptuousness was there in great numbers. So was Edi Strauss, conducting. So were Herr and Frau Sacher of the hotel and torte, laughing together and thus dispelling dismal rumors about their marriage. So were the unexcelled ladies' favors, this year's being silver sachet balls.

Even such merriment was overshadowed by the *Donaudampfschifffahrtsgesellschaftsball*, an evening with the longest name and the most panoramic decor. For this Danube Steamship Company's Ball the entire premises of Harmony Hall turned into a giant steamship, complete with the swash of real water, the sounding of real foghorns, with sailors, sea nymphs, and a waltz band revolving vertically on a titanic paddle wheel. At the height of the nocturnal "voyage" the real Chief Admiral of the Austro-Hungarian Navy appeared on the "bridge" and watched gentlemen launch a number of ladies in "lifeboats" into the "sea." But nobody really disembarked before 6 A.M.

It wasn't only the upper classes that caught the brightening beat. On January 15, the Master Bakers' Ball swept through the halls of the Sofien Caterers. Male salt sticks whirled about with cleavaged apple strudels to an orchestra in chef hats, white aprons and black bow ties. "The gayest evening yet," said Max Schlesinger, the *Wiener Tagblatt*'s senior ball critic, a man of uncompromising standards.

A few days later the workers' district of Hernals had its famous Laundrymaids' Ball. Not just dressed-down duchesses came to frolic, but real pinch-'em laundrymaids in their working clothes of sleeveless bodices, pert head kerchiefs, and striped stockings visible to the knee during the faster waltzes. The aristocracy adored finding little adventures here.

And then toward the end of January started the Gschnas Balls, with which Vienna's carnival outdistanced all other cities still further. *Gschnas* was an ultralocal word, pronounceable and comprehensible only to the Viennese. Perhaps the closest semantic kin of *Gschnas* was the original meaning of the English *glamour* — namely, false magic. It was the kind of magic for which the Viennese had a heavenly weakness. Run by the city's artists' associations, the *Gschnas* fests celebrated with many-colored genius the defeat of gray reality.

In January 1889 the outstanding *Gschnas* was the Fourth Dimension Ball, permitting no costumes or decorations that were even remotely rational or true to "regular" life. A lovely rose garden bloomed upside down from the ceiling with pre-Dadaist blitheness. At a banquet, lovely live witches in negligees rubbed up against knights made of solid wax. In a room called "Peking by the Danube," scenes from Austrian history were enacted in the style of Chinese Opera. Waltzes jumbled into gongs and twangs.

Throughout the city there was neither end nor limit to the *Faschingslust* — to the carnival-urge — to phantasmagoria, to the obsessive joy in sheer ecstatic make-believe. In the general stores, the food stalls up front were replaced by stands full of Japanese lanterns, masks, dominoes and fans. Dress shops turned into costume bazaars. At St. Stephen's Square before the cathedral, the huge Rothberger clothing emporium stayed open all night to sell or rent tailcoats at any hour until dawn, with fitters at the ready — except, of course, for the night when the fitters had their own Fitters' Ball on January 20.

The ball season was also profitable for businessmen like Sigi Ernst, a name so proverbial that many of his advertisements did not need to specify what merchandise he sold. Everyone knew that Herr Ernst offered the best selection of condoms in the Imperial capital. On January 27, he informed the readers of the *Neue Freie Presse* that "in response to requests from his estimable clientele" he was opening an additional, more discreet entrance to his establishment in the inner courtyard of Kärntnerstrasse 45. We do not know whether he enjoyed the custom of Dr. Arthur Schnitzler (whose diary records a total of 419 unions with Jeanette by January 31) but one senses that the crush of business left Herr Ernst little time for waltzing.

A number of physicians were also a bit pressed in savoring the joys of carnival, being so preoccupied with servicing its sores. Their advertisements mingled with those for masks and costumes. The same January 27 issue of the *Neue Freie Presse*, for example, featured a Dr. Hartmann's announcement that a second "sequestered" waiting room had been set up at his office on Lobkowitz Platz 1, to accommodate patients with "secret diseases."

For Theodor Herzl that January was precisely what it was not for most others. For him it was a rather straitlaced time. He loved going to balls, both social ones and professional like that of Concordia, the journalists' fraternity. Yet he always went with his "little" Julie. He was monogamous half a year before his marriage. In 1889 a *Fasching* night out meant to him not dissipation but dressing up to match some magnificent ensemble of his fiancée.

He had, at any rate, little time for revelry. His ambition was still to have a play produced in the new Court Theater's first season. But Hugo Wittmann, his co-author of their half-finished comedy *Love Poachers*, found himself overburdened. Wittmann, as chief cultural correspondent for the *Neue Freie Presse*, had had to deliver copy on Sarah Bernhardt as well as on scores of other esthetic urgencies throughout the winter. Time wasn't the only lack. Presently Wittmann saw no way of solving the principal problem in *Love Poachers* — namely to lend a stale boardwalk intrigue a fresh twist — and wanted to give up his side of the partnership. Herzl had to write him a panicked letter: "I couldn't let you go under any circumstances. . . . You have pulled our common cart, as I have, pulled it through the worst. We cannot part before we have either failed or succeeded."

In the end Wittmann persevered, not knowing that Herzl had become, secretly, so doubtful about *Love Poachers* that he thought of shifting from part-time dramatist to full-time journalist. He decided to approach the *Berliner Tagblatt*, which had published him before. In a carefully drafted proposal to its editor he noted that he had been offered fifty gulden per article from Moritz Szeps at the *Wiener Tagblatt*, that he received forty gulden per piece from the *Neue Freie Presse*, but that he would accept less from the *Berliner Tagblatt* in exchange for a formal, long-range commitment appointing him cultural correspondent in Vienna.

The letter was never sent. At the last moment Herzl decided to go on risking it as a split-level free-lancer, half comedy manufacturer, half serious feuilletonist. He would keep up the *fortwursteln* after all: he wrote a long, complex, wonderfully stylish and trenchantly perceptive defense of Zola's latest novel (*Le Rêve*) in the *Neue Freie Presse*; and spent Christmas and New Year's finagling new plot complications for *Love Poachers*.

And so Herzl danced few nights away during the carnival's first month. He and Wittmann were toiling their play to a finish. Officially, *Love Poachers* was not submitted to the Court Theater until February 4. But Wittmann, being culture chief of the *Neue Freie Presse*, was rather cozy with the theater management and the play reached the *Direktor's* office informally around the third week of January.

The verdict: all very well and good, but let the authors reword some of their suggestive language.

This judgment was handed down while carnality ranged barefaced through *Fasching* Vienna, sporting frankly at balls, in newspaper advertisements, on street corners. But on the Imperial and Royal stage even the most indirect mention of sex was impossible. No matter how compromising the intentions of a libertine character, his lines must be lily-white if spoken in the Court Theater.

Herzl and Wittmann did some quick laundering. Example: scene three of the second act. Here a father and a daughter (their true relationship unknown in the resort hotel that is the setting) pretend to elope together; actually the father wants to help the daughter to escape from her engagement to a man she loathes. The "unexpurgated" scene:

> THE FATHER (to the hotel concierge): The next express to Cologne leaves at one A.M. doesn't it?
>
> CONCIERGE: Yes sir, at one A.M.
>
> FATHER: I need a sleeping-car compartment for the lady and one for me.
>
> CONCIERGE: Very well, sir. I shall reserve by telephone instantly.

Mentioning a man, a woman, and sleeping compartments in *one* sentence? The Court Theater regarded conversation of the sort ribald, and never mind how chaste the framing circumstances. Messrs. Herzl and Wittmann had to clean up the sound of the situation. Their new lines read:

> FATHER: The next express for Cologne leaves at one A.M., doesn't it?
> CONCIERGE: Yes sir. At one A.M.
> FATHER: I need one place in the ladies' car, and one place for me, first class.

After such changes the Court Theater accepted the play, with an anonymous by-line as the authors requested. It was scheduled for early production and indeed rehearsals began within a month. The Court Theater retained its purity, Herzl exulted, the carnival swelled on and so did the boom in condoms and secret diseases.

Was Vienna overdoing it? Wasn't there too much laxness? And too much official hypocrisy under whose cover the laxness continued uncorrected? A few citizens thought so. It was an opinion shared, for example, by some of the older fathers sitting around the rim of the International Trade Ball, a substantial burghers' festival which in theory was not supposed to be overdone.

The fathers thought that this season's *Fasching*, which had started so slowly, now looked as if it were accelerating too fast. It was getting a bit out of hand. Where was Steffi?

The fathers shook beards in unison with Steffi's father. Where in God's name was Steffi? Steffi had had her dance card filled out nicely in advance by young men, all of whom were known and well regarded. And she had danced off nicely with Partner No. 1 on Dance No. 1. But then the Gentlemen's Island had gone into action.

The Gentlemen's Island consisted of a dense black cloud of tailcoats at the center of the dance floor, an unpredictable core around which the dancers turned. Every so often a tailcoat would shoot out toward a pair, touch heels, bow, and take the lady away from her partner. Partner No. 1 had lost Steffi to such a depredation. And that was all right, that was *Fasching*, it couldn't be helped.

But when would the predator return her? Or had he in turn lost her to yet another rogue from the Gentlemen's Island? It was now Dance No. 4. What was going on?

This year many Steffis seemed to be getting lost more often and staying lost longer. The other fathers didn't like it any more than Steffi's. It was an example of what was going wrong in the city. They began to talk about it, lighting grave cigars. They agreed it was a lack of discipline. That's what kept the Empire from progress: a lack of discipline in morals and in politics. Elsewhere the carnival proceeded in saner fashion, and so did life in general. Other countries were on the move; right now in January they were executing cunning strategies, while Austria whirled about heedless. The recent engagement of Princess Alice of Hesse, now there was an instance. The fathers saw clearly through that one. They agreed that it was Bismarck himself who had sabotaged the Princess's tender relationship with Prince Battenberg, the Austrophile. Why? So that she could become affianced to the Crown Prince of Russia. It was an alarming hint of Berlin's tilt toward St. Petersburg, away from the Austrian alliance. Why did Parliament bicker instead of legislate when even Japan was about to regenerate itself with a new constitution modeled on Prussia's? And speaking of Germany, that new military agreement between the Germans and the Italians — did anyone at the Foreign Ministry here in Vienna keep an eye on that? Who paid attention in Austria? What waltzing statesman or goblet-happy politician? Except for the ever sober and watchful Emperor — poor man, long may he live! — who couldn't attend to everything himself? And who had, uh, Steffis, though not necessarily of Steffi's sex, in his own family?

But the less said about that, the better. The fathers exchanged glances of deep knowledge and dark resignation, grimly content to share such problems with the All Highest father. Then they addressed themselves to Schönerer, the right-wing fanatic who took a good point like the excess of Jews in the intellectual professions and exploited it for hysterical self-promotion. No telling what unrest the man might create now that he had just been let out of jail. Then there were the Social Democrats who had just organized themselves into a party with a near-seditious manifesto condemning private property and class privileges. Not to mention those hotheads in Budapest lately who were trying to abolish German as the language of command in the Imperial and Royal Army. The Hungarians were out to destroy the Monarchy's most important unifying force. And where was Steffi?

Yes, where? The mothers wanted to know, too. They kept their gold-handled lorgnettes poised for a sign of the girl. It was getting to be a bit much. What had happened to Steffi? The fathers banded together to search for her at the buffet. The mothers sipped tea and blamed Johann Strauss. In their youth this sort of thing had happened rarely. And in *their* mothers' day — the pre-waltz day, never. The minuet, the quadrille, the cotillion, hadn't that been much more graceful, easy, thrilling and yet safe? The ladies shook their coiffures. They could remember the waltz when it had still been hopped instead of sinuously glided as it was now. This polka-like hopping betrayed the waltz's true origin. It came from the peasants! The ladies recalled their parents' shock when those bouncy embraces had broken the gallant symmetry of a minuet into rank couples, if not couplings. But of course — and the ladies were all of one mind here — it was just the lasciviousness of the waltz which had attracted the nobility. That's why Johann Strauss had lent his divine melodies to the waltz: to please the aristocrats and, incidentally, to corrupt youth — heavens, there was Steffi at last.

High time, too. The gas chandeliers had already been turned down for the last five half-lit numbers. But there was Steffi, looking excited and exhausted at the same time, the egret feather in her hair a bit askew, pressed close to some inscrutable mustache from the Gentlemen's Island. If Papa saw her! Perhaps it was best that Papa himself had, for some reason, still not returned from the buffet with the other fathers. Mama kept her eye on Steffi and shook her head over Johann Strauss.

Johann Strauss could have shaken his head over himself. If the *Fasching* was anybody's, it was his. And yet it was not for him. He did not go to any of the thousands of balls where many hundreds of thousands of couples swirled to the melodies which had first sounded in the solitude of his study. He never danced himself, did not know how. He had become too rich and too preeminent to be a regular conductor like his brother Edi. And he was too tired to undergo again and again the Johann Strauss role of the honored guest. Above all, that resistant opera of his had to be seen through, and the best time to get on with it was at night.

But at least he was over his "phase." He could bear the sight of other people again. So the billiards instructor came back to the palais in the Igelgasse to improve Adele's cue positions for a better game with him before lunch. Afterwards the cartooning teacher arrived to show Johann how to make a funny drawing of Johannes Brahms. Various friends called for an evening of tarok in the Coffeehouse Room.

After they left, and while the city reveled, he sat alone by the harmonium, playing and penciling, penciling and playing another aria for his opera *Pazman*.

When he did go out, he avoided the carnival and went to the Ronacher, the big cabaret-revue theater.

"Unfortunately I've already ordered a box at the Ronacher," he wrote his friend Adalbert Goldschmidt who had proposed a dinner with Anton Bruckner. "I would like to cancel it for your and Bruckner's sake. But I cannot change my plans because I have a rendezvous there [at the Ronacher] with friends. I hate the very idea of such an evening. Just now I have a lot of work, and such get-togethers always last much longer than seems necessary. They keep me from my task. Evenings like this start at the Ronacher and end at Brady's [Brady's Wintergarten, a popular nightclub] and usually don't see me returning home before dawn — which I hate. Then I get very upset over my frivolity, and get so very angry at what can no longer be undone that I can't accomplish a thing in the days which follow. I just pace up and down in my study and can't concentrate. I can only work when I have no petty upsets. . . ."

The carnival lit up Professor Bruckner's isolation. After his Christmas sojourn in Kremsmünster he was back in Vienna, teaching at the Conservatory, playing the organ at the Palace Chapel, re-reworking the Third Symphony, sketching out the Ninth, and being alone. He saw very few of his colleagues. Johann Strauss was one of his remote celebrity acquaintances; but when plans were made for a meeting, something always happened to abort them.

He suspected that "something" might be the Brahms-Hanslick clique, his shrewd enemies with whom Johann Strauss cultivated friendships. He feared he wouldn't feel welcome at most of the city's *Fasching* affairs. He felt very awkward with the sophisticated dissipation at which Vienna was so good.

On January 11, Bruckner did go to one affair: the Upper Austrian Foresters' Ball at the Blumensaal. As the city's most prestigious Upper Austrian, he had been invited as honorary guest. For the occasion he had asked his Frau Kachelmayer to fish out black socks instead of the customary white from the disorder of his clothes cupboard. The foresters were mostly employees of Viennese magnates with Upper Austrian possessions. In a way they were salaried hicks like himself; they spoke his dialect. At their urging he finally took a dirndled maiden by the waist and for the length of an oom-pah-pah *Ländler* bobbed around the hall with her.

Then he was done, thank God. That January he was more uncertain with women than ever. During his Christmas stay at Kremsmünster another adorable young girl had confounded his blood. Her name was Mathilde Fessl, a lawyer's daughter, and she had asked him nice questions about music in the most pleasing way. But then they'd started talking about Lent. And he couldn't believe his ears. She was a *freethinker!* An infidel! An atheist girl of seventeen! To Bruckner the world was more incomprehensible than ever. No wonder it was the kind of world that celebrated Brahms but acted so meanly towards him. It was not the kind of world which set him dancing.

Brahms did no dancing at all, his countless ball invitations notwithstanding. *Fasching* amused him, as the Viennese did in general, but it was much too unbuttoned a joy for his North German temper. Besides, he never changed his regimen of rising at 5 A.M. And even if the carnival had kept more sensible hours, say, right after his nap in the early afternoon, Brahms would still have been too busy for extracurricular gaieties in January 1889.

There was fancy work to be done. Joseph Joachim, the violin

virtuoso, was in town again, preparing another Brahms concert. The composer himself would accompany on the piano in his newly published Violin Sonata in D-minor. For such personal appearances Brahms left absolutely nothing unprepared, down to the bows he planned to take. For these he preferred the conductor to pull him, with gentle force, out of his hiding place behind the curtain. He liked to tune his applause as if it were a fine piano. That was *his* carnival.

During *Fasching* Dr. Sigmund Freud hid himself with much more conviction. He was more of an outsider than ever, taking no part at all in the carnival. The city sang with a million throats, danced with millions of legs, but he was deaf to rhythm. Quite literally. Frau Freud suggested that they take advantage of post-Christmas sales and buy a piano, so that little Mathilde could play it one day. But the master of the house laid down a veto which lasted into his most prosperous years. No piano, no violin, nothing of the kind. He proscribed music in the world's most musical city.

Carnival disrupted his one conviviality, the Saturday tarok game. Dr. Rie and Dr. Königswärt, card partners and fellow physicians at the Pediatric Institute, went to balls on some tarok nights. Freud had no room for *Fasching* in his budget. He had to husband money and time for more essential concerns. At this season his late-afternoon walks around the Ringstrasse often took place in a darkness crowded and brightened by people in evening dress on their way to excitement. "What a stage for the sparkling, beauty-minded, thoughtless world. . . . It's a marvelous tumult in which to be alone. . . ." A teenage Freud had written that about Vienna's World's Fair in 1873. Now it was still true for him as he strode through the carnival of 1889. He'd arrive in his study at the Maria Theresienstrasse, a continent away from the masked faces that passed laughing below his second-floor window. And the paper on hysteria, waiting for him at his desk, removed him still further. Not even friendly colleagues like Breuer or Chrobak could keep him company here. His paper took him on a journey longer and more unauthorized than he realized himself.

He began that paper as a neurologist. He ended it as a psycholo-

*Jeanette Heger, accommodating and much betrayed,
the original of the "Sweet Girl" character Arthur
Schnitzler made a byword in his stories and plays. In
1888–89 Jeanette accommodated Arthur to four
hundred sixty-four acts of love.*

gist. In crossing this watershed he had to separate himself from the great fathers of neuropathology — Helmholtz, Brücke, Meynert — titans whose books had been his scripture, whose ideas he had admired. To them, and therefore to nineteenth-century science, man's consciousness was firmly embedded in the anatomy of the nervous system. Freud started his paper with that premise intact. But as he went on he arrived at an insight which subverted the ground on which his mentors stood: He saw that consciousness was a world unto itself, a world of depths that could outwit and over-rule the anatomical verities of traditional medicine.

Freud worked on this paper before, during and after the carnival of 1889. The title: "Quelques Considerations pour une Étude Comparative des Paralysies Motrices, Organiques et Hysteriques" ("Some Points in a Comparative Study of Organic and Hysterical Paralyses"). He wrote it in French, perhaps logically so, since he aimed to publish it in *Archives de Neurologie*, edited by Jean Charcot. But the mind is indeed a devil of deviousness that sneaks essence into incidentals. It was no accident that Freud lived piano-less in a rigorously musical town. That he wrote in a language no one else was talking around him. And that he, apparently deaf to the abandonments of *Fasching*, had begun to listen to an unheard-of wantonness inside the soul.

A thousand meters down along the Ringstrasse, Arthur Schnitzler did have traffic with *Fasching*. There was no way to avoid it, even if he wanted to. It poured right into his house. On New Year's Day his father gave a house ball. The date was a bit premature since officially carnival didn't begin until five days later. But the fete was held to toast the forthcoming marriage of Arthur's sister Gisela. And when Privy Councillor Professor Dr. Johann Schnitzler invited, the world came. Fiacres with the great stars of Court Opera and Court Theater drew up to Burgring 1. Charlotte Wolter and Katharina Schratt were there, as were others of Professor Schnitzler's patients and friends. Naturally Arthur attended. But he could not bring his sweet girl, Jeanette.

Arthur kept busy with other *Fasching* matters, also directed by his father. Professor Schnitzler, in his capacity as head of the Polyclinic, had charged his son with preparations for the Polyclinic Ball and all the tediousness that involved. Early in January, tedious became downright unpleasant. It turned out that a member of Arthur's ball committee, acting on his own, had placed an advertisement for the affair in the _Deutsches Volksblatt_, an anti-Semitic sheet. Young Schnitzler called a meeting and after some ugly exchanges obtained a vote which declared the man's action arbitrary and out of order. The affair was settled . . . for the moment.

At the same time something more cheerful happened. On January 15, Arthur's first contribution to a prominent literary weekly broke into print. _An der schönen blauen Donau_ finally published "My Friend Ypsilon." It was a slight, arch piece about an oversensitive writer who in the end falls victim to the nemesis he'd invented for his protagonist. Oddly enough, the opening of the tale describes this author as being "sad when he was working on a sentimental theme . . . for example . . . about a prince who died of a broken skull . . ."

At the month's end that last phrase would take on reverberations sounding to the ends of the Empire.

Chapter 20

The final week of January, Rudolf's name kindled a sensation in Budapest politics even though he himself remained in Vienna.

Leading up to the shock was a more familiar overture, namely Hungarian students screaming for their country's autonomy. At Budapest University, demonstrations had been as regular as lectures. This January, however, some fire-eaters shouted for the end of the common customs union between the two halves of the Empire. The demand struck at the lifelines that kept the Dual Monarchy breathing.

Newspapers and coffeehouses buzzed in Vienna. Then it seemed as though the commotion would subside again. *Fasching* waltzes closed over the unsuitable assonance. Only people like Gustav Mahler were seriously inconvenienced by it. That's why State Secretary Baron Bernizcky kept a close watch on him from Vienna. After all the Baron, in charge of all of His Majesty's theaters everywhere, had appointed the young Austrian head of the Budapest Royal Opera House. Nobody knew better than Bernizcky that in those overheated precincts music was apt to turn political if not downright martial. Mahler had to run his Opera as though it were a castle under siege. So far, thank heaven, the boy was doing well.

Actually Mahler had engaged the problem at the very outset of

his tenure. Magyar irritabilities must be placated; Magyar caprices, pampered. Mahler reined in his own touchiness. He took Hungarian language lessons and made the most of two Jewish Hungarian friends who helped him assimilate. He had Moritz Warman decorate his hotel apartment *à la Hongroise*. And Sigmund Singer, through his connection to the Hungarian nobility (less anti-Semitic than its Austrian counterpart), briefed Mahler on the cultural tastes of local aristocrats. Within five days of his arrival in Budapest in the fall of 1888, Mahler dined with Count Albert Apponyi, a power in the Budapest Parliament.

Yes, in Vienna Bernizcky could report good things to the Emperor who was also King of all Magyars. With characteristic speed Mahler had learned to adopt Hungarian urgencies overnight and promptly voiced them in his first speech to his staff. Henceforward, he said, there would be no more truckling to foreign stars at the Budapest Opera. No more prima ballerinas like Madame dell'Era, who had demanded and received a six-horse gala coach with a Negro page at her disposal for her entire three-week engagement. No indulging a Pauline Lucca who would only sing if eight new costumes were made specially for her according to her bizarre specifications. No more foreign-star cult. From now on the Royal Budapest Opera House would develop a Hungarian ensemble and draw more on Hungarian talent in singing, dancing, designing and composing.

Almost instantly Mahler had managed to initiate the magyarizing of the casts for the fall productions. By January the house was in a fury of activity under the leadership of this gnarled young prodigy, this odd little Austrian giant, with his jerky-gaited hurry, his stuttering eloquence, his driving ubiquity. Official Vienna noted it all with satisfaction.

He was bending the stupendous range of his energies to a task that demanded them: the creation, for the first time ever, of a Ring Cycle sung in Hungarian. He didn't let himself be distracted even by the Vienna premiere of his own opera, *Die Drei Pintos*, on January 18, nor by the rather viperish treatment he received at the hands of the Viennese press.

One would have thought that the Viennese reviewers could —
like State Secretary Bernizcky — appreciate that the man's mu-
sicianship had smoothed Austro-Hungarian relations. One might
have hoped that the carnival at least had sweetened the critics'
tempers. Not a bit. They were in no *Fasching* mood when it came
to Mahler's contribution to the Weber-Mahler opera.

The Vienna *Salonblatt* despised Mahler for "exploiting with his
concoctions the divinely gifted author of *Der Freischütz*." The
Abendpost accused Mahler of monotonous rhythms and a pseudo-
Wagnerian garishness which distorted the charm of Weber's melodies. The supreme Hanslick in the *Neue Freie Presse* allowed that
"Herr August [sic] Mahler" showed some skill in orchestration
and in the mimicking of several Weber idioms. But he sniffed at
Mahler's cumbrous use of percussion and found his brass tones
heavy for a light opera like *Die Drei Pintos*. He also noted that the
public seemed rather bored during the second act.

Mahler hadn't even come to Vienna for the occasion — all too
wisely as it turned out. He forged ahead with his Ring Cycle in
Budapest. But here, too, the critics started to complain. The Royal
Opera was being magyarized, yes. But that meant the banishment
of the very divas who had given the house a cosmopolitan glitter
and pulled in the landed grandees from their *puszta* manors. Now
the grandees no longer came so often, for what was being offered
was just plain good music. The Princesses Esterházy and the Princesses Palffy, if they did appear at all, no longer dressed up as much.

That was one side of the carping. On the other, nationalists
growled that this new German-speaking conductor imposed the
ultra-Teutonic Wagner on the Magyar tongue while Hungarian
opera composers were still being criminally neglected.

Official Vienna now had less reason to rejoice. Mahler forged
ahead. He couldn't help it if Princess Esterházy wore her second-
best stomacher to *Rigoletto*. Nor was it his fault that neither Mozart
nor Verdi nor Wagner had been born in Debrecen. He persisted,
ignoring some very sour ironies. For example, one of his nationalist
scourges, the Budapest journalist Maurus Vavrinecz, had so poor
a command of Hungarian that he wrote his anti-Mahler anti-

Gustav Mahler
1888

Gustav Mahler at twenty-eight, the new director of the Court Opera at Budapest, where this photograph was taken

German maledictions in German, then had them translated for publication in the fanatically Magyar journal *Fövárosi Lapok*.

Mahler forged ahead. Day and night he rehearsed the Ring Cycle; lived, slept, ate in the opera house: threatened, begged, seduced, overwhelmed his singers and musicians. On the twenty-sixth of January he got into his tailcoat, shuffled to the lectern, bowed, and lifted the baton for the world premiere of *The Valkyries* in Hungarian. The music surged, the Rhine Maidens soared — and the audience screamed in panic. One of the Maidens suddenly sagged in the ropes. She had fainted in midair because she had seen flames licking toward her. A fire had broken out on stage.

People cried, some stampeded. Mahler, monomaniacal as ever, kept conducting and compelled the orchestra to contain the terror with the sheer force of great sound. The fire was put out. The performance proceeded. Mahler forged ahead.

At the final curtain the entire house stood up to shout its homage as only Hungarians can. In the newspapers the next day most critics jubilated. Even Vavrinecz's translated gruffness had to dole out some praise.

The glory was Mahler's in Budapest that week. Yet Rudolf, indirectly, dominated the news. Suddenly opera was upstaged by Parliament.

On the twenty-fifth of January — that is, on the eve of the magyarization of Richard Wagner — Count Stefan (Pista) Károlyi rose to make an astounding speech to his fellow deputies. He attacked the new Army Bill which required Hungarian reserve officers to pass a German-language examination. Others opposed the bill, too, of course. But — *Károlyi!* Károlyi was known to be among Rudolf's closest hunting companions. In fact, the Budapest papers ran his speech together with the report that he had been asked by the Crown Prince to host a reception for a common friend returning from an African safari.

Until now the Crown Prince had publicly and passionately upheld German as the single, unifying language of command in the motley-tongued Empire. Count Károlyi would never assume the contrary view without his high friend's encouragement. Had

Rudolf joined the Magyar nationalists? Was the rumor true that he would let himself be crowned Hungarian King? That he would turn against Franz Joseph and take away the royalty from his Imperial and Royal father? What had happened to Rudolf?

Chapter 21

Many things had happened to the Crown Prince. Among these the most insidious might have been a twinge of hope.

He had spent the final days of 1888 in Austro-Hungarian winter chic at Abbazia, the Monarchy's Cannes on the Adriatic. It was warm there and sunny and very archducal and dull. Orchids, palms, exotic shrubbery ornamented the gardens of the Villa Angiolina where the Crown Princess resided and where he could stand it for barely forty-eight hours. He sat through the ennui of one soiree with the Grand Duke of Toscana and went on the obligatory trip on Archduke Johann's yacht *Bessie*. Then all the talk about horse races and dog breeding and King Milan's old bedroom problems with Queen Natalie in Serbia became too much. On the twenty-ninth of December he took the night train back to Vienna.

In the capital the cold air pricked him into new life. He did not yet take flight into new trysts with Mary Vetsera. He felt like standing his ground. On January 1, an Army Command Conference took place to discuss revisions in promotion procedure. He was the Inspector General but his presence had not been requested because (so the War Minister explained) His Imperial Highness was thought to be in Abbazia. Well, His Imperial Highness was no longer in Abbazia but appeared, invited or not, at the conference. He spoke out in favor of curtailing aristocratic privilege as a factor in rank promotion. There seemed to be the impression that the generals listened. On January 2, he answered cheerfully New Year's greetings from Berthold Frischauer, Moritz Szeps's right hand at the *Tagblatt*: "May the year 1889 not be too bad for all of us. May it bring us stirring, interesting months. I hope we shall meet again this year on a few interesting political expeditions."

Yet the first expedition he was summoned to was apolitical, uninteresting, debilitating. He had to join the Emperor's hunt at Mürzsteg in the province of Styria. Rudolf liked the chase, but not with his father's retinue, which consisted of just the kind of archducal dunderpates Rudolf had escaped in Abbazia. The Emperor's formality with him, and the various highnesses' endless asininities, pressed on his nerves. Just two years ago, on this very shoot in Mürzsteg he had almost shot his father by mistake.

This time the Mürzsteg hunt passed harmlessly, except to animals. It was on Rudolf's return to Vienna on the sixth that January turned difficult. Carnival had begun. This year it flung over his shoulders a sort of epauletted straitjacket.

The season was much more oppressive for him than in previous years. Usually Emperor and Crown Prince would appear at a number of balls together, an assignment not altogether onerous for Rudolf. At least his father would never linger on such occasions. As soon as Franz Joseph had done his duty at the *cercle* (the reception), having strolled the round, having extended the favor of minimal chats, he would turn to the ball president with the ritual nine concluding words: "*Es war sehr schön. Es hat mich sehr gefreut.*" "It was very nice. I enjoyed it very much." Then His Majesty would depart to fanfares along an avenue of bowed heads. Afterward Rudolf could either leave himself, free for the rest of the night, or stay on without the constriction of the All Highest presence.

In January 1889, however, Court Mourning eliminated all balls from Franz Joseph's schedule. Instead the monarch gave a great number of dinners which Rudolf must attend in their entirety. In addition, Franz Joseph instructed his son to host further dinners himself. And that was even harder for a Crown Prince already wracked by protocol and emptiness.

Again and again he had to sit all evening long tethered to one gilded chair or another, bound over to the wrinkled prattle of some duchess to his right, some jeweled bore to his left. Highnesses from abroad thronged to Vienna for the season and he had to labor through the posturings of high hospitality. On the sixth of January he must give a dinner for Leopold of Bavaria. On the night of the seventh he must take Leopold to the Ronacher Theater for a cabaret revue he had seen three times before. The evening after that must be spent at his father's state table; the Emperor was entertaining Russian potentates. On the night following he must dine the Russians — the Russians whom he so hated, of all people — at his own apartments.

And that was just the beginning. More princes had announced their visits. He became the prisoner of his Lord Chamberlain's schedule, of sashed, bemedaled drudgery. Court dinners, diplomatic dinners, cabinet dinners also lay ahead. And as if that weren't enough, Crown Princess Stephanie arrived from Abbazia on the ninth. She just adored playing the hostess with tiara and long train. One could count on her to prolong hours excruciating to Rudolf.

Sometimes during those endless evenings he managed to stroll away for a quick glance from the window. Outside, the *Fasching* ranged through square and street, free as the wind. Figures flashed up in the lantern light, in the masks of their dreams. People outside were playing tag with their most drastic fantasies. He, the Crown Prince, who was himself the fantasy of many others, could only go back to the confinement of his dinner seat.

The middle of the month brought other Army Command Conferences, this time on a revision of drill. Again Rudolf made sure to participate. He spoke up, and his Uncle Albrecht, the Archduke and Field Marshal, gave a slight smile. It was to Albrecht's smile, not to Rudolf's words, that the generals responded. Their orders were to salute and to ignore the heir apparent.

The inanity of his vacuum became less and less endurable. He had a puissant mind, made more powerful still by an excellent

The "Empire Salon" in Rudolf's palace apartments, where he had to give the ponderous receptions that so bored him

education. He had an imperial temper and the impatience of an unemployed talent of thirty. Everywhere people hymned his charm, his grace, the certainty with which he would lift his realm to greatness — someday. But right now he must do nothing, touch nothing, say nothing, think nothing, move nothing. He was charged up and tuned up, and forced to glisten in emptiness, a coroneted marionette.

Politically his impotence continued. In Serbia, for example, King Milan, the crumbling Austrian satrap, crumbled still further. But the Austrian government did not — as Rudolf advised in still more memos on the subject — shift support to a more popular alternative. Here, too, the Crown Prince must look forward, helplessly, to inheriting yet another avoidable danger.

Even his social position was laughable. He was the Emperor's first and most glamorous subject. Yet he could not sponsor a ball for his favorite cause. Together with Vienna's great surgeon Dr. Theodor Billroth he had founded the Rudolfiner Association bearing his name. It aimed to provide nursing care outside the limitations and prejudices of the Catholic Sisters who had controlled nursing almost exclusively so far. Despite resistance from clerical forces around the Emperor, the Rudolfiner had become a respectable institution. But it had never obtained all the funding it needed. The camarilla undercut it quietly and effectively. Rudolf, at whose feet were laid the protectorships of numberless fetes, deserving and undeserving, this same Rudolf found himself unable to launch one carnival event on behalf of his Rudolfiner.

Those were the walls that shut him in. He was growing tired of pushing against them. He no longer used Mayerling as a retreat in which to frame anonymous articles for the *Wiener Tagblatt*. Writing had always been his best recourse. By January he lacked not just the time but the energy and the concentration to take firm hold of his pen.

And he could cope less and less with inner pressures. There was an old gonorrheal infection whose recurrence he feared. He took morphium for that persistent cough. And a bit more morphium and more champagne-laced-with-cognac against all those hours, dawn after palace dawn, when he could ring for his footmen to bring him everything except sleep. "I am," he sometimes said to friends, "the most nervous man in the most nervous century."

Of course there was a quick way out of the nineteenth century. For quite a while now the suspicion had been with him that he would be ground up slowly but wholly, long before the coming of the twentieth. He'd been strolling toward that other, faster exit. And then away from it again. And then around it. It led beyond a dark rim, into the mystery of the Prague Jewess on whose grave he had dropped the too-late roses and whose face he saw exhumed in the features of Mary Vetsera.

"I must make a confession . . ." Mary Vetsera wrote her nurse on January 14. "I was with him yesterday evening, from seven to nine. We both lost our heads. Now we belong to each other, body and soul. On Saturday I hope to get away from a ball, and then I'll rush back to him."

Immediately after writing this, she went to Vienna's most expensive gift shop, Rodeck's, and ordered a gold cigarette case with the inscription, *January 13 — in gratitude to destiny*. It was a present to her lover.

Lovers they had finally become on the evening of the thirteenth. Very soon they became still more: partners in an ultimate pact. Actually Rudolf had proposed the idea of suicide to another woman first. Mitzi Caspar, whom he still saw, had heard it the month before. But Mitzi did not live as close to the cliff as he. She had laughed at the suggestion — surely it was a joke — and he pursued it no further.

Mary Vetsera did not laugh. She cried, she hugged him, she merged the idea into their passion. It made her glow. She was already the queen of fashion. But fashion staled so fast. Soon her name would assume a luster that decades could not tarnish: *Mary Vetsera, Crown Princess before History*.

After the decision was talked out, agreed to, covenanted, he felt different about her. He no longer needed to be so very secretive about their relationship. The liaison between his flesh and hers was less important now than the affair ahead, between their skeletons. The skull he kept on his desk: was it important what hair it had once worn? No, only the bones of Mary Vetsera were unique to him. The life washing around them was more ordinary, the life of a girl among the many other girls he had known.

And that in itself he found freeing. He was not infatuated — had he ever been? — with the breathing Mary. Anything touchable could bind or betray him no longer. And he discovered another freedom. He played his own life as if it were a mere gaudy flashback from a much more solid and enduring vantage point. After the Decision in mid-January, the world had turned into a cascade of make-believe which would expire very soon . . . as quickly as *Fasching* vanished on Ash Wednesday.

From then on he had his own secret carnival. The roles assigned to him by his official heraldic life — they all became costumes worn by a rogue to different brief balls. Henceforth all his enemies would be stalemating nothing but a mask.

In the last two weeks of the month Rudolf managed to impersonate flawlessly several disparate men. On January 15, the deposed sovereign of Bulgaria, Prince Alexander Battenberg, arrived in Vienna. Rudolf screwed on his Crown Princely countenance and bore the full brunt of etiquette. He visited Battenberg in his suite at the Imperial Hotel; was at home for the Prince's return visit to the Palace; with Stephanie gave a dinner for Battenberg in his apartments; took the Prince to see *Wilhelm Tell* at the opera and to eat *Tafelspitz* at the Sacher.

He did all this so well that on February 1, i.e., on the other side of the brink, Battenberg wrote an amazed condolence: "I had the good fortune of seeing His Imperial Highness fit and well and in his fullest prime, of talking to him, and of deriving pleasure and delight from being face to face with this magnificent prince."

But Rudolf also seemed fit during more odious rigmaroles in mid-January. With the Crown Princess he bowed and smiled during a dinner they gave for high Court officials; during another dinner tendered to ambassadors of the diplomatic corps; during yet another where the guest of honor was Prime Minister Taaffe, his second most effective frustrator. And with number one, the Emperor, he attended a ballet evening. They saw *Puppenfee* and *Wiener*

Waltzer, sitting together in the Imperial Box of the Court Opera on January 22: smiling, smiling, smiling at ovations tendered them by their subjects.

He appeared alone at the Carl Theater on January 15 and applauded von Suppé's operetta *La Vie Parisienne*. And on the twenty-third he went to the Theater an der Josefstadt for *Die Gigerln von Wien*, the comedy success of the season. A great cheer broke around him when he was discovered in the audience. He deserved it, too, if only for his contribution to the play's theme. A *Gigerl* was a Viennese gay blade, absurdly chic and sportive in costume and in manner, a caricature of the ideal represented by the Crown Prince himself.

In those January weeks he carried the ideal to wonderful extremes. If his evenings unrolled luminously at soirees and entertainments, he was on his feet again at sunrise with rifle and binoculars. Despite the cold, he put up a good show in Lower Austrian shoots. He brought down six wide-tailed eagles at Mannswörth on January 13; bagged three more at Orth on the twentieth and again three on the twenty-first. On the twenty-third he killed five antlered deer and two marten; and on the twenty-fifth, stalking some ice-free ponds in the Danubian swampland with Archduke Otto, he got no less than twenty-six ducks.

But he also found time for work on the second volume of *The Austro-Hungarian Monarchy in Word and Picture*. In such activities he was the amazingly informal people's prince. Unlike other archdukes he never summoned commoners through his Lord Chamberlain. To ask his co-editors for a conference he sent each a cordial handwritten note on plain unmonogrammed stationery: an unaffected straightforwardness which Hanslick, music consultant on the project, thought "characteristic of the Crown Prince's attractive and modern simplicity of manner."

Perhaps it was also "modern" of Rudolf to conclude at another Army Command Conference on the afternoon of January 22 that he, Crown Prince, Field Marshal-Lieutenant and Inspector General, was being ignored once too often. Perhaps in his "modern" alienation he let himself be drawn by Hungarian friends into an adventure which would explode with Count Károlyi's speech before the Budapest Parliament on the twenty-fifth. Or, more likely, he wasn't really in it at all. Flirting with sedition was just another mask-thin part. Politics was pretense, costume paint, now that it no longer had substance or hope. His plan with Mary Vetsera had reduced the world to vapor. To phantasmagoric preamble at best.

For others, like Franz Joseph, the world remained painfully real. Painfully real were the reports of certain agents; and so were some wire messages Rudolf had dispatched to Hungary and elsewhere. The Marquis of Bacquehem, as His Majesty's Commerce Minister, ran the Imperial and Royal Telegraph Service and kept a meticulous file on all of Rudolf's cables. Copies of significant ones were submitted to the monarch before they were destroyed. By the end of January Franz Joseph appeared to feel that his son, incomprehensible to him in recent years, might now have become dangerous. The young man must be brought to his senses.

But by the last week of the month Rudolf spun in an orbit beyond the reach of even the All Highest command. During those days the two Lipizzaners of his phaeton seemed never to stop trotting. Even the fast Bratfisch was not fleet enough for the Crown Prince. His carriage kept flitting in and out and through the city. On Thursday, the twenty-fourth, he met Mary Vetsera on a deserted Prater meadow. They set the date for Mayerling for the coming Monday, for a hunt to which Rudolf had already invited a couple of shooting companions. After that he drove to the Palace to dress, and from the Palace to the opera to see Mahler's *Drei Pintos*.

An odd double conjunction marked the week. In Budapest the next forty-eight hours would see the Mahler premiere of *The Valkyries* sung in Magyar, together with the parliamentary bombshell of Rudolf's friend Count Károlyi. But in Vienna, too, there was an intertwining of the fortunes of Gustav Mahler and Rudolf Habsburg. On the night of the twenty-fourth Rudolf did not remain alone in the Court Opera's Imperial Box. At the last moment the curtains were drawn aside. Franz Joseph entered.

Nobody had expected him. The monarch hardly ever partonized musical events. He much preferred the Court Theater — even before the advent of Frau Schratt — and only ballet could attract the All Highest Presence to the opera house. Yet he came that night to the Weber-Mahler opus so tepidly received by the critics. His entrance during the overture upstaged that of any of the singers, and many in the audience kept watching the way the Crown Prince rose to kiss the Emperor's hand; how the two whispered intensely in what appeared to be a very serious and sustained conversation; and how, after the second act, the Emperor left most abruptly — but not before the Crown Prince had risen to part the curtain for his father.

It was a historic whisper to which Mahler's harmonies soared, even if its content has been lost to history. One thing is sure. By that evening Rudolf had assumed one more mask, one of the final ones: unyielding correctness vis-à-vis his father. Let the Emperor dam him for his Hungarian rashness or for his Vetsera escapade. He would accept censure impassively, imperviously, with a face into whose pallor his youth and the fresh blue of his eyes had vanished. He would give his father the surface of respect, no less, no more. He had already surrendered himself to something much grander than a dual crown. And toward *that* he charged now with the unceasing tingling somnambulist energy of the insomniac.

The next day, Friday, the phaeton whirled out of the Palace gate again and drove fast, too fast, east beyond the Prater into the Danubian swamps for more hunting. Then Rudolph drove back into town, to Hodek's the taxidermist at Mariahilferstrasse 51. At Hodek's they were stuffing his recent trophies; drawing the correct simulation of life over the hollow corpses of six wide-tailed eagles in various facsimiles of flight. He liked that. He complimented the craftsmen, walked out into the street, was recognized with cheers, drove back to the Palace, changed into the uniform of a general of the Infantry, drove to the Gusshausstrasse, to the studio of the artist Taddheus Ajdukiewicz where he sat for a portrait showing him on horseback in the supple, slightly bent-forward casualness the *Gigerln* so admired. He posed with a steely patience for *his* taxidermist: the painter coloring animation over a core that was nothing but speed galloping over a thousand byways toward Monday in Mayerling. Session finished, he drove back to the Palace for a dinner.

The next two days, Saturday and Sunday, he kept plunging through the winter air in his open carriage: hunting, Hodek's (which stayed open for him on weekends), the painter's studio. On Sunday afternoon he raced from the portrait session to the Palace; changed into civilian clothes; drove to the tradesmen's entrance of the Grand Hotel; hurried up the back stairs; met Countess Larisch in her suite to discuss how she would manage things for him on Monday with the Vetsera family; hurried down the stairs, leaped into the phaeton for a drive to the outer Prater; found Mary on the appointed meadow; had quick words on final arrangements; scudded back to the Palace where the valet waited with his next uniform. And that was how the days drummed away with Lipizzaner hooves.

The nights were harder, particularly the last two of the week. Both were devoted to celebrating his enemy, Kaiser Wilhelm of the Prussians. On Saturday at 6 P.M. Franz Joseph summoned the Court to the great marble hall in the Palace for a dinner honoring the German Emperor's birthday. Rudolf had to appear as Colonel of the Second Brandenburg Uhlan Regiment, had to lift goblets, had to smile for hours through toasts and speeches glorifying a bounder. But he bore up well — as well as any of the spruce and glass-eyed creatures at the taxidermist's.

The next night, Sunday, he had to wear the Teuton uniform again. Prince Reuss, the German Ambassador, gave his own reception to mark his suzerain's anniversary. It was a *de rigueur* gala for the Austrian Imperial Family (and "an unenjoyable prospect" as Franz Joseph wrote Frau Schratt). But at least it was held late, at 9:30 P.M., which gave Rudolf more time to run his phaeton through the day, preparing for what was to come tomorrow.

At the German Embassy not only the Court and government members converged but the elite of Vienna's *haute bourgeoisie* — and therefore the Vetsera clan. For one moment in the course of the *cercle* a confrontation came to pass: the girl who exulted in an august triangle, and the wife who suspected and despised it. Crown

Princess Stephanie in a regal gray gown, with diamond tiara, stood face to face with Mary Vetsera, who had met the Crown Prince in the Prater grass only a few hours earlier and who now glowed fiercely in her pale-blue ball dress with yellow appliqué. For one moment — later there were reports that it was more than one — it looked as if the Baroness would not curtsy to Her Imperial Highness. But then she did . . . and the chatter resumed in the Embassy salon.

Throughout the reception Rudolf was as quiet as he was pale. If he talked at all it was mostly to the sculptor Viktor Tilgner, one of the few commoners present. During an otherwise bland chat the Crown Prince suddenly twitched his shoulders, as if to shake off the silver epaulettes. "This whole uniform is distasteful to me," he said to Tilgner. "Unbearably heavy . . ."

It was less than an outburst. It passed quickly. Rudolf noticed Count Hoyos among the guests, admonished him, jocularly, not to forget their hunting date at Mayerling. Franz Joseph departed. Rudolf kissed his father's hand, bowed to Mary with whom he had exchanged only glances, bowed to the other Vetseras, made his various good-byes, and within minutes sat once more in his phaeton. Again hooves sparked against cobbles, wheels spun and bowled around midnight corners to Heumühlgasse 10 where Mitzi Caspar received him.

He now had twelve hours left in the capital he would never inherit. He used the time to rehearse once more, in sovereign, summarizing speed, all the roles he had enacted in Vienna.

At Mitzi's simple flat he drank his cognac-laced champagne, bantered and caressed, and incidentally remarked that tomorrow before noon he would leave for a hunt, forever. He said it lightly, with his quick offhand charm, and of course he had said something like that before. It made her laugh; it was so absurd. But she was surprised that he, an unbeliever, made the sign of the cross on her forehead when they parted at three A.M.

By seven in the morning he was up and about again in his apartments in the Palace. A copious agenda waited for him. He dealt with it briskly, item by item. He studied the telegrams (monitored before delivery by his father's agents) on parliamentary skirmish-ings about the Army Bill in Budapest. To his staff he expressed vivid but carefully neutral impatience that voting on the issue had been postponed. He received Berthold Frischauer of the *Tagblatt*, who brought him the latest bulletins on the French elections, cabled to the newspaper's offices during the night. Next came Prince Battenberg, about to leave for Venice. He thanked the Crown Prince for being so accomplished a host; but Rudolf, like any accomplished host, smiled away Battenberg's gratitude and only regretted that his guest's plans would not let him join tomor-row's hunt at Mayerling.

After that, Lieutenant Colonel Albert Meyer had an audience. Meyer was Chief of Staff of the 25th Infantry Division which Rudolf nominally commanded. The Colonel brought him dozens of orders to be signed — a figurehead's busywork. This done, there was still another meeting on the schedule, with Archbishop Count Schönborn-Buchheim, as well as a conference to be attended at the Army Museum. But then the clock on Michaeler Tower struck 11 A.M. The Crown Prince called in an adjutant to cancel his last appointments.

He was now ready. He summoned his Note Bearer, a faithful soul named Püchel. The man was instructed to have Rudolf's Palace quarters ready again by 5 P.M. the next day, when he would be back to attend a family dinner given by the Emperor. Rudolf repeated the same intention to Stephanie and to his little Elisabeth when he said good-bye to them in their apartments. Püchel held the horses as he leaped into the phaeton. He drove a few paces toward the Palace gate, but turned and came back.

"Did I hear you say something, Püchel?" he asked his servant of many years. "Can I do something for you?"

"No, Your Imperial Highness, I said nothing," Püchel said. "Good shooting at Your Imperial Highness's hunt."

The Crown Prince nodded. The Crown Prince was gone from the Palace.

That was at half past eleven in the morning on Monday the twenty-eighth of January, the Crown Prince's progress through the city being routinely reported by Special Agent Wiligut in a telegram to Police Headquarters. Yet one essential fact eluded Wiligut and his superiors. They had no idea that Rudolf's phaeton was at this point only part of a precisely timed maneuver already in progress.

Somewhat earlier, at 10:30 A.M. Mary Vetsera and Countess Larisch had left the Vetsera mansion on the Salesianergasse. They would — so they told Mary's mother — do an errand on the Kohlmarkt, the smart shopping street. The public fiacre they hailed took that direction. But after two blocks the Countess leaned out the window and gave the cabbie a different address: the Augustiner Bastei, one of the remoter bastions of the old part of the Palace. Here the ladies skipped out and were swallowed up by an iron door left open for them. Rudolf's ancient valet Nehammer stood behind it, ready to guard the ladies until fifteen minutes later when, exactly on time, Bratfisch arrived. It took two seconds for Mary Vetsera to step out of the iron door into the fiacre. At 11 A.M. sharp her journey began to the Vienna Woods.

At 11:30 Rudolf departed with his phaeton.

The two vehicles rolled along the same route, separated by a distance of about ten miles. The first was pulled by Bratfisch's black steeds; the second by the Crown Prince's light-gray Lipizzaners. They moved down the Ringstrasse, its historic gestures and heroic contours woodcut-sharp in the clarity of the chill day. They wheeled past the Court Opera to the quay of the River Wien, crossed the Wien over the Rudolf Bridge, named after the Crown Prince, and then headed south past Schönbrunn Palace, south into the first meadows of the Vienna Woods, and toward a grove of beeches where the Rotes Stadel, the Red Barn Inn, lay sequestered. Here the first fiacre stopped. The inn was closed for the winter. Mary Vetsera waited inside the cab. Bratfisch whistled a slow sweet waltz and to its rhythm beat his arms against the cold.

It took about twenty minutes for a man in a fur-collared overcoat to appear, strolling among the trees. The Crown Prince. When his phaeton had passed a thicket a bit farther back, he had handed the reins to the accompanying coachman, ordered him to turn the carriage around, and jumped out. The police, trained on the phaeton, followed it as it emerged from the thicket and headed back to Vienna. His pursuers gone, Rudolf walked to the Rotes Stadel. He climbed into the fiacre with a jest: Had he kept Their Lordships waiting too long?

They laughed. Bratfisch's tongue clicked the horses into motion. Whistling, he steered through the mounded snow. The white hills and the black trees glided by slowly. No hurry, the Crown Prince said. No need to arrive before dusk fell on Mayerling.

On this Monday night of the twenty-eighth of January 1889, the sun set at 4:52 P.M. The planet Venus, which had been curving toward earth for months, was now marvelously close. Its brilliance struck the naked eye in early twilight, by half past four. Icicle-like, it pierced a sky lucid and violet.

The official *Abendpost* was moved to remark on the phenomenon that week. And Rudolf and Mary had leisure to admire so rare a brightness from the billiard-room window of the lodge. The hunting party would not arrive until next morning. And not until the next night would they consummate their great departure. Meanwhile they were alone with a few servants, with flames purring in the fireplace, and with the frozen peace of the Vienna woods.

Fifteen miles away, in the carnival city, a hundred orchestras tuned up. Thousands of gentlemen knotted white ties. In boudoirs the ladies scented their décolletages. Only at the Palais Vetsera did *Fasching* grind to a halt on Monday, twenty-four hours before it would suddenly founder through all of Vienna.

About 1 P.M. Countess Larisch had arrived at the Salesianergasse. Suddenly a great spasm of guilt had seized her. Certain hints Rudolf had thrown out, cryptic but dark, curdled into panic. Perhaps her help to the pair was a terrible complicity. She burst in on Baroness Helene's lunch. She had lost Mary, she stammered to Mary's mother. She had lost Mary on her "errand" — lost her perhaps to the Crown Prince — and she was scared.

She could not or would not clarify much further, but her fear terrified the mother. Twice that afternoon the Baroness sent Larisch to the Police Commissioner of Vienna, Baron Franz von Krauss.

Once Larisch went by herself; the second time with Alexander Baltazzi, the lost girl's uncle. Each time they returned, nonplussed by the Commissioner's iron prudence.

The little Baroness was gone? he had said. The famous little fashion personality? Well, the little Baroness would come back from her outing. No, he would not advise filing a missing-person notice. Not if His Imperial Highness was involved. No point to that at all because the police force, even the highest-ranking detectives, were constitutionally prohibited from investigating or touching any premises of the Imperial Family anywhere. No, any information relating to such matters went only to the Emperor himself — nowhere else. No, the Commissioner would advise waiting till tomorrow when the little Baroness would no doubt return. After all, girls will be girls and Crown Princes will be Crown Princes, and in the end even lofty irregularities like these would regularize themselves nicely.

And the next morning, on the twenty-ninth, everything did indeed look regular at Mayerling. Count Hoyos and Rudolf's brother-in-law, the Prince of Coburg, arrived at the lodge for the shooting party. The blinds of all four windows of Rudolf's ground-floor bedroom were drawn, but then they often were. In the billiard room, Rudolf greeted his guests, alone, in his dressing gown. A silk scarf was casually slung around his neck, and he gave one of his flawless performances of princely charm. He said that his nose had the impertinence to have contracted a cold; it would keep him from the hunt. But it didn't prevent him from sharing a gay and hearty breakfast. He asked his friends what news they had heard from Budapest, the merry mess in the Parliament there? Even the birds in the trees here in the Vienna Woods were carrying on about that. They laughed, they enjoyed the coffee poured by Loschek, Rudolf's valet, and then the Crown Prince cheered the others on their way to the chase.

For the Prince of Coburg it was a short hunt. He came back to the lodge at 1 P.M. so that he could return to Vienna in time. As Rudolf's in-law he had been invited to the family evening at the Imperial Palace. Surprisingly Rudolf announced that he himself

Mayerling as it looked during Rudolf's last days, before its rebuilding

would stay at the lodge. It was his impertinent cold, he said; it had had the nerve to get worse instead of better. So far it was just a nasty trifle, but the freezing ride to town might provoke it into pneumonia. Would Coburg be a dear? Would he tell the Emperor that his son respectfully kissed his hand and begged to be excused?

Coburg promised and Coburg left. Shortly afterward Loschek sent one of the lower servants trudging to the nearest telegraph office at Alland village.

> TO HER IMPERIAL AND ROYAL HIGHNESS THE MOST SERENE LADY THE CROWN PRINCESS ARCHDUCHESS STEPHANIE, VIENNA, IMPERIAL PALACE.
>
> PLEASE WRITE PAPA THAT I ASK HIS PARDON MOST OBEDIENTLY FOR NOT APPEARING AT DINNER, BUT BECAUSE OF A HEAVY COLD I WISH TO AVOID THE JOURNEY THIS AFTERNOON AND STAY HERE WITH JOSL HOYOS.
>
> EMBRACING YOU ALL MOST WARMLY, RUDOLF

Rudolf's impeccability continued when Hoyos returned from the fields in the evening. They chatted in the billiard room. The day's bag was meager. But Rudolf, playful, absolved his friend from poor huntsmanship. Hungarian politics must have scared off the game. That's why he wasn't cross with his cold for making him stay indoors all day.

They sat down to a dinner of *pâté de foie gras*, roast beef, venison and red wine. The Crown Prince ate heartily, drank moderately. He showed Hoyos some of the messages he had received during the day. (With good reason, the staff of the telegraph office at Alland village was always tripled during Rudolf's stays at Mayerling.) Most of the cables came from Budapest and brought inconclusive news of the Army Bill imbroglio. Rudolf shrugged his shoulders at rumors linking him to some of the firebrand oratory there. He compared the parliamentary caprices of Magyar counts to the quirks of first-rate gun dogs. He liked his Károlyis and Telekis; there was nobody less dull. But on the whole it was easier to deal with four-legged thoroughbreds than the other kind.

They smiled. They toasted each other with good Baden County

wine, lit cigarettes. "The Crown Prince," Hoyos would later say, "turned on me the whole beguiling force of his personality."

At 9 P.M. Hoyos retired to his quarters in the former farm part of the estate, about five hundred yards away. Only then did Mary Vetsera emerge from Rudolf's bedroom. Her "shopping dress," worn since early the day before, was wrinkled. She was hungry. It hadn't been possible to bring her food while she hid behind discreet blinds. None of it mattered.

Loschek served her cold venison. He sat out new goblets before her and Rudolf, put new candles in the candelabra, new logs in the fireplace, hauled champagne from the cellar, rapped against the door of Bratfisch's room in the servants' wing. Bratfisch came out, knowing what was expected of him. Rudolf and Mary applauded his entrance into the billiard room. He settled himself on a stool in cabdriver's position, and began to sing and to whistle all the tunes the pair knew so well and of which they could not get enough: the sad songs about Vienna long before the Ringstrassse, lost and dear; wistful songs about good wine drunk long ago; funny songs like the fighting-lovers ditty from *Die Gigerln von Wien*; sentimental songs about the nut tree dying slowly by the Danube; and last but not least the song about Archduke Johann who had married a postmaster's daughter back in the eighteenth century — yes, especially that one, because it was Rudolf's and therefore Mary's favorite.

Bratfisch sang deep into the night, until the logs were ashes, the champagne drunk, the candles burned, and Venus faded. Then that was over, too. Hand in hand, Rudolf and Mary went to the bedroom.

Behind them Loschek carried a final set of tapers. Rudolf instructed him: at 8 A.M. breakfast alone with Hoyos and with Coburg who was due back from Vienna early in the morning; after that, another hunt which Rudolf might join. "Meanwhile," the Crown Prince said smiling, "don't let anyone into my room, even if it is the Emperor."

The Emperor did not come. But sleep came to Loschek, most loyal of servants, for by then it was already after 2 A.M. He did not sleep long. At 6:30 steps waked him. The Crown Prince stood by the bed, hands in the pockets of his dressing gown, the silk scarf still slung about his neck. He ordered Loschek to call him at 7:30 for breakfast and to have Bratfisch ready with his horses at the same hour. Then Rudolf walked back to the bedroom, whistling softly one of last night's tunes.

Loschek dressed, alerted the kitchen staff, and went to see about Bratfisch. At 7:30 sharp he knocked at the Crown Prince's door. He knocked again. Outside, ravens cawed on snow rosy with the dawn sun. Loschek knocked. Wind sounded in the great black firs. Loschek knocked louder. Usually the Crown Prince slept lightly. Loschek knocked louder still. "Your Imperial Highness!" he called, *"Your Imperial Highness!"* The ravens cawed. Loschek ran up the main stairs of the two-story lodge, and down a small spiral staircase leading to the back door of the bedroom. He reached the back door. He knocked there. Ravens cawed. The pack of hunting dogs, alerted by the noise, had started barking. Loschek knocked. He knocked as hard as he could. He knocked and called. He screamed to wake his master. He ran up and down the staircases again, to the front door of the room. He grabbed a log of firewood and began to beat it against the door.

By then the other servants had gathered in the back of the ante-room. Bratfisch kept them from coming close. Count Hoyos came running from his quarters. Almost immediately afterwards the Prince of Coburg raced up, just arrived from his overnight stay in Vienna. Both noblemen joined in the knocking and the calling. Then they stopped. They couldn't believe this was happening. They ordered Loschek to break down the door. Loschek, out of breath, half crying, whispered that he had to inform Their Serene Lordships that a lady, that Baroness Mary Vetsera was staying in His Imperial Highness's room.

Coburg and Hoyos recoiled. They retreated to the billiard room. They had to make a decision. Loschek kept knocking and calling. A kitchen maid began to whimper. Within a minute the two stepped from the billiard room, pale, and repeated their order. Break down the door. Some servant had already brought a wood-chopping axe. Loschek raised it to smash the lock. The lock resisted. Loschek hacked away at the white-painted door panels. The axe crashed, the panels splintered. Ravens fluttered up from the snow outside. The dogs barked and howled to the echoing blows. Loschek hacked out a gash. The gash became a hole. Framed in jagged wood, smoky with burned candles, dark with the drawn blinds, the room inside was visible.

Only then did Loschek drop his axe. The silence that followed changed the Empire.

❧ Chapter 22 ❧

At dawn of this same Tuesday, January 30, a footman stood close to the door of the Emperor's bedroom, listening. It was his duty to stay there the night through, until he heard the right sound. It came punctually at 4 A.M.: a sudden crisp creaking of the springs.

His Majesty had risen from his iron bedstead. The footman knocked; entered; bowed deeply; and walked with candlestick, sponge and towel to the simple washstand. Franz Joseph, who disdained more modern bathroom conveniences, was already waiting there. In chaste sequence he began to fold back his nightshirt here and there, exposing to the sponge one part of his body after another. Segment by segment the footman moistened the monarch, soaped him, rinsed him, dried him; sometimes steadied himself on him too, for the night's vigil was long and beer a not so secret fortifier. Franz Joseph submitted calmly. He was used to being his subjects' pillar.

The footman finished. Bowing again, walking backwards with his face toward the Emperor, he retreated to the door — and sleep. His shift was over. For Franz Joseph the day had started.

Pachmayer, the chief valet, arrived next at 4:20 A.M. with the first of the day's several uniforms. The Emperor dressed, had a cup of coffee and a crescent roll at the table by his bed, and walked to his rococo desk in the next room before five o'clock in the morning. Most of his realm still slept; his cities snored from the Swiss to the Turkish border. But the candelabra already flickered on both sides of his rosewood desk.

Franz Joseph sat down to what was bound to be a better day for once. On Monday he had undergone a gruesome number of audiences; they always piled up when he was about to leave town. Last night, Tuesday evening, there had been the annoyance about Rudolf's absence from the family dinner. But this morning his eye quickly found the lovely item on his schedule. It jumped at him from the calligraphy of the huge agenda sheet clipped to the top of his portfolio. The entry said: "11 A.M. — *His Majesty's visit with Her Majesty.*"

In that one sentence lay not only delight but convenience. It meant that he wouldn't have to drive all the way out to Schönbrunn Palace to meet Katharina Schratt. He needn't walk the icy gardens at 7 A.M. and neither would she, poor thing, have to be all dressed up and coiffed at an unearthly hour, fit to meet her Imperial swain by prearranged accident. Only such detours made it possible (and decent) for commoner to meet Majesty outside the formalities of an audience.

But today it would be much simpler. With the Empress's help the pair could take advantage of one of her rare stays in the palace. Officially Frau Schratt's Court position was "Reciter to Her Majesty." Today the actress would be calling on Elisabeth in that capacity. And during this recital Franz Joseph would happen to visit his wife — at 11 A.M.

But a world of chores must be done before that desired moment. At five o'clock in the morning couriers began bowing their way to the Emperor's desk. The entire apparatus of state had learned to hum at the wee hours to suit the All Highest early habits. It hummed red-eyed to carefully supressed yawns, but it hummed. The Adjutant General of the Imperial Chancellery appeared to receive his assignments. The First Lord Chamberlain came to pay his respects.

At 7 A.M. the Chief Secretary brought to the monarch's desk the business that would occupy him through the morning. It was a sheaf of recommendations concerning the forthcoming sojourn in Budapest of Franz Joseph and his Court. His personal popularity — and especially that of his wife — was to appease Hungarian turmoil and float the government Army Bill through the snares and rapids of Parliament. But the Imperial charisma must be deployed with care, and there was nobody more careful than the Emperor. His genius for detail was well known to the officers of state involved in the Budapest business — his Minister of War, his Hungarian Prime Minister, and the Hungarian Palatine. Hence they had worked out a set of suggestions for all phases of the All Highest residence in Hungary: the meetings over which Franz Joseph, as the Apostolic King of Hungary, was to preside; the audiences to be granted, the honors to be conferred, the appointments to be made; the dinners, déjeuners, receptions to be decreed and arranged; the lists of guests to be invited; the accents of protocol to be stressed, softened or subtly modulated.

It was an exhaustive dossier whose proper treatment demanded a thousand decisions, some large, most small. Much of the morning Franz Joseph did what his ancestors had done before him, through many generations. He ruled and overruled with utter confidence, with axiomatic competence, and without the slightest inspiration. Inexorably the royal pen scratched on. He turned page after page, gathered rapid overviews, crystallized quick judgments. Every paragraph on every sheet received an All Highest comment on the margin. He approved wholly or partly or conditionally, on precisely stated terms; or demanded amplification or further advice from experts; or vetoed until further notice; or canceled instantly, outright and irrevocably. He seldom hesitated and he never stopped until shortly before 11 A.M.

At about 10:58 he rose from his desk to walk past the salutes of adjutants and guards. Each one he returned meticulously, almost smiling. After all, he was striding toward his wife's apartments, and therefore to Katharina Schratt.

Before the Empress's salon stood Baron Nopsca, her First Lord Chamberlain. The courtier bowed as the monarch approached; strangely enough, he also seemed to shake his head. Stranger still, he did not step aside as the Emperor came close, just shook his head still more. At last he straightened up to show a face made of wax and tears. The Emperor saw it at the very moment that he heard sobs from inside. He reached for the golden door knob, but the Baron held his arm. And then Franz Joseph faced a situation he could not grasp. For the first time in his life, a door before which he stood failed to open.

Elisabeth the Empress and Queen had also risen at an early hour. Her Palace routine was quite different from her life away from Vienna — and she spent most of her year abroad.

At fifty-one, Elisabeth remained a legend for her pallid beauty, for the diet and exercise with which she chastened her body into an exquisite attenuation, but most of all for her restlessness. She roamed half the world incognito as the Countess Hohenembs. Often just one lady-in-waiting accompanied her on the most unpredictable forays. Nearly as often she was alone, galloping through the Scottish heather, or taking a six-hour hike up a Bavarian Alp, or wandering veiled through bazaars at Smyrna, rowing a boat in the sunset sea off Amsterdam, or sitting on an empty Adriatic dune, the point of her parasol inscribing strange verses into the sand.

She rarely lived palatially, except during her random sojourns in Vienna as in the weeks just before and after New Year of 1889. On that Wednesday morning of January 30, she rose at 6:30 to take a long scented bath in the tub attendants had carried into her room. Her masseur, a specialist from Wiesbaden, soothed the neuralgic sensitivities of her joints. Then it was the turn of the "hair maid." By 8 A.M. the "hair maid" (discreetly excising some gray filaments) had finished combing what was still among the most lustrous manes of Europe. A chambermaid brought a breakfast of herb tea and toast. In her gymnasium a few steps away her fitness-physician, Dr. Kellgrün, awaited her and advised Her

Majesty on some new exercises at the chinning rings and on the mat.

At 10 A.M. her dressers helped her change from her gym clothes. She was toned up, ready for her Greek lesson. Her instructor, Monsieur Rhoussopholous, had already been ushered into the salon. He began to read a passage from the *Iliad* describing the character of Achilles. The Empress followed her custom of writing in her little leather notebook questions she wanted to ask the instructor about Homer's language. The poetry was very beautiful, but it was also difficult, and a knock on the door annoyed her. The knock came too early. Her watch said 10:45 — fifteen minutes before Frau Schratt's time.

It was not Frau Schratt, however. It was a lady-in-waiting, Ida von Ferenczi, who begged Her Majesty's pardon to report that her First Lord Chamberlain, Baron Nopsca, had an urgent message from Count Hoyos. The Empress said curtly that the message would have to wait. At this moment the Baron entered without obtaining permission. Elisabeth rose in anger. But then she saw the Baron's face. The little leather notebook dropped to the carpet. Her Majesty's day, even more inviolable than her husband's, stopped.

Gradually everybody's day stopped. On the same Palace floor the Crown Princess Stephanie was taking a singing lesson. Her music instructor, Frau Niklas-Kempner, was vocalizing the refrain of a Rumanian folk ballad — but the rococo door burst open, and she never finished.

Nor did Prime Minister Taaffe complete his conversation with Galician deputies in a conference room at Parliament on the other side of the Ringstrasse. Shortly after the noon hour a page began making gestures at him which asked him to step away. The Count decided not to respond. This might be nothing more than another message about the missing Vetsera girl. The mother had already bothered him about it last night. But he would not let it disturb a busy afternoon, especially not an afternoon when the new electric illumination would be tried out in Parliament to shine on, among other things, the Prime Minister's witty new cravat.

So he waved the page away. To his surprise the fellow not only refused to go but actually bent down to whisper at his ear in the most forward fashion. Whereupon one saw a rare sight: the Prime Minister jumping up and running off, so suddenly that he forgot his trademark topper and his dashing overcoat.

The disruption spread deeper and lower. On the Palace grounds a regimental band marched in together with the changing of the guard. After them trailed the usual crowd of oom-pah-pah lovers who didn't mind the cold or the pickpockets working their trade. Shortly before 1 P.M. the band had just launched into "The March of the Huguenots," when a palace official approached the leader. He cut off the tune with two sharp raps of his baton.

The music stopped. In the street the people couldn't believe it. When had that ever happened before? But the music stopped everywhere. It never even got started in the lofty hall of the Musikvereinssaal where Johannes Brahms was strolling toward the dais with Joseph Joachim, the violin virtuoso. Composer and soloist thought they were about to rehearse the second Vienna performance of Brahms's Double Concerto. They were wrong. Before their incredulous eyes, the orchestra was leaving its seats. The concertmaster, when they reached him, was baffled. A secretary had just come running in from the front office to say that the rehearsal must be stopped, the performance was canceled.

All over the city telephones rang with the same injunction: *Cancel.* They rang in the management offices of the Court Opera, of the Court Theater, of music halls, cabarets, ballroom establishments, and on the committee desks for *Fasching* events. Where there were no telephones, telegraph boys and messengers appeared. Some of them already wore black bands on their sleeves, without knowing for certain yet just what great death was abroad in the city. Rumors swirled like locusts down the streets; in minutes they had devoured the carnival.

By midafternoon a gigantic though still uncertain whisper flooded the town. It carried the Crown Prince's name on the crest of disaster. But still nothing conclusive was known. From everywhere crowds converged on the Palace. The guards stood impassive. Their rifles flashed as they presented arms to Court car-

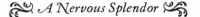

OUR CROWN PRINCE DEAD

Front page of the Wiener Tagblatt *for Thursday,
January 31, 1889*

riages. More and more archducal carriages raced toward the portals. Toward evening Venus rose through the cold half-light, as brilliant as on the night before.

Finally, in the morning, the horror congealed into print. Every front page on every newspaper was a scream.

OUR CROWN PRINCE DEAD!

Dead at thirty, of a stroke. Dead of a heart attack, another edition said, quoting another official source. Dead of an accidental gun-shot wound, said a third — and was confiscated instantly.

On February 1, the evening edition of the *Wiener Tagblatt* broke out into a black-framed monumental headline: THE MOST HORRIBLE TRUTH. It was the official suicide announcement. Crown Prince Rudolf had been found in Mayerling, alone, killed by a pistol he himself had fired.

But what *was* the truth? What lay behind all these dazing re-versals? The Viennese, who could obfuscate so gracefully, who could paint such rosettes and cherubs over the dreary real — they were stunned not only by the event but by the clumsiness with which the government had tried to doctor it. Suddenly the myth was a shambles. Only days ago the Crown Prince had danced his Lipizzaners down the Ringstrasse. Now something awful had fallen on the Empire.

Chapter 23

Terrified millions guessed at the truth. But only three men had seen it in its rank immediacy: the Prince of Coburg, Count Hoyos, and Loschek the valet. In Mayerling, at 8 A.M. on Wednesday, they had stared at it through the jagged fragments of a door. They had seen the couple on the bed, fully dressed, with their brains blown out. The girl stretched out, hair flowing loosely, hands cupping a rose. The man half-sitting, leaning against a night table whose mirror had helped him take aim at his temple. He was still bleeding from the mouth. His and her blood mingled partly dried on the white sheets.

The Prince of Coburg collapsed at the sight. Hoyos ran with Bratfisch to the fiacre. They arrived at the Baden depot of the

Southern Railway in time to stop the Trieste express by a special emergency signal from the stationmaster. At 9:18 A.M. Hoyos jumped onto the train. At 9:50 A.M. he jumped off at the Vienna Southern Railway terminal. He ran for a cab and reached the Palace just before 10:15.

Here his nerve left him. What he had seen was too terrible to be telegraphed. But now he felt it was also too monstrous a thing to say. Never could he say it to His Majesty's face. He stumbled into the office of Rudolf's First Lord Chamberlain who led him to Baron Nopsca. With Nopsca's help he gained admittance to the Empress, stuttering that Mary Vetsera had poisoned the Crown Prince and then herself. This was the slightly mitigated ghoulishness which the Empress sobbed out to Franz Joseph as he entered.

At the same time the news spread from the Baden train depot. To stop the express train at the local station, Hoyos had been forced to give the stationmaster a hint of the extremity. The stationmaster promptly telegraphed the railroad's owner, Baron Nathaniel Rothschild. That afternoon the stock exchange, like all public institutions, closed abruptly. But thanks to Rothschild it closed a bit more knowledgeably than the others. Most traders dumped. But soon long-term calculation won over short-term shock. On Thursday, when the death of the Imperial leftist was official, the stock exchange opened in a buying mood.

After the first crushing moment Franz Joseph appeared to absorb the blow almost as well as the market did. He was stunned, and being stunned was an armor against agony. Stunned, he consoled his wife. Katharina Schratt arrived and tried to console them both. Then he went back to his study to stun himself further with work. He worked late and at 10 P.M. that night telegraphed his Hungarian Prime Minister to take resolute measures against any further disturbances over the Army Bill.

At 4 A.M. he was up as usual, ready to work once more. Soon afterward, with dawn reddening the Palace windows, he received the chief Court physician, Dr. Widerhofer, just back from Mayerling. The doctor could not withhold what he had found. And now came the full, throttling news: The Crown Prince, he reported, had not been poisoned. His Imperial Highness had killed Mary Vetsera with a revolver shot about two hours before killing himself with another bullet.

But that wasn't all. There was also the matter of Rudolf's last letters. Only one of these had been written in Mayerling, with Mary already dead beside him. "I have no right to go on living," said the letter to his mother, "I have killed," and then requested that he and Mary be buried together at Heiligenkreuz Monastery near Mayerling.

In another letter Rudolf advised his sister Valerie to emigrate after Franz Joseph's death, "for what will happen then in Austria is unforeseeable." To his wife Stephanie he wrote that she was now liberated from his presence and the burden he had been to her; she should be kind to their little daughter. He left letters to Baron Hirsch and to Mitzi Caspar which the Emperor read but whose contents remain a Habsburg secret. To his valet Loschek he wrote a letter requesting him to fetch a priest as his last order and thanking him for many years of loyal service.

For his father, the Emperor, there was nothing. No letter. Not the briefest note. Not a line. Nothing.

It was an appalling, eloquent omission. Dr. Widerhofer had to convey it to Franz Joseph, that very early morning of Thursday, January 31. The two men stood alone on hard marble in the palace dawn, monarch and physician, and the monarch sank slowly to the floor, and cried.

He refused help. He must be left there, to lie shaking. He stopped shaking. He stood up again. He asked if the body had been returned to the Palace and placed in Rudolf's bed, as ordered. He was assured the order had been carried out. He then instructed his son's Adjutant General to put white officer's gloves on his son's hands. He girded himself with his saber, pulled on his own white gloves. He walked to his son's bedroom.

Here the Crown Prince lay, gloved hands crossed over a blanket pulled up to his neck, forehead covered by a snow-white bandage — all as ordered. Franz Joseph stood straight, immobile, sculpted, throughout a fifteen-minute vigil. In accordance with custom and regulation, he was saying good-bye to a brother officer.

The son had completed his only possible and desperate insurgence. Outside the Palace, Vienna had begun to quake with it. But inside, the last confrontation took place on the father's terms — correct down to the color of the gloves.

The ceremony restored paramount perspectives. Franz Joseph became himself again. Majesty re-entered his veins. Once more he was his people's central symbol. Such symbols do not weep. They are structuring and orienting energies. They radiate order into the world's grievous chaos. Even this, even the abomination of Mayerling, must be ordered into a proper scheme. Here lay the Emperor's task: to bureaucratize the unspeakable, to resolve it into administrative responses and thus render it more tolerable to himself and to his subjects.

Two imperatives loomed above everything else: A Catholic burial must be obtained for Rudolf, circumstances notwithstanding. And Mary Vetsera must be erased from public view — her name, her death, her body. The last necessity was the most urgent of all.

Mary's mother felt the pressure first; that is, to the degree that she could feel anything at all. Throughout her life the older Baroness had been a woman of burnished will. Her great wardrobe, her command of fashion, her jewelry, her social arts, her parties, her daughters — Mary most of all — had always been aimed upward. And now those heights that had been her aspiration and unflagging pilgrimage — they suddenly came down on her like a vile avalanche. Her Mary had been swallowed up by them. Now they crushed her rights as a mother. They came crashing down on her life's purpose.

She had been at the Palace Wednesday morning, searching for her daughter. Quite unexpectedly she'd found herself received by the Empress. A lifelong dream came true, as nightmare. Her Majesty told the Baroness that both their children were dead. Numb, the Baroness returned to her home. Immediately the Emperor's Adjutant General called to say that Mary had poisoned the Crown Prince. The mother must leave Vienna before nightfall to escape the wrath of the populace.

There wasn't enough life in her now to ask questions, to object, even to comprehend. She left for Venice the same afternoon but stepped from the train midway, at a station in the Alps, to turn around. Not in resistance, but out of the dumb insensate urge to be with her daughter's body. A northbound train took her back home. Instantly the heights struck at her again. She found her palais surrounded by police agents. It was suggested strongly that she leave once more.

In one last instinctive convulsion the social climber in her reared: She would entertain such a proposal only from a suitable high emissary, sent by the Emperor himself.

Within an hour the Prime Minister Count Taaffe arrived, gallant and merciless, with top hat and cigar. He was most suitable indeed — the only man in the capital to draw a certain acrid savor from the day. The Crown Prince had never been his cup of tea.

His Apostolic Majesty, Franz Joseph, as photographed in 1888

But this crisis was. It demanded the highest kind of *fortwursteln*.

The Prime Minister began by conveying to the Baroness his personal condolences. The tragic situation, he said, had now been clarified as a double suicide by gun. It was therefore in everybody's interest that the Baroness depart from the capital at once, at least for the duration of Rudolf's obsequies. That she consent, also at once, to her daughter's secret but Catholic interment in an inconspicuous grave at Heiligenkreuz Monastery. And furthermore, the Baroness must not draw attention to the burial site either by her presence or by any other sign until a time in the future when public curiosity might have vanished. If the Baroness agreed, His Majesty's government would be grateful; indeed it would release to her brother-in-law Count Stockau, and therefore to her, her daughter's last letters found at Mayerling. In saying all this he was expressing the All Highest will. He was quite sure that the Baroness, being the lady she was, would not run the risk of obstruction.

Count Taaffe, leaning back with his Havana, had trained on her the murderous smoothness feared in Parliament. The Baroness had nothing left but acquiescence. That day she was given poor Mary's farewell words. She read them. Like the Emperor, she cried.

"Dear Mother," Mary wrote. "Forgive me for what I have done: I could not resist love. In agreement with him I wish to be buried by his side at the Alland churchyard. I am happier in death than in life. Your Mary." The letter to her sister recommended that she marry for love; and Mary asked that a gardenia be placed on her grave every January 13, the day Rudolf had become her lover.

But through the macabre came glints of the high-spirited belle, the Turf Angel queening it over the races, the gay, conquering beauty. "Bratfisch whistled wonderfully," said her postscript to her sister. And the letter to the Duke of Braganza, one of her more favored admirers, was one long tease about willing him her famous boa so that he could hang it above his bed. "Cheers, Waterboy!" Rudolf added to that letter — "Waterboy" being Braganza's nickname because he sported neckerchiefs like the boys who watered horses at the cab stands.

Cheers! . . . the gaiety from on high. Its laughter came echoing through a ghastly veil. The Baroness cried and departed.

Chapter 24

Mary Vetsera's body was now abandoned to the Imperial machinery whose gears had already begun to grind. The All Highest family stood constitutionally beyond the reach of police or judiciary. Under the Emperor's direction the so-called Lord Marshal's Office (*Obersthofmarschallamt*) executed the legal business of the House of Habsburg with supreme authority, not reviewable by any court in the realm. This Lord Marshal's Office processed the Mayerling case.

Mayerling would be a difficult job, even for so lofty a bureau. Mary Vetsera, not being a Habsburg, was subject to common authorities in life or death. If these authorities declared her a murder victim — which she assuredly, though willingly, was — a homicide report would have to be filed with the district attorney in Baden, to incalculable consequences. But if Mary Vetsera were to be declared a suicide, then the Crown could not honor its pledge to give Mary a Catholic funeral; then the consecrated earth at Heiligenkreuz Monastery would be denied her. That is, under ordinary circumstances.

The Lord Marshal's Office telegraphed Abbot Grünböck at the monastery. In addition Rudolf's First Lord Chamberlain wrote him a letter, conveying an All Highest wish. A police courier galloped off with it to Heiligenkreuz in the Vienna Woods. Double-pressured, the Abbot made an extraordinary accommodation. His graveyard would receive the body.

Thus the true manner of Mary's death could be legally obliterated. Next came her physical disappearance.

In the afternoon of the same day, January 31, Alexander Baltazzi and Count Georg Stockau, Mary's uncles, went to Mayerling. They drove in Stockau's unobtrusive carriage, avoiding the main roads. A representative of the Lord Marshal's Office followed, together with a Court physician. They passed the armed guards, the unquiet ravens, the howling dogs. Inside the lodge they removed an Imperial seal put on a certain door. Behind it, under a heap of old clothes, lay Mary Vetsera, now forty hours dead. Her discolored fingers still clutched the wilted rose.

"Had I read about such a scene in a penny dreadful," the Lord Marshal's agent, Heinrich Slatin, would later recall, "I should have regarded as an extravagant nightmare what I was now experiencing."

The agent's official findings read as follows: "On the morning of January 30, 1889, a female corpse was discovered in the village area of Mayerling. The Court physician Dr. Franz Auchtenthaler diagnosed undoubted suicide by means of a firearm. . . . The undersigned Herr Georg Count Stockau as well as the co-undersigned Herr Alexander Baltazzi identified the body as that of their niece, Marie Alexandrine Baroness von Vetsera, born in Vienna on March 19, 1871 . . ."

While the agent drew up the document, the physician washed caked blood from the corpse. Then it was dressed in coat and hat, in boa, veil and shoes. It was stood up. The two uncles linked arms with their niece and walked her slowly out into the night, past any possible suspicious eyes, through the howling winds, past Rudolf's barking dogs, to Count Stockau's carriage. A hearse would, of course, have given away too much and provoked too much attention in an area that might at any moment become infested with journalists.

The two uncles lifted Mary into the carriage, propped her into sitting position, wedged her between them, pushed a broomstick between her dress and her spine to keep her erect. A detective climbed in as well.

Then the carriage began to move, lit by a single lantern. The agent from the Lord Marshal's Office followed in a second vehicle with the Court physician. The shadows of horses and wheels moved past those of leafless trees. And so the cadaver that, alive, had made the boa the rage of Vienna, still bore the chic trademark. And so Mary Vetsera, spark of so many costume balls, starred in a final masquerade. And so Alexander Baltazzi, who had won the English Derby in 1876, must content himself with slower horsemanship, that night of January 31, 1889.

Slowly, over icy ruts, in sudden, driving rains, the small caravan bounced and creaked along byways through the dark. Drops whipped against the window. Mary swayed to every jolt. The horses kept slipping. Often the drivers had to stop to caulk their hooves. Though the distance wasn't great, the carriages labored longer than planned. They arrived not much before midnight at the churchyard of Heiligenkreuz Monastery. A group of high-ranking police awaited them.

Mary's carriage stopped at the burial chapel where her uncles placed her in a makeshift coffin hastily nailed together by a carpenter. The Lord Marshal's agent proceeded to the abbey itself where the district governor signed the death deposition and completed other paperwork which provided a veneer of legality along with utter secrecy.

And then it was time to hide Mary in the earth. But the rainstorm had grown so cruel, the darkness so drastic, that the gravediggers would have needed too many lanterns for their work. Too much visibility would have been created. The commanding police officer, Commissar Gorup, telegraphed in cipher to police headquarters in Vienna. There a special council was meeting in an all-night session. Commissar Gorup obtained permission to postpone burial until daybreak.

The officials therefore adjourned to the abbey's cellar for refreshments. Since the abbey's wine was famous and since the importance of the mission was in itself intoxicating, the mood became animated.

So animated that years later the Lord Marshal's agent still remembered such *Gemütlichkeit* with distaste. As the night wore on and the jollity increased, a monk had to speak sobering words.

Finally the rain's color changed from black to gray. In the wretched, pouring dawn a huddle of umbrellas bobbed over wet snow patches to the grave site. A prior pronounced a blessing while his hassock grew sodden. A body sank away. At 10 A.M. Commissar Gorup sent a telegram to police headquarters which, deciphered, said: ALL FINISHED.

It was all finished except for the death certificate which was never issued. And except for the entry into the parish death registry, which would not be made for many weeks. Otherwise it was all finished officially as far as the person of Mary Baroness Vetsera was concerned. Overnight she vaporized into virtual tracelessness. In all the far reaches of the Dual Monarchy her name reached print just once again, in a provincial sheet called *Illustriertes Grazer Extrablatt*. It ran a story claiming that young Baroness Vetsera, a social figure in the capital, had died in Venice and was now resting in the family tomb in Pardubice, Bohemia. Somehow the article had bypassed the censor.

But apart from this stray fantasy, her name never appeared again in any book, magazine or newspaper published in Austria-Hungary. No printed mention was ever made of her death or even her life. It was as though nobody remembered that she had walked the earth. Her existence as daughter, sister and niece, as flirt or lover, as ballroom magnet and race-course presence, her whole career as glamour princess in the fashion columns of the daily press — all extinguished from the root, all finished. It had never happened. It had never begun.

It was all finished, and it was not all finished. Her extirpation completed only half the business in which she had been involved. If Mary's buriers must be thieves in the night, Rudolf's interment must be a daylight pageant, with every pomp of church and state.

Toward that purpose an autopsy was performed on the Crown Prince. At 8 P.M. on January 31, while Mary's uncles dressed her for her bizarre ride through the Vienna Woods, Court officials were busy in the Palace with her lover. A chamberlain opened the door of Rudolf's bedroom to admit the autopsy commission. It consisted of Professor Hermann Widerhofer, physician-in-chief to His Imperial and Royal Majesty; Privy Councillor Dr. Eduard Hofmann, director of the Institute for Forensic Medicine, and Professor Hans Kundrath, director of the Institute for Pathological Anatomy.

These distinguished scientists dissected and examined the Archduke until 2 A.M. They spent the night drawing up their report. It stated that His Imperial and Royal Highness, the most serene Crown Prince, had died as a result of the shattering of his skull and the anterior parts of the brain. That a bullet fired from a medium-caliber revolver had produced the injuries described. That His Imperial and Royal Highness himself had fired the shot. And that, lastly and most importantly, certain pathological formations had been found, such as "the clear flattening of cerebral convolutions, and the distensions of the ventricles which . . . are usually accompanied by abnormal mental conditions and therefore justify the assumption that the deed was committed in a state of mental confusion."

In short: Rudolf had not been quite lucid when he placed the revolver against his temple. By the lights of the Catholic Church he was not a suicide. Hence he could be buried, after the Habsburg manner and with Habsburg solemnity, in the crypt of the Capuchin friars, like all his ancestors before him.

Did the physicians bend the facts to allow this conclusion? In Austria many a coroner's report adjusted the truth in such a manner. Vienna, as we have seen, was a city of Catholic suicide-artists. Its doctors often exercised much deftness in discovering brain pathology which would allow a religious funeral. In the baroque climate truth was a holy game, not a narrow pedantry.

For the Imperial Family, the truth was especially malleable. Just as the Habsburgs' legal transactions transcended the judiciary, so their spiritual way stations lay high above parish or diocese. The Court Chaplain, Dr. Laurenz Mayer, was not subordinate, like other priests, to the Archbishop of Vienna. He stood directly under the

Pope himself. He wielded the independent authority of a cardinal. At the same time he was a member of the Court, ready to do his suzerain's pleasure. Now his verdict on Rudolf's burial was grounded on the autopsy report: it granted the Crown Prince obsequies with full ecclesiastical honors. Only at the Emperor's request did Dr. Mayer go through the additional motion of having his opinion ratified by the Nuncio, and through him by the Holy See.

There was quick growling at this among the Empire's hierarchs, especially the Archbishop of Prague, Count Schönborn. Rudolf, that liberal free-thinker, had never been a friend to the faith. Nor had he shown any affection or understanding for the hereditary aristocracy, many of whose members were princes of the Church. Why endow this dead libertine with a privilege he had not earned?

Because the Emperor so demanded. Or, to be more precise, because the Emperor had already so decided. On February 1, His Majesty's Chief Master of Ceremonies presided over a meeting in the Palace attended by the Court Chaplain, the Guardian of the Capuchins in charge of the Imperial Crypt, the Master of the Horse, the Master of the Music, the Chamber and Court Farrier, and the Commander of the Imperial Guards. This meeting, recorded in the official chronicle of Palace events, planned the ceremonial of a church funeral, "as approved of by His Majesty *on the previous day* [italics added]."

This approval is also recorded and dated in the Protocol of Ceremonies. It was given even earlier than "the previous day" which would have been January 31. Franz Joseph approved of, and therefore decreed, a church funeral "on the afternoon of January 30," more than twenty-four hours before the autopsy and before the "decision" of the Court Chaplain.

Now the sad command must be executed. Now solemnities must unfold, day after day, rising toward the climax of the actual entombment. While still breathing, Rudolf had been a refractory marionette of state. His corpse was a much more obedient object.

Three times it lay in state, on three successive days, in three different places. On January 31, it reposed in his own bedroom for

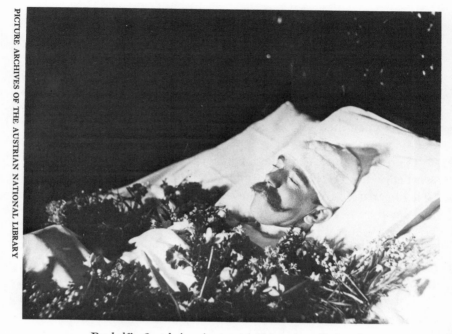

Rudolf's first lying-in-state in his palace bedroom

vigils of the Imperial Family alone. On February 1, following the autopsy, its broken skull was sealed with wax; its hair combed; its innards removed, mummified, put in a special vessel and placed, after Habsburg custom, in a special vault under the High Altar of St. Stephen's Cathedral; after the same custom, its heart, similarly enshrined, joined many ancestral hearts in a little crypt at St. Augustin's, the Court parish church.

What remained was embalmed and incensed and carried to a bier in a reception room. It was dressed in the white uniform of a general of the Army, the tunic starred with decorations and ribboned with the red-and-green band of the Order of St. Stephen. A cross of white ivory was pressed into the cold fingers. For two days it was displayed here, where incense, candle smoke and flower scents commingled into an unearthly mist. Here members of the Court came to pray, threading their way past kneeling priests, Imperial Guards keeping vigil, and countless wreaths. Hundreds of emperors, kings, presidents, potentates temporal and spiritual, had sent floral tributes through their ambassadors. So had thousands of cities and towns, guilds and corporate bodies throughout the realm, including the journalists' brotherhood, Concordia, whose wreath was dedicated much more simply than the others, "To the writer Crown Prince Rudolf."

On February 3, at 9 P.M. a black-robed group appeared. Singing Palestrina's *Miserere*, the Court Chapel boys' choir accompanied the body to yet another lying-in-state. It was moved to the Court Chapel which had been turned into a sacramental black cave. The pews, altar and oratory were draped in black, the floor black-carpeted. On a black-draped pedestal seven feet high, Rudolf's body floated white on a black cushion under a black canopy. His crown as Imperial Prince, his archducal hat, his Imperial sword and general's saber, his Order of the Golden Fleece, all lay on black velvet bolsters surrounding the body. Out of an underbrush of still more wreaths rose a forest of black candelabras. Pale flames flickered on candles longer than bayonets. Officers of Rudolf's regiment, drawn swords at attention, were black-sashed sentinels. From an invisible recess came the sound of dirges, one group of chanters spelling another without cease.

At seven o'clock the next morning, the chapel opened. For the first time the public could view the body. But the public, that is, the whole city of Vienna, had been tiding toward the corpse for many hours. There had been a general convergence through the snow which had begun dropping heavily from a dark heaven. From the inner districts and from the outer suburbs, from Ottakring and Erdberg, groups had been heading for the Palace. They moved in tramways, in carriages and by foot. They came in black. They had shopped the stores clean of black garments. Some had black carnival masks tied adroitly around their arms to look like mourning bands.

But there was nothing adroit about the crowds themselves. All grace of manner had gone from the streets. These crowds trudged heavily on the trampled snow. They were no longer Viennese. They stumbled against one another in the half-dark under massed black banners. Black flags hung so thickly from windows and roofs that some narrow streets looked like sinister tents and others like tunnels. House gates, lanterns, store signs were swathed in black.

Whole families were on the march through the snowy gloom, from grandfathers with canes to tots in prams. Space had been set aside for them around the Palace and along the Ringstrasse. But the area could not contain them. The pressure of their numbers overturned barricades and pushed aside cordons of Palace gendarmes. When the Court Chapel opened there was an oceanic forward crush. Children screamed, women fainted. Whole rows of pews were broken. Police shouted and soldiers tried to form a phalanx. Not till the Cavalry appeared would the crowd move back into more orderly formations. Ambulances had to be called; medical-corps men carried off twenty-odd casualties. A number of women suffered violent sobbing fits and had to be led away for treatment.

Meanwhile the viewing started. Multitudes passed in and out of the Court Chapel. Greater multitudes replaced them. There was no let-up, even toward evening. At 4 P.M. the police announced to the still swelling throng that the chapel would be closed for their own protection. Everyone should go home.

Nobody did. Nobody moved. The crowd stood motionless in the snow that had started melting into a drizzle. Thousands stood wet and immobile as the statues on the Ringstrasse roofs. A low, sepulchral chorus began to spread: *We want to see our Crown Prince. . . . We want to see our Crown Prince. . . .*

After an impasse, police on horseback proclaimed a message: The Emperor himself had intervened. At the All Highest command, viewing would be continued for another three hours.

Franz Joseph intervened everywhere, orchestrating even the minutiae of grief. His wife lay in bed sobbing, devastated. His daughters were in shock, nursed by their ladies-in-waiting. But he, being Franz Joseph, sat at his desk. He was doing his duty. His pen moved over papers. More than ever, he had overcome the personal father in him to turn wholly into all his people's patriarch; into the all-resilient, all-sheltering archbureaucrat. Rudolf, his successor, had killed himself, but he was at work integrating the death itself into Imperial continuity. In his hands disaster must become ritual; and ritual, a dynastic celebration. He never stopped, writing, summoning, conferring, commanding.

With his First Lord Chamberlain he charted the dimensions of Court Mourning: The first month, Deepest Mourning. The second month, Deep Mourning. The third month, Limited Mourning. Each phase provided different dress rules for different ranks, from the black jewelry of archducal ladies and the black scabbards of lord privy councillors in the first month, to the black visors and white gloves to be worn by Imperial and Royal ambassadors abroad, in the third.

Franz Joseph attended to that. He ordered the two coffins: the temporary wooden one, and the ornate metal sarcophagus craftsmen would work on for months. He inspected countless condolence telegrams from heads of state around the globe, and he minutely annotated countless acknowledgments drafted by secretaries in his chancellery. The thank-you cable to the King of Greece, for example, had to be corrected; it was not addressed in terms of *du* (the familiar second person singular). On the other hand the reply to the former Empress Eugenie of France must be redrafted because it did not apostrophize her as "Your Majesty."

The stampede of events may have overwhelmed his subjects. But Franz Joseph bore his sadness firmly. His overview encompassed not only the sea of messages from crowned chiefs and highnesses abroad but from district governors and little burgomasters throughout his domains, even from myriads of tiny hamlets like the one in southern Hungary which telegraphed its All Highest Lord:

THE HUMBLE INHABITANTS OF A SMALL REMOTE VILLAGE WITH THEIR TEARS SWELL THE SEA OF SORROW.
COMMUNITY OF BÖGÖZ

Franz Joseph saw to it that even such were answered by return wire, but not by himself, of course.

HIS MAJESTY'S THANKS FOR THE TOUCHING PROOF OF SYMPATHY.
PRINCE HOHENLOHE,
FIRST LORD CHAMBERLAIN

Finally a delicate telegraphic maneuver must be brought off. Just about every chief of state in Europe wanted to rush to Vienna for the funeral. They must all be kept away, ceremoniously. The monarch instructed his Foreign Minister to send identical dispatches to all his embassies. Again he supervised the phrasing himself.

UPON ALL HIGHEST COMMAND I INFORM YOU THAT HIS MAJESTY THE EMPEROR, MOST DEEPLY MOVED AND BOWED BY SORROW OVER THE TERRIBLE MISFORTUNE WHICH HAS BEFALLEN HIM AND HIS FAMILY, HAS DIRECTED THAT THE OBSEQUIES WILL TAKE PLACE IN THE CLOSEST FAMILY CIRCLE AND THAT ALL REQUESTS AND INQUIRIES CONCERNING THE POSSIBLE ARRIVAL HERE OF FOREIGN DIGNITARIES ARE TO BE ANSWERED ON THE LINES THAT HIS MAJESTY IS MOST SINCERELY GRATEFUL FOR ALL PROOFS OF SYMPATHY BUT DESIRES TO HAVE AROUND HIM, AT THIS PROFOUNDLY MOVING CEREMONY OF MOURNING, NONE BUT THE CLOSEST MEMBERS OF HIS FAMILY.

In some cases this wasn't enough. To the German Kaiser, Franz Joseph had to word a bald request in his own name.

YOUR WARM WORDS OF SINCERE PARTICIPATION IN OUR GRIEF HAVE DEEPLY MOVED THE EMPRESS AND MYSELF AND DONE OUR SORROWING HEARTS GOOD. ACCEPT OUR WARMEST THANKS FOR YOUR LOYAL FRIENDSHIP AND ALSO FOR YOUR INTENTION TO COME HERE. IF I ASK YOU NOT TO DO SO YOU MAY JUDGE HOW DEEPLY CRUSHED MY FAMILY IS IF WE HAVE TO ADDRESS THIS REQUEST EVEN TO YOU.

FRANZ JOSEPH

It would have been too much — the Prussian's muted gloating at Rudolf's bier. But a crush of other potentates would have been too much as well. The Empress was in no condition to bear the formalities engendered by such presences. Or, for that matter, to endure the low inquisitiveness this death aroused in highborn minds. Franz Joseph, who could endure anything, had another reason for not wanting his peers by his side: The funeral must be of uncluttered opulence, centering on father and son. If Rudolf's death was a major disruption of Franz Joseph's reign, his burial must be one of its major pageants, controlled and dominated by the monarch alone.

And that is precisely how it was staged. Thirty years earlier, in 1858, a select audience in the old Court Theater had watched a performance honoring the Crown Prince's birth. In 1889 a similar audience watched the drama of his death rites in exactly the same spot. On the demolition site of the old theater a gigantic grandstand, draped in black, was erected. Notables of the Empire took their seats here at 3 P.M. of February 5. It was the best place from which to observe the procession.

All around them the masses gathered. They came in even more tremendous numbers than for the lying-in-state. The overflow reached so far to the northern part of the Ringstrasse that Johann Pfeiffer, King of the Birds, had to retreat into a courtyard with his cage. Many in the crowd had been camping on cobbles for days — so important was it for them to catch a last good glimpse of their Crown Prince. They used field latrines put up by the Army. They lived on provisions they'd brought along, or bought sausages from hawkers. Other vendors offered them black-framed drawings of the high deceased, hastily printed booklets with his biography, and crape-edged nosegays of *Maiglöckchen*, lilies of the valley, his favorite flower.

All the milling and selling stopped on Tuesday afternoon, February 5. The black hats and wan faces which choked the streets all began to turn in the same direction. Every window along the funeral route brimmed with faces. Some young men actually balanced on the staffs from which black flags hung. The sun shone. Yes, after days of wet and snow, the sky had cleared for this crescendo. The sun shone hard, cold and clear. The crowds shuffled; they heaved and waited. Occasionally there were hoofbeats, muffled calls. Mounted police had to keep a path open from the Court Chapel along Michaelerplatz, Josefsplatz, Augustinerstrasse, Tegetthoffstrasse, to the Capuchin Church on the Neuer

Markt. Onto these streets a silence dropped, the heavy silence of a multitude.

At four o'clock sharp, the bells of the Court Chapel began to toll, slowly. Slowly, preceded by slow-riding Hussars, the ancient black mourning carriage of the Habsburgs drove out of the inner Palace courtyard, drawn by a pair of black steeds. The Emperor sat inside. For once the sight of him drew no cheers. Thousands of hands removed thousands of hats. Numberless heads bowed in silence, soldiers presented arms. Bells tolled, not only those of the Court Chapel now, but that of the cathedral and of all other churches in the metropolis, all beating together slowly, all in one tremendous, melancholy pulse.

Archducal carriages rode out next, coachmen sitting, footmen standing, in black tricornered hats, black livery, black stockings and black-buckled shoes. Then came a single Lipizzaner with a rider in formal Spanish mourning dress. Then a six-horse carriage occupied by Rudolf's Lord Chamberlains and the principal officers of his personal Court. And then came the hearse itself, a black baroque sculpture, pulled by six Lipizzaner grays. Under a black canopy held up by fretted black columns, surmounted by Rudolf's arms in gold, the coffin floated through the ringing of the bells. Bells, bells, they rang slowly from ten thousand and one steeples throughout the realm, from Lake Constance on the Swiss border to the wilds of Transylvania. You were never out of earshot of metal, moaning.

On both sides of the hearse moved burning torches. Pages in feudal dress held them aloft, marching in single file. Riding in single file to their right were six Arciere Honor Guards with white plumes on silver helmets, their crimson coats studded with gold; to the left, six Hungarian Honor Guards on white steeds, in silver-laced red tunics, tiger-striped capes fluttering off one shoulder. Then came, also on horseback, medieval bodyguards with halberds and black panaches. Then came, marching stiffly, a battalion that was a mosaic of the Monarchy's armed prowess — one company of the Imperial and Royal Army, one of the Austrian Militia, one of the Hungarian National Guard, one of fezzed Bosnian Sharpshooters, and one company of Marines in the uniform of the

Austro-Hungarian Navy. Then came the lesser figures of Rudolf's entourage on foot, and finally a rearguard squadron of Hussars.

Yet other presences traveled in the cortege, neither visible nor audible, yet flamboyant in the minds of the staring masses. These were the rumors about the Crown Prince's true end: that he had been shot by a poacher, knifed by a girl's outraged brother, assassinated by a foe at Court, fallen victim to a gallant duel . . . As the bells tolled, the torches flared, the Hussars' horses pranced, these stories grew beyond scandal. They merged into the pageant, magnifying it. They misted into a heraldic frieze, new embroidery on the old Habsburg myth by which the city had lived for seven hundred years.

And now, as had happened in so many generations, the myth was punctuated once more by a high death; by the halt of an august procession before the small, plain Church of the Capuchins.

Karl Count Bombelles, Rudolf's First Lord Chamberlain, disembarked from his carriage. With a golden staff he knocked against the simple portal. The dialogue began, ancient and brief.

"Who is it?" a friar demanded from inside.

"His Most Serene Imperial and Royal Highness, the Archduke Crown Prince Rudolf of Habsburg."

"We know him not."

The door remained closed. Again the golden staff knocked.

"Who is there?"

"The Crown Prince Rudolf."

"We know him not."

The door remained closed. Once more the golden staff must knock.

"Who is there?"

"Your brother Rudolf. A poor sinner."

The door opened. It admitted the casket, which black-clad lackeys had lifted from the hearse. The Emperor entered after it.

Inside, the narrow church was packed with splendor: The Prince Cardinal of Vienna; the Papal Nuncio; the Austrian bishops in their ceremonial vestments; the ambassadors and plenipotentiaries extraordinary accredited to the Court, all in formal dress with swords; the highest aristocrats; the Emperor's cabinet; the governors-general of the realm's component states; the chiefs of its great cities, including a giant white-bearded and fezzed grandee, Beg Mustapha Fazli Paschic, the Lord Mayor of Sarajevo.

Franz Joseph walked to his pew in the first row, next to the King and Queen of Belgium, the one royal pair whose coming he had not been able to prevent. They were, after all, parents of the widow. With the others in the church the Emperor listened to the Cardinal's prayer. He chanted, knelt, crossed himself. And when the service was over he did a thing the Court could not believe. He, the chief ikon of dynastic ritual, broke out of the rite.

This moment came after the footmen lifted the casket. Rudolf's First Lord Chamberlain was leading it into the crypt to hand over his master's remains, together with the casket keys, to the perpetual care of the Chief Friar. Ceremonial demanded that the First Lord Chamberlain perform this final act of his office alone — and ceremonial was violated by Franz Joseph himself.

On sudden impulse, he walked with the Lord Chamberlain down the steps. Not only that, but when the casket came to rest in the crypt, he dropped to his knees, kissed the wood of this still-temporary coffin, weeping, and, weeping, whispered the Pater Noster. For one minute he was the broken, heedless, poor sinning father of a poor dead sinner.

Then he rose to his feet without assistance. He took out his handkerchief, applied it to his face. He walked out, dry of eye and firm of step. He was by God's grace the Emperor of Austria and the Apostolic King of Hungary, ready to rule another twenty-seven years. The episode was over.

Chapter 25

"Throughout these heavy days," reported the German military attaché in Vienna, "the Emperor kept to his schedule of military briefings, political decisions, and the dispatch of executive decrees. . . . After January 30, his work proceeded at the same pace as before."

Franz Joseph had purged himself of private calamity through meticulous pyrotechnics of public grief. His capital could not recover so efficiently. Spectacle failed the city, perhaps for the first time. The day after the funeral Vienna awoke as from a dismal jag. The sun was gone. From the funerary pageant only street litter was left, and Lipizzaner droppings rimed with frost.

The show was over and the fact sank in. How could it have happened? What exactly was it that yesterday's great dark circus had tried to celebrate away? What had turned this fairy prince, this arrow toward greatness — into a corpse? Nobody knew for sure. Everybody distrusted everything, particularly official bulletins. Many people believed the forbidden, that is, newspaper stories printed abroad, beyond the reach of censorship.

It hadn't escaped the foreign press that a young lady of social fame had vanished just when the Crown Prince died. Outside the Empire, front-page sensations exploded like gushers and then poured across Austrian borders. It became the job of the police to confiscate a flood tide. On a single day, February 19, they impounded 4790 copies of various foreign journals in Vienna. Still, a black market of Rudolf revelations developed fast. Most fiacre cabbies — those eternal foilers of authority — kept a Mayerling lending library under their seats. The fee was forty kreuzers, and the maximum loan period ten minutes. For that long you could wolf down a copy of Munich's *Neueste Nachrichten* whose headline contained the word "Vetsera."

But double suicide with the Baroness was by no means the only popular plot line. Another was put forth by a book published in Bavaria only fourteen days after the funeral. It had a pregnant Mary as the Prince's murderer, and his bodyguards as her executioners. Yet other versions saw Rudolf as the victim of Mary's brothers, or of the Duke of Braganza, or of a forester avenging the seduction of his wife, or of a cunning dagger hired by the Crown Princess, by the Crown Princess's brother, by the Jesuits, by the Freemasons, by Bismarck, by the German Kaiser, by the Tsar's secret police. . . .

These rumors did not really titillate. They disturbed. The funeral itself, with its daubs of high color, only added to the bafflement, now that one looked back at it in cold retrospect. Empress Elisabeth, the Crown Prince's own mother, had not participated. Nor had his widow, the Crown Princess Stephanie. Why? The official *Wiener Zeitung* stated that the shock had endangered the health of these august ladies. Their doctors had not permitted them to attend. Neither Loschek nor old Nehammer, Rudolf's most intimate servants, had been in the procession. The newspapers explained that Loschek suffered from an abscess on the neck and that both were incapacitated by grief. But Bratfisch, whose stamina matched the Emperor's — where was he?

And there had been a more crushing absence of much greater official weight. The Cardinal Archbishop of Budapest had not come. Nor was he the only gap in church ranks. Pope Leo XIII had approved of the funeral and telegraphed his condolences. Yet at the solemn requiem mass held for the Crown Prince in the Church of Santa Maria dell-Anima in Rome on the day of the funeral — the Vatican's entire College of Cardinals had stayed away.

Austrian newspapers didn't publish the fact. But all Vienna knew it by the next morning. Vienna also knew very quickly that at Trient, in South Tyrol, the requiem had been read only in mutilated form; that in Merano a defiant priest had tried to close his church on the funeral day; that in Linz only the Protestant churches had rung bells in Rudolf's memory; and that even in the Emperor's favorite Alpine resort of Ischl, the parish priest had kept the bells silent during the Crown Prince's burial.

Of course many ecclesiastics considered Rudolf, not without reason, a radical, an Imperial infidel come to a heathen end. But he was no longer a danger. His official memory was now the Emperor's property. Why should that property be defaced — even by cardinals? Had Rudolf's life been so unforgivable? Or his death? Something seemed to have gone awry between Church and Crown. These two had been the joint impresarios of the great Austrian centuries. Together they had cast over reality's daily mud an authorized fantasy that was palliating and redemptive. Now a rift had cut between them. The hope of the future had become a painted cadaver in a crypt. A crack ran through a fundamental premise of the realm. The city shivered.

"I have lived through the saddest catastrophes in Vienna," wrote Eduard Hanslick, the supreme music critic of the *Neue Freie Presse*. "I have lived through revolutions, the loss of lands, murderous devastations by flood and fire — nothing of all this is comparable to the horror of January 30. . . . The disconsolate, desperate turbulence which ripped through the entire population is indescribable . . ."

And yet, slowly, a semblance of normality had to be attempted. On February 10, the Court Theater resumed performances. Through unfortunate scheduling it reopened with Grillparzer's *Sappho*; that is, a tragedy featuring premeditated suicide, the very thing the government had been at pains to exorcise from the Rudolf melodrama.

On the same day an official portrait of Archduke Franz Ferdinand, Franz Joseph's nephew, was issued. Many newspapers published it. Franz Ferdinand's father, as the Emperor's next eldest brother, was by Habsburg house law next in line for the throne. The father had not yet officially relinquished the claim to the son. Still, the ubiquity of the son's portraits foretold such an act, as did the announcement that the Emperor had received Franz Ferdinand in a long audience. Unofficially, the young Archduke was the new Crown Prince.

But who was this Franz Ferdinand? Court intimates spoke of his weak lungs, his jagged temper, his clerical disposition. The *Wiener Tagblatt*, which ran his picture, also wrote an editorial about the fate of Europe's great liberal princes: the passing of progress-minded German Emperor Friedrich, who reigned only ninety days before his death, had put Kaiser Wilhelm into power. And now Rudolf's tragedy in Austria had brought Franz Ferdinand to the fore. "A nemesis seems to pursue those men fit for rule not only by birth but by ability . . ."

Nemesis hung over the roofs. On February 11, Franz Joseph with his Empress and his entire Court traveled to Budapest for an indefinite stay. True, the move had been planned before Mayerling; indeed Magyar politics demanded it. And yet the capital felt forsaken. The same week Archduke Ludwig Viktor left for Kleesheim, his castle in Salzburg. Archduke Karl Ludwig went to Merano for a cure. Archduke Albrecht had military business in Arco where he joined Archduke Karl Salvator. Archduke Eugen sojourned in Olmütz, Bohemia, on some prolonged official occasion. Franz Ferdinand, the de facto heir apparent, returned to garrison duty in Prague, and the Crown Princess Widow Stephanie (as she was styled henceforth) must for her health's sake take to the sun at Miramar on the Adriatic. The *Neue Freie Presse* summed up all these trips in one laconic sentence: "For the first time almost no members of the Imperial Family are present in Vienna at this season."

But "this season" was no longer The Season. Carnival had died. The ballrooms were closed, the great chandeliers remained unlit, the orchestra stands empty, the waltzes undanced. Why linger?

Many high aristocrats followed the All Highest example. Every day, luxury sleeping cars had to be added to trains leaving the Southern Railway terminal. The compartments filled up with Their Serene Highnesses, the Princes Lobkowitz, the Esterházys, the Windischgrätzes, with their trunks and their retinues. "Suddenly many of our great nobles find it necessary to go south," said the *Wiener Tagblatt* on February 21. "Wintertime is not merry enough for them this year. Let the lower echelons in Vienna do all the mourning. The people of our city, who must absorb the grievous death of the Crown Prince, will survive this blow too. But they won't forget it either."

"The Crown Prince" still meant Rudolf. In the popular mind that name and that office were still so intertwined that even a grand-opera funeral could not part them. It was not: *The Crown Prince is dead — long live the Crown Prince!* It was: *The Crown Prince is dead* . . . Silence. Emptiness. Grandees scatter, maggots twitch. And the cold wind blows.

"In the annals of 1889," said a financial article, "our true Ash Wednesday will be fixed not on March 6 but on January 30."

The death of our Crown Prince necessarily entails the demise of our carnival. This signifies a material loss to Vienna which its inhabitants will bear with the same selflessness with which they are bearing the moral loss. Thousands of ball preparations, agreements, contracts, budgetary allocations by corporate and private parties have been canceled overnight. The huge entertainment *établissements* will suffer, but their damages are easier to bear than the ones sustained by innumerable other trades, from those concerned with the manufacture of ladies' favors to fashion workshops producing evening gowns or specializing in masquerade costumes. Leather-goods firms are particularly hard hit. Their carnival novelties are usually ideas of the moment and cannot be used again next year. A great loss has been suffered by charities who will not receive the proceeds they expected. This applies to the balls of the White Cross, the Red Cross, the Railway Employees' Benefit Ball, and dozens of District Welfare Balls . . .

For some the catastrophe resulted in overwork. Three seamstresses fainted on February 10 in a plant in the Ottakring District. They had sat for fourteen hours straight at sewing machines stitching mourning clothes together. For many more workers the opposite held true: Mayerling meant neither an overtime windfall nor a perfumed Grand Guignol — it meant no food on tomorrow's table.

On February 16, Dr. Rainer von Reinöhl, an economics professor at the University, published statistics showing that two hundred thousand of Vienna's less than two million lived below the starvation level. That for a majority of Viennese workers the expenses of raising a family resulted in the beginnings of malnutrition. And that the so-called Greater Vienna Plan would only aggravate the destitution: If the working-class neighborhoods outside city limits were to be incorporated into the City of Vienna, then their poor inhabitants must pay city taxes and thereby have less money than ever for food.

This study used findings obtained before Mayerling. Afterward the picture became still grimmer. Carnival-connected firms cut back, employees were let go, at least for the time being. Charity funding dried up. And, to complete the wretchedness, in mid-February the temperature fell to the year's brute low point, eleven degrees below zero Celsius.

In slum districts like Ottakring and Erdberg — candidates for inclusion in Greater Vienna — many hundreds shivered their way to the *Wärmestuben*. These "warming rooms" were maintained at government expense for the indigent who either had no roof or could not afford coal and kindling wood for whatever shelter they had. But the *Wärmestuben*, soon crammed beyond capacity, had to turn back half the people pressing against their doors.

On February 20, a woman was hauled into court for living with her little son down in the windproof sewers, close to the warm effluents. The charge: endangering her child's health. The defense: there was no other way to keep the child from freezing. The judge acquitted her and condemned society. The result: mother and child were free to go out into the cold again.

✤ Chapter 26 ✤

Franz Joseph, residing in Budapest, seemed to have averted his face. Rudolf lay in his temporary coffin. The aristocrats raced their greyhounds in sunny Abbazia. Only the people were left in the city, to starve, to shiver and to grieve. Some turned angrily away from Habsburg to Hohenzollern — to the north, toward Germany. Pan-Germanism was a soiled sentiment since von Schönerer's jailing. Nevertheless it enjoyed a sturdy life underground as well as above. In bad times it could ignite unexpectedly. On February 7, it singed Hugo Wolf.

On that date one of the first cultural events after Mayerling took place. It was a *Lieder* recital and as such not out of key, having not a merry but a serious nature. The Wagner Society gave an evening largely devoted to Hugo Wolf songs, performed by the great baritone Ferdinand Jäger. The young composer himself sat at the piano, but hardly in the state of elation he ought to feel on "his" evening. He was irritated by a quarrel with his publisher, worn out by the secrecy of his affair with Melanie Köchert, depressed by the funereal atmosphere in the city. In addition, a false rumor had been making the rounds in the Wagner Society. It whispered, to his vexation, that Wolf was a Jew.

So he acknowledged the opening applause with a glare. But it

wouldn't have helped him if he had been in a better mood that
night. Herr Jäger was singing *"Heimweh"* ("Homesickness")
based on an Eichendorff poem. An ovation broke loose when he
came to the line *"Grüss dich, Deutschland, aus Herzensgrund!"*
"A salute to you, oh Germany, from the heart's depths!" The
applause here took no note whatsoever of Wolf's music. It was a
purely political noise. Nor would the clapping and the stamping
cease. Finally the Society chairman had to get up and remind the
audience that the song was not finished. Herr Jäger began from
the start again. Again he was interrupted at the same point by a
pan-German demonstration. Wolf slammed his music sheets together, cursing. Pandemonium. Calls for the police on the part of
the nonpolitical music-minded. Herr Jäger threatened to leave, and
would have, if the Teutons hadn't marched out first in closed
formation.

During those frigid weeks they made their presence known
everywhere. A pan-German sheet called *Kyffhäuser* printed a
warning: Let Jewry stop its machinations; it no longer had protectors in high places. The same sheet had printed the news of the
Crown Prince's death as a small item in the "Miscellaneous"
column.

Young Dr. Schnitzler ran into a related viciousness. The Polyclinic Ball had already taken place and the Ball Committee met at
an inn to review finances. A member got up, the same one who
earlier had placed a ball ad in an anti-Semitic paper and been
rebuked for it by Schnitzler. Now he rose to accuse "this Jewish
gentleman" — Schnitzler — of a felony committed during the ball:
The Jewish gentleman had had the gall to ask the orchestra leader
to repeat a waltz instead of letting the music go on to the quadrille
scheduled next in the dance program. The accuser grew increasingly vehement and finally demanded a formal and humble apology
from "the offender." Even more astounding than the virulence of
the charge was the vote of the committee when the Jewish gentleman refused to drop to his knees. Only the month before they had
voted with Schnitzler to rebuke the anti-Semitic member. Now,
on the question of forcing Schnitzler to apologize, they voted
five-five. Whereupon the committee chairman broke the tie in

favor of the Jewish gentleman, presumably because his father controlled the Polyclinic.

There was an outbreak of veiled thrusts. In Parliament, German-nationalist deputies proposed a complicated bill which, without spelling out the issue involved, would make it hard for Jews to change their names. And from the Winter Palace of St. Petersburg — always Rudolf's *bête noir* and the most anti-Semitic of all courts — came curious news.

Apparently the Tsar had permitted a break of the etiquette observed by all other crowned heads in Europe. Barely a week after obsequies for the Austrian Crown Prince, a court ball had been held in the Russian capital. To be sure, it had been a "black ball." The master of ceremonies had wielded a black staff. The ladies had danced in black decolletage dresses with long black trains. Decorations had been black and Lucullan dishes were served on black china. The Tsarina had worn a virtual cap of diamonds set off stunningly by her black gown. It had been a most piquant and animated affair. Something very different. Among the guests only one diplomat had appeared. No others had been invited. That one had been the Ambassador of His German Majesty, the Prussian King.

By then the word *Mayerling* had already begun to phosphoresce throughout the world. Abroad it tingled and thrilled. In Vienna it was like some hidden hell machine of which nothing was known except that it was made of gold. Now and then the city tried to shake off the giant riddle that undermined its boulevards. There erupted rumors of some rational solution. At one point word spread that Johann Pfeiffer, King of the Birds, had heard his parrots speak the truth of what had happened in Rudolf's hunting lodge. A crowd formed at the Schottenring. The police brought the man and his black-craped cage to a precinct house. But the birds just blithered and jabbered in panic, and their King lost his renowned humor. The bafflement continued.

In the second week of February a Monsignor Luigi Galimberti drove up to Mayerling itself. Ordinarily nobody could enter the estate. Guards kept the gates barred. But the Monsignor was Papal Nuncio to the Empire. He had to be admitted.

At the lodge the Lord Marshal's agent, Dr. Heinrich Slatin, was still busy, drawing up an inventory of assets and objects for the Emperor in his capacity as Rudolf's executor. Slatin had to stop work when the Nuncio walked in, his corpulence beautifully caped, his hands folded. Since he didn't speak German, he and Slatin communicated in an awkward mixture of Italian and Latin. The Nuncio conveyed blessings from the Holy See and then expressed the desire to sanctify "all the unfortunate places" with humble prayer. He asked that these be pointed out to him, with appropriate explanations of what had transpired where in this most deplorable tragedy. He particularly wanted to pray over the spots where the bullets had struck after leaving the poor flesh. "*Quam multi globuli?*" he asked in his Church Latin. "How many bullets?"

Dr. Slatin realized almost too late what was afoot: he was being ushered, euphoniously and piously, toward a trap. If he admitted to more than one bullet, he might also be admitting the possibility of more than one death and therefore the killing of Mary Vetsera. "Since I never had the Crown Prince's revolver in my own hand," he would write in a memoir published after his own death, "I could truthfully answer, '*Nescio*, I don't know.' Otherwise I would have fallen into the snare of this cunning and jovial prince of the Church."

Characteristically more blunt in his curiosity about Mayerling was Johannes Brahms. But uncharacteristic for the normally cool North German was his perturbation over the suicide. He even took time off from his rehearsal with Joachim. Because of Mayerling the premiere of his Third Sonata for Violin and Piano must be delayed anyway. In the meantime the master shot off to his publisher in Berlin what was for him quite a shaken letter: "The saying that 'everything has happened before' has been dashed to pieces. It is new how emperors and kings kill themselves. They explode, they drown [an allusion to King Ludwig of Bavaria], they kill themselves. And now, in addition to all this, our Imperial tragedy. . . . Would you send me newspapers from your side of the border — but in an envelope, please . . ."

At the other end of the musical and emotional gamut, Brahms's antagonist suffered the same shock still more intensely. Anton Bruckner was not merely affected by Mayerling. He was consumed by it.

On an icy mid-February morning, somebody knocked at the door of Bruckner's young musician friend Friedrich Eckstein. Outside stood the master's housekeeper, the incomparable and much-tried Kathi Kachelmayer. She had a message. Professor Bruckner had got it into his head to go sleigh-riding in the Vienna Woods with Herr Eckstein, if Herr Eckstein would share the expense, and that's why she had to go chasing through the cold streets at this unearthly hour. What did Herr Eckstein say to such an idea? The Professor was dying to know in his usual sudden fashion.

Herr Eckstein had a well-to-do father as well as an unquestioning reverence for genius. He was one of Bruckner's very few true friends. An hour and a half later the two boarded a train at the Southern Railway terminal. Bruckner, in his usual broad-brimmed hat and loden cape, pulled at his enormous scarf and, peculiarly distracted, exclaimed over and over again at how wonderful the fresh snow looked and how marvelous the landscape would be still deeper in the woods. They got out at Baden. Here Bruckner fussed tremendously over the right kind of horse and the suitable sort of sleigh, and it was not until he told the driver to head toward the Monastery of Heiligenkreuz that Eckstein grasped the reason behind the frenzy.

"Here it became obvious," Eckstein wrote in his memoirs, "what the true subject of Bruckner's thought was, and the object of his trip. It was about the event that had occupied him so much during the last few days, the entirely unexpected death of Crown Prince Rudolf, the catastrophe of Mayerling. It was barely a week since these things had happened that had filled Bruckner with the deepest horror. Now he began once more, perhaps for the one hundredth time, to discuss the matter with me and to ask my opinion of it. He confessed that the true purpose of the sleigh ride was not his need to breathe fresh air or to enjoy the winter scenery, but the insatiable, overwhelming desire to visit the site of all these horrors, to inspect closely the area itself, and, if possible, to learn from persons living there details about the uncanny events.

"Therefore he had decided to visit first the Monastery of Heiligenkreuz, to find out details from some of the monks, or perhaps even from the Abbot himself, who was his personal friend, and of whom it was said that he had performed the last rites over the corpse. . . .

"After lunch we entered the monastery. Bruckner asked a monk to announce him to the Abbot, who greeted Bruckner very respectfully. . . .

"The conversation was general at first: the seriousness of the times, certain ecclesiastical issues, the musical situation in Vienna, etc. Not a word about the Crown Prince or the catastrophe of Mayerling. Bruckner began to show obvious signs of impatience. I saw that he was getting tired of all this diplomacy. And sure enough he burst out. Really! Would the Abbot not ever mention anything about those certain occurrences! Those critical days at Mayerling?

"The Abbot, so suddenly interrupted in his small talk, actually seemed not to have heard the question. But Bruckner repeated it and became more importunate. The Abbot, at bay, had to give a serious reply.

"Yes, he said, he had given final blessings to a corpse under unusual circumstances, at an unusual hour; but he was still so shaken by the events that it was entirely impossible for him to talk about it. [This was the Abbot who had buried Mary Vetsera.] In addition, he could not grossly violate the silence to which he had been sworn.

"Bruckner, very disappointed, now gave up his effort. We returned to small talk, and before taking our leave, Bruckner had to agree to the Abbot's request to play the great organ of the monastery for the evening's blessing.

"Soon afterward I had the good fortune to hear the master make this venerable powerful instrument come alive in the deepest silence of the forest. Bruckner fantasized for a while variations on a choral theme which preoccupied him just at that time, and he knew how to get the most moving effects out of this very simple melody. . . .

"At 6 P.M. we climbed into the sleigh again, but to my surprise Bruckner asked the driver not to return to Baden, but to drive first to Mayerling itself. We reached it after a marvelous journey through wooded gorges now swathed in darkness. Bruckner had hoped to meet a local here or there, and to get him to talk, or to look at the site of these murderous events from up close. Again he was disappointed. The sequestered hunting lodge was quite dark, all entrances locked and barricaded, no human being anywhere. We climbed out of the sleigh to look at the place more closely, but saw no movement. But as we walked along the building, we noticed a feeble light in the last window on the ground floor. Inside we spied a few nuns in black veils who were reading their breviaries by candlelight or whispering prayers. This unexpected sight was so spooky that Bruckner vehemently clasped my arm.

"Now it was obvious that we had no business being there, and that we had no alternative but to return with our purpose unful-filled. Silently, we returned to our monastery in order to warm and fortify ourselves with its wine. This drink chased away the ghosts of night. . . ."

They did not stay chased very long. Back in Vienna, Bruckner stood in front of the Imperial Palace and counted, over and over again, its many hundreds of windows. At home he tried to find a letter from his friend August Göllerich in Regensburg. It had answered his request to total up the exact number of embellish-ments on Regensburg City Hall — turrets, weather vanes, gar-goyles, etc. Bruckner's counting mania had come upon him again, as it sometimes did in times of stress: the need somehow to order and structure and contain a great amorphous doom.

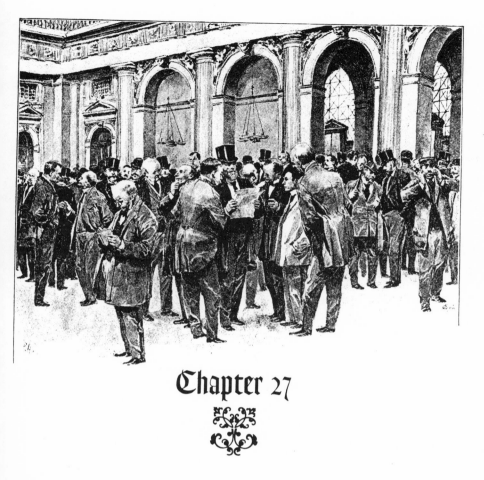

Chapter 27

The whole city had become a hive of paroxysms and aberrations centered on the new body in the Capuchin Church. Despite the cold, lines lengthened daily at the crypt entrance. With almost hourly regularity, stretcher-bearers carried out women who had fainted before Rudolf's coffin. A delegation of gypsies arrived to lay a wreath with the inscription: *Oh, great prince, our zithers will moan for you!* On the same day all the gold leaves vanished from the giant wreath left by the French press. The widow Rosalia Franzl, praying by the casket, was robbed of her pocketbook with the savings of a year.

Peasants from Dalmatia and the Tyrol came straggling on foot into the city, hoping they would still be on time for the funeral. Some of them mistook the Stock Market for the Palace. This was quite natural. No life stirred at the Palace. But the Stock Market, a neo-Renaissance splendor on the Ringstrasse (diagonally opposite Freud's house), swirled with top-hatted gentlemen in mourning clothes. With pensive countenance they maintained the firm upward trend in prices.

It was weeks since Rudolf's death, but grotesqueries would not stop. A special Chinese funeral flag had been sent express from the Emperor at Peking, and the Chinese Ambassador couldn't be dissuaded from climbing onto the roof of the Hotel Imperial to hoist it personally. He almost fell off. Within two hours the wind tore the flag loose; like a gaudy eagle it floated above the streets. It was joined by a melee of black kites in the sky, for many of the regular funeral flags had pulled free as well.

And the suicide season in Vienna, which had paused for a while as if in awe of superior company, began again. In fact, it took off with almost competitive flamboyance. On February 8, a railway employee named Franz Caspar climbed into a giant copper kettle in the courtyard of the Technological Institute. Not a drop of liquid could seep out of this vessel. Here Franz Caspar cut both his wrists as well as his throat. When he was found, the doctors weren't sure what he had died of, his wounds or drowning in his own blood.

Two days later a jeweler's assistant, Joseph Enderle, set for himself and his five children a sumptuous Sunday table of high tea: coffee, cake, cookies, whipped cream, gingerbread — treats quite beyond his threadbare means. Sunday night the six were dead. Herr Enderle had laced the coffee with strychnine.

Two days later still, a soldier pointed a gun at himself and pulled the trigger. His act would not have received very prominent notice, especially since he survived his severe wound. But he had tried to kill himself while doing sentry duty at Laxenburg, Rudolf's summer residence.

Soon things began to happen that showed how deeply the Crown Prince's fate had stained the imaginations of young men. One of these was David Mosé, a gifted art student of eighteen. He obtained permission to sketch the Crown Prince's lying-in-state at the Court Chapel. His drawing attracted the approval of the monarch himself, and the Lord Chamberlain's Office acquired reproduction rights for twenty gold ducats. Mosé collected the honorarium at the bureau of the Palace Paymaster; on his way home — he lived at Berggasse 22 — he suddenly lapsed into delirium. To passers-by on the Ringstrasse he shouted his name, and that of his parents, and "Mayerling." An ambulance carried him away.

Another painter, Georg Hartmann, was well embarked on a successful career. He enjoyed commissions from the highest aristocracy. The news of the Crown Prince's death, though, pushed him into nervous exhaustion. He took to his bed. The only sentence he would speak to visiting friends was "I am also thirty years old. . . . I am also thirty years old. . . ." After a week he went back to the easel. But he changed the half-finished landscape on his canvas to the portrait of a young man lying in state. Then, within the space of a week, he stabbed himself with a scissors, slashed himself with a razor, and jumped from a third-floor window. On the sixteenth of February he was committed to Professor Meynert's psychiatric clinic at the University.

This was the clinic to which Dr. Freud had not been admitted as a physician. By 1889 Freud had drifted away still further from the neurological orientation of his old teacher Meynert. And he was not the man to hide either drift or rift. He had the inner armor to take both the penalties and the rewards of the outsider.

But he was no maverick when it came to being a Habsburg subject. The Imperial charisma touched him as it did others. It was not insignificant that his mother had translated her birthday from the Jewish to the Christian calendar so that it coincided with Franz Joseph's on August 18. Freud himself transmitted to his children this fascination with the Crown. His son Martin recalled fond stories his father told about the Emperor. And: "We Freud children were all stout royalists, delighting to hear or to see all we could of the Royal Court. We were always entranced to see a Hofwagen, a coach of the Court, and we could tell with precision the extent of the passenger's importance by the color of the high wheels and the angle at which the magnificently liveried coachman held his whip."

Freud's principal biographer, Ernest Jones, relates that Freud was "greatly shocked" by the drowning of King Ludwig of Bavaria in 1886. Even the death of a more remote prince like that of Alfonso XII of Spain in 1885 made (again in Jones's words) "a deep impression." Yet Freud was quite provoked by his own disturbance: "The complete stupidity of the hereditary system is seen through a whole country's being upset by the death of a single person."

What, then, did Dr. Freud say about the suicide of the Crown Prince, whose Palace lay fifteen minutes away from the Freud residence? What did a cataclysm so heavy with psychiatric overtones signify to him? What did he, inevitably sensitive to Imperial symbols, insignia and anecdotes, think about Mayerling?

Nothing whatsoever, in print. Not a syllable of comment has come down in any book. Not one word about it in any article, monograph, published letter or even oral mention chronicled by others.

It would seem a remarkable feat of abstention — *except*. Except that the subject muffled in this Freudian silence bulks unnamed but imperfectly neutralized and quite unmistakable in the work that occupied the young doctor during the days of Mayerling, as well as before and after it: the paper he wrote, and kept rewriting, in French on the cause of paralysis.

It was a stringently scientific tract, framed in scholar's language. Yet in it can be heard eerie echoes of the hunting lodge in the Vienna Woods. For example, it explores at length the difference in brain disease between organic and hysteric paralyses. Hysteria, the paper said, produces a so-called functional lesion which is "indeed a lesion but one of which no trace can be found after death." These lesions, "although they may not persist after death, are true organic lesions even if they are slight and transitory."

This sounds like a furtive postscript to the autopsy report on Rudolf. Echoes of Rudolf become still stronger as the paper examines the problem of an arm that refuses to move.

"I will give a suitable example," Freud wrote. ". . . I only ask permission to move on to psychological ground — which can scarcely be avoided when talking about hysteria. . . . I will begin with some examples drawn from the social side. A comic story is

Dr. Sigmund Freud in his passport photograph for 1888

told of a loyal subject who would not wash his hand because his sovereign had touched it. The relation of this hand to the idea of the king seemed so important to the man's psychical life that he refused to let the hand enter into any other relation. . . . Savage tribes in antiquity, who burned their dead chief's horse, his weapons and even his wives along with his body, were obeying this idea that nobody should ever touch them after him."

In the same way, Freud wrote, a hysterically paralyzed arm "is not accessible to conscious associations and impulses because . . . [it] is saturated with the memory of the event, the trauma which produced the paralysis."

And as if the undertow of this weren't strong enough, Freud then proceeded to a discussion whose terms exactly fit the psychic aftermath of the Rudolf-shock. He dealt with the "surplus" feeling an event may produce through "subconscious associations." The surplus can be "abreacted," i.e., discharged. "If the subject is unwilling or unable to get rid of this surplus, the memory of the impression attains the importance of a trauma and becomes the cause of permanent hysterical symptoms."

Here Freud used for the first time the word "subconscious." For the first time he employed the crucial principles of repression and abreaction — so new to himself that he was naming them for the first time. For the first time he used examples from anthropology to flesh out his ideas. For the first time he fully unloosed an intuition that was encyclopedic, heterodox, unpredictable; ranging from neurological scholarship at the start of the paper to nuances scooped "from the social side" at the end.

The paper, with its Mayerling subtext, was a seedbed of psychoanalysis. What's more, in doing all this Freud may also have shored up his own sanity against the demons roaming the streets since January 30. There is a therapy to which only the creative are privileged. Freud "abreacted" his Mayerling trauma by using it to construct an insight — about abreaction. And when it came to publishing the paper, he repressed the abreaction. "For accidental and personal reasons," as Freud put it, without ever explaining, the paper did not see print until 1893.

Two weeks after the Crown Prince's death Franz Joseph took a number of steps which proved Dr. Freud a precise case-historian of Mayerling and, incidentally, Anton Bruckner an accurate spy.

Rudolf's testament bequeathed Mayerling to his little daughter Elisabeth. The Emperor lost no time in buying it from her, very quietly, sometime in mid-February. A few days later the Lord Marshal's Commission, still taking inventory at the lodge, found itself interrupted again. Now it was not the Papal Nuncio but another spiritual personage: Maria Euphrasia Kaufmann, Prioress of the order of Discalced Carmelites at Baumgarten near Vienna. She was accompanied by the architect Josef Schmalzhofer. It was His Majesty's command, Herr Schmalzhofer said, to build a new Carmelite nunnery on the site. For that purpose he had to do some surveying here. And very soon, even before the arrival of masons, the Carmelite Sisters began to take over Mayerling. Bruckner had glimpsed their dark, hooded figures that winter night. He may have been among the first outsiders to know a fact which was not announced until April 9.

The architect's instructions were to bury the hunting lodge

under the convent. The walls of the bedroom that had enclosed Rudolf's end were pulled down, and the parquet floor ripped up. The spiral staircase was demolished together with the rarely used matrimonial bedroom to which it led. On the roof, the chimneys were plucked away. All the outer contours of this wing were changed and enlarged so that it might serve as the convent church, with altar, sacristy and side chapel. Suitable remodeling in the rest of the building provided for the nuns' dormitory and for dining and reception rooms, etc. Even the garden was replanted and its dimensions changed. All the fences around the property were rebuilt to a greater height.

The endowment patent which funded the project declared: "This endowment shall be known as the Emperor Franz Joseph Endowment of the Carmelite Convent at Mayerling. . . . The Carmelites are to pray daily for the salvation of the late Crown Prince the Archduke Rudolf." A church would be built where the Crown Prince had died so that, in the words of the head of the Lord Marshal's Commission, "this room and the air space above it can never again be used for profane purposes."

What was it again that Freud's paper had said? The one he was working on while the convent was being built? How did he explain the condition of a hand — that is, of an area that had been "touched by a king," a spot congested with "surplus" emotion? This is how he explained it: "The relation of this hand to the idea of the king seemed so important to the man's psychical life that the man refused to let the hand enter into any other relation" (so that it could never be used again for ordinary or profane purposes). The area is "saturated with the memory of the event, the trauma which produced the paralysis."

Only one thread connected the new convent to the world. In a house just outside the nunnery proper, the Sisters managed a foresters' old-age home. From here a telephone wire ran to the village post office at Alland. But after a few months it was disconnected, like a nerve end decommissioned by paralysis. Before long the old-age home itself was relinquished to another order of nuns. The Discalced Carmelites perfected their encapsulation. They devoted themselves wholly to The Memory of the Event: living in strictest claustral retirement; veiled forever in black; keeping vigil and praying for Rudolf daily, week after week, year after year, decade after decade unto this day.

On their refectory table, in front of the Prioress's seat, lay a round bone with two sockets, just like the one Rudolf had kept on his desk. A skull.

Meanwhile the Crown Princess Widow Stephanie had added Rudolf's "bachelor apartment" to her quarters in the Palace. Since most of the rooms' appointments were "considered unsuitable for her," as the announcement phrased it, the furniture was removed to other Imperial residences, and from there still further to the official mansions of Austrian ambassadors abroad, to Rome, Belgrade and elsewhere. Court carriages scattered the Crown Prince's substance to the four winds. The Palace had to be scrubbed clean.

Yet further erasing and muffling must be done. In the Emperor's name and her own, Stephanie conferred the Order of the Iron Crown Second Class on Dr. Widerhofer who had examined the scene in Mayerling. Rudolf's First Lord Chamberlain, Count Bombelles, received the Grand Cross; his valet Loschek, the Gold Merit Cross with Crown plus retirement with full pension. The rest of Rudolf's more intimate retinue was also either rewarded or decorated into silence. The regiments which bore the Crown Prince's name received new designations.

By the end of February the true Rudolf had been laundered away, as far as the Court was concerned. It had both solemnized and bowdlerized his image. "Dear Bombelles," Stephanie wrote, perhaps with a straight face, to a man long familiar with her hopeless marriage. "It is a dear duty to send you the oldest saber of my unforgettable husband. Keep it as a souvenir of my precious Rudolf. . . ."

❧Chapter 28❧

February ended amid ice and ashes. Rudolf, the hope of rejuvenating Vienna, had been blasted away together with the glitter of the season. Over cold pavements blew whiffs of burned-out promise. The Ringstrasse kept announcing greatness to eyes and ears stopped up with gloom.

But the town was still trying to recuperate. It helped that in the last half of February the weather let up now and then. Some mourning flags were furled. A number of ball committees met to weigh a partial resumption of the carnival. The demands of mourning had to be balanced against considerations of charity and economic necessity.

Schwender's Colosseum, the city's biggest *Fasching* machine, had already reopened with its ladies' band, its tunnel of love, and its Turkish coffeehouse featuring *tableaux vivants*. The Alpine Club bravely staged a delayed ball with a huge glacier, a roaring waterfall, and an eagle circling over a freshly shot chamois on a boulder.

Few came to any such affairs. Commoners were still too unnerved for revelry. The aristocrats were not there at all. Their Graces, Their Highnesses and Lordships, the Lobkowitzes, Esterházys, Schwarzenbergs et al. preferred to do their celebrating far away in the castles of their estates.

A dark sort of energy did seep back into town. People suddenly began to steal the streets — at least symbolically. In poor districts like Ottakring, street signs and house numbers were unscrewed during the night. The thieves sold them to scrap dealers. Only a few months before, the sweatshop tailors and the jobless cobblers had drunk up their last gulden in the wine gardens, singing the sweetness of Vienna. Now the legend had frozen brittle. Why not dismantle it and sell the rusty parts for junk?

Perhaps everything that wasn't stealable was pointless.

"Why hast thou lived, why hast thou suffered?" demanded Mahler's Second Symphony, still unfinished in 1889. It was a question Mahler himself must have been asking — not in Vienna, nor in Budapest (where his Royal Opera had resumed after a week's mourning for the Crown Prince), but in his home town of Iglau. At Iglau he sat by the bedside of his dying father.

"*Why dost thou live?*" Young Schnitzler brooded on the theme, though he had a very healthy and prosperous father. He had his Jeanette with whom he had been to bed four hundred and thirty-three times by February 28. He had other girls as well. He had his by-line at last in the prestigious *An der schönen blauen Donau*. But on February 25, he wrote his friend Olga Waissnix with a self-irony far more severe than his earlier and warmer despairs,

> . . . things go as well with me as they go badly. The spirit of medicine is easily caught. Hence I have no patients. Apollo gave me song's sweet lips. Hence I am not produced at the Court Theater. Life is scarcely the highest good of all; which doesn't seem to keep me from continuing existence.

There seemed to be little point in living and trying in vain. "*I am not fit for society!*" Hugo Wolf flung at a friend about the same time. The sentence is from a letter which was a malediction, a curse against the very drive for greatness on which Rudolf had foundered.

> Do I wish to become a famous man? Yes, I was in a fair way of striving toward that goal. Folly! Madness! Idiocy! As if the satisfaction of common vanity would offer compensation for the manifold sacrifices, worries, infamies and outrages that are bound up with the attainment of such an aim! Ten thousand devils may fetch me on the spot if I ever encumber my brain with such anxieties again! The devil of vanity and inordinate ambition will not catch me by the forelock again, and you can depend on that.

Another man disencumbered himself of such anxieties to the extent of giving up his crown. On March 6, Vienna's ally in Serbia, King Milan, abdicated. He had no obvious reason. Nominally his twelve-year-old son succeeded him. Actually an anti-Austrian current began to move to power — the first whirl in a vortex which, a generation later, would pull the Empire down into World War I.*

---

* It was the equivalent of the CIA in this new, hostile Serbia that instigated the assassination of Franz Ferdinand, Rudolf's successor, at Sarajevo.

More immediate and private was the impact of Milan's act on the House of Habsburg. The ex-King traveled to Budapest to report to Franz Joseph and Elisabeth just why he had given up his reign. The events in Vienna, he confessed to Their Majesties, had upset him unbearably. He was depressed to the point of doing away with himself. Rudolf's example had made him fear for his sanity. He did not want to die a suicide on a throne.

It was all Elisabeth needed. She'd already sunk into a neurasthenic trough before Milan's arrival. Rumors about her condition darkened as they multiplied. The Court was forced to issue a denial: Professor Krafft-Ebing, the great psychiatrist from Graz, had *not* been summoned to the Empress's bedside.

Whatever the truth, a general derangement kept Krafft-Ebing busy. The end of *Fasching*, March 4, was the traditional date for the gala in Vienna's insane asylum. Milder cases were allowed to participate, usually in costumes they had made themselves. This year the Mayerling miasma seemed to have produced a horde of gory apparitions: executioners, cannibals, Bluebeards, Jack the Rippers, all hopping about frenzied to an all-inmate band "playing" waltzes on papier-mâché instruments. The entire staff of doctors joined in to control the merriment and so did Krafft-Ebing who had just been appointed to take over the University's psychiatry chair later in the year.

The life returning to town was either mad or it was death-ridden. The Fiacre Ball held in early March always attracted not only cabbies but young nobility making a cult of the raffish drivers. This year a huger crowd than ever spilled beyond the doors of the Blumensaal. But they hadn't come to drink or eat or flirt as in other years. They came to listen. They came to hear one man in particular. Patiently they showed appreciation for various favorite vocalists in the fiacre trade, known by such nicknames as "Hungerl" and "Schuster-Franz." Then the moment arrived for which everybody had been waiting.

In a swallowtail coat Bratfisch mounted the dais. He sat down on a stool like a coach seat, so ingrained was his habit of performing from the driver's seat. He began to sing and to whistle — the crowd's favorites and his own and those of his dead master. One

*Bratfisch, Crown Prince Rudolf's private horse cab
driver*

song in particular he had to repeat over and over again. It ended with the refrain, *"Wo bleibt die alte Zeit und die G'müthlichkeit? Pfirt di Gott, mein schönes Wien!"* "Where is the old time, the *Gemütlichkeit?* Fare thee well, my beautiful Vienna!" The entire crowd applauded and wept together, the bakers' apprentices in their rented dinner jackets cheek to wet cheek with playboys in their silken lapels.

As March went on, the darkness in the city became more abrasive. By the middle of the month Josef Bratfisch was not only heartbroken but furious — furious enough to sue.

An anti-Semitic paper in Vienna had published a story stating that Bratfisch had auctioned off articles he had received from "a high personage." At the same time a certain Johann Hartmann addressed a letter to the Fiacre Guild accusing Bratfisch: "He has sold certain articles to Jews. And other Jews, seeing the high prices these fetched, began to sell a great number of items which they called 'Bratfisch items.' This was done with Herr Bratfisch's permission, and he received a percentage of the profits of these faked presents." Bratfisch filed a libel suit against Hartmann as well as against the anti-Semitic sheet.

Anti-Semitism grew to be a dominant note of that March's nastiness. It boiled over during the City Council elections on the eighteenth of the month. Dr. Karl Lueger, the rising young Jew-baiter who was a representative in Parliament, commanded a gang of bravos in his local district of Margareten. They had identified in advance voters known to cast a liberal vote. *"Jew! . . . Jew lackey! . . . Jew!"* they chorused to scare such people away. And Lueger's candidates won not only in Margareten but in other districts too.

As usual, the hard times were convenient times for a demagogue — in this case Lueger. And the times were bad during those March weeks. Strife and stress increased everywhere. People complained that the city could not bear the tax load and that welfare costs had gone out of control. Bankruptcies multiplied. The *Neue Freie Presse* cited an invidious statistic on the front page: Budapest, though a smaller city, ate three paprika chickens for each *Backhendl* — fried chicken — consumed in Vienna.

It wasn't funny. To the Vienna burgher the fried chicken was his Bird of Contentment, an emblematic species presently endangered. No wonder there was a hiss in the streets. A new, ugly sound along the streetcar tracks.

Only a few months ago the horse tramways of the town had still been rolling drawing rooms. As you boarded, the conductor bowed and wished His Lordship good day and wondered if perhaps His Lordship were in need of a ticket. You said, yes, you would be pleased to have one. The conductor handed you one with a chamberlain's flourish and received in return not only the fare to which a tip had been added, but also a counterflourish. The conductor bowed a fine arc and thanked His Lordship, and you bowed a bow only a shade less deep, accompanied by a hand wave implying that such gratitude, though overgenerous, was appreciated all the same.

Now the streetcars had turned sullen. The Tramway Conductors' Ball did poorly. But a series of midnight meetings of drivers and conductors pulled large and increasingly wrathful throngs throughout March. They'd had enough, their leaders said. Enough of a company rule penalizing drivers who took more than forty-seven minutes to traverse the route from the Währing district to the Prater; which made no allowance for delays caused by funeral parades or blocking freight coaches. They'd had enough of a fourteen-hour day filled with hard work, enough of grubbing for puny tips with incessant courtesies. They wanted more than starvation wages and more than a half-hour lunch break. And they wanted it now.

The company gave them — an evasive statement. Whereupon trouble started in the tramway garage on the Kronprinz Rudolf Strasse. Strikers beat with clubs at nonstrikers who wanted to enter. The police were called, the paddy wagon came galloping, arrests were made. Nonetheless the streetcars stopped running on a number of lines.

It was only the start of what promised to be an evil spring. Rudolf's still-temporary coffin in the Capuchin crypt was robbed again and again of precious decorations — in mid-March, of seven silver leaves from the great laurel wreath. Criminal hands desecrated something else held dear by the city, namely its wine. Thieves kept breaking into the trains bringing Lower Austrian vintages into town, drained half the barrels into their own receptacles and then filled up the barrels with water.

On Ash Wednesday children playing in a cemetery found the dug-up corpse of an old woman, its breasts sliced off. The perpetrator was believed to be suffering from some weird superstition. And the malevolence continued into Lent. It was not limited to crooks and fiends. It lived in the souls of very civilized young men.

"Gisela M. is boring," notes Arthur Schnitzler's diary on March 19. "She made mistakes in her dress, which disgusted me. I was brutal with her and bothered no more about her. Jeanette bores me too. I prefer a prostitute to her, anything, new lips, a new sigh. The 'third pillow' lies beside us . . . the invisible pillow on which lies another head, and I embrace another when Jeanette holds me tight. . . ." By the end of March, the diary records, Jeanette's boring thighs had held him tight four hundred and sixty-five times.

Impatience, callousness, violence simmered in the most upright circles. It was in March that two of young Schnitzler's crowd, both bucks of the *haute bourgeoisie*, clashed blades in fencing practice. The exchange grew heated. The foil-tip of one partner — Max Friedmann — broke through his opponent's mask, punctured an eye, pierced the brain, and killed the man on the spot.

"At the time Max Friedmann and I were seeing a lot of each other," Schnitzler wrote. "Often we went to masked balls together. I therefore considered it my duty to visit him the day after the accident and to commiserate with him. I was strangely affected by the fact that not only in conversation with me but also with others, Max dealt hardly at all with his unfortunate victim but seemed solely occupied with the question of whether or not the courts would find him in any way delinquent. . . . The investigation was terminated a few days later because of a lack of incriminating evidence; and sooner than any of us would have thought possible, friend Max was back in the fencing arena."

Newspaper reports of the incident struck Bruckner, who knew none of the parties involved but was a connoisseur of death. His niece had just died, and on March 14, he wrote a short note to his sister, enclosing twenty gulden to help meet expenses for the funeral. With no logical connection to his preceding lines he added: "P.S. Yesterday a young officer son of a very rich burgher was stabbed to death at a fencing exercise."

His preoccupation with the beyond did not in the least exempt Bruckner from the aggressiveness in the world all around him. He and his small band fought defensive skirmishes against archfoe Brahms and against Brahms's redoubtable artillery general Hanslick. During those harsh bellicose days the underdog Brucknerians even tried a counteroffensive. At the end of February their organ, the *Wiener Allgemeine Zeitung*, had neatly chewed up a recent recital of the enemy's songs:

> Though Brahms often writes with genius, he just as often reaches for the pen when he has no inspiration. Four out of five songs . . . were not good. . . . Despite Brahms's personal participation the performances were received rather poorly. Some time ago one could read black-on-white in a newspaper of high repute [i.e., Hanslick in the *Neue Freie Presse*] that Herr Brahms's *Zigeuner Lieder* had dropped to earth like a gift from heaven. This meteorological event can be less easily documented than one that is more remarkable still: At the Bösendorfer Hall yesterday, during the rendition of those Brahms *Lieder*, the audience fell from the clouds.

A few weeks later the *Zigeuner Lieder* were sung again, this time in the big Musikvereinssaal, and again the *Wiener Allgemeine Zeitung* assaulted the great Brahms bravely. And in another article on the same page you could read:

> Our famous native composer Bruckner has made such rapid progress with his Ninth Symphony that it may be ready for

performance next season. The first movement and the scherzo are almost finished. The second movement, a serenade, is already sketched out. The master believes that this new symphony will give him his greatest satisfaction. It seems probable that the new symphony will be first performed abroad — naturally. This is the fate of all our native composers. [Brahms of course, was German, not a native of Austria.] Our own artists receive recognition only if they are first valued beyond our borders.

Freud, around the corner from Bruckner, was much younger and less experienced in being an unappreciated prophet. But that spring he too jumped into a feud, all the way.

For that he took time off from his study on hysteria. He finally had to make a stand against Theodor Meynert. As stands go, this one was reckless and, to use a still uninvented word, oedipal. Privy Councillor Professor Meynert was not only the founder of the Vienna Psychiatric Clinic and one of the leading alienists of his time; not only a man of ecumenical culture and of advanced politics (piano virtuosos played Mozart in his salon and he had written poetry about the French Revolution); not only a huge force at the University and one of its most powerful lecturers; in addition, he had left a very early and very deep personal impression on Freud. In Freud's own language, Meynert was "the most brilliant genius I have ever encountered." He was "more stimulating than a host of friends."

And just this man the young doctor now dared make his enemy. In 1889 things came to a boil, but trouble had been heating up for many months. During 1885–86 Freud had gone to Paris on a grant to study with Charcot. He had returned very excited about the potential of hypnosis, both as therapy and as diagnostic art plumbing the psychic origins of neurological disturbances. To Meynert, however, hypnosis only induced "an artificial form of alienation." It would be unfortunate if "this psychical epidemic among doctors" were to spread.

Insubordinate, Freud had spread it. He had continued to practice and to champion hypnosis. On another subject he had also been heretic. He had treated hysteria as an affliction not limited to women and which behaved "as if there were no anatomy." To Meynert this was nonsense. Hysteria was an exclusively female phenomenon (*hystera* being the Greek word for *womb*) caused only by nerve lesions. Theorizers like Dr. Freud verged on quackery.

For a long time Freud had borne this conflict mutely. But even his silent disobedience had excluded him from the laboratories Meynert controlled. He had been forced to restrict his already very limited University lectures to anatomy, and any kind of participation had been denied him at the Psychiatric Clinic. His work at the Kassowitz Pediatric Institute, which was small and outside the University framework, had really been banishment.

Now in 1889 the situation — like many such situations in Vienna — became envenomed. Speaking to a group of doctors, Meynert referred to his former disciple as "only a hypnotist."

During the post-Mayerling spring of discontent, Freud decided to hit back, in print. The Vienna medical weekly, *Wiener Medizinische Wochenschriften*, had just asked him to review a book on hypnotism. There was his forum. Freud went to work as bitterly as the circumstances warranted, as cleverly as the eminence of his adversary demanded.

In his review Freud conceded that among the opponents of hypnotism figured men like Privy Councillor Professor Meynert who had acquired weighty authority. Freud further conceded that it was difficult for most people to conceive that scientists like Privy Councillor Professor Meynert, who enjoyed great experience in certain regions of neuropathology and who had given proof of great acumen, should have *no* qualifications on other problems. Freud conceded yet further that respect for greatness, especially intellectual greatness, was among the best characteristics of human nature. But even more important than such respect was the respect for facts. One needn't be afraid to say so openly, if one set aside one's dependence on authority in favor of one's own judgment arrived at from a study of the facts. . . .

It was, Freud went on, fitting to make some allowance for the frequent intolerance on the part of great men. Therefore he would not inquire into the reasons which led Privy Councillor Professor Meynert to attack him. He did want to state that as the victim of such attacks he was in good company — *vide* the author of the excellent book under review, Dr. August Forel. Dr. Forel was a brain anatomist of high repute and yet saw hypnosis as something other than "a piece of absurdity," to use a term Privy Councillor Meynert had employed. . . .

Since this reviewer appraised the book positively, Freud continued, Privy Councillor Meynert might be confirmed still further in his judgment that Freud had returned from the wickedness of Paris in a depraved state. But the reviewer, Freud, was still obliged to correct Privy Councillor Meynert's recent definition of him as "a local practitioner of hypnosis." This might create the impression that he did nothing else but hypnotize. On the contrary the reviewer was "a local nerve specialist" making use of *all* therapeutic methods, if Privy Councillor Meynert would be gracious enough to acknowledge that. . . .

"*Where is the old time?*" Bratfisch had sung. "*Where is the Gemütlichkeit?*"

One man knew where it was. At least he was among the few who could produce old-fashioned smiles in the teeth of modernity, of truth and of death. That man was Johann Pfeiffer, King of the Birds. He still performed on the Schottenring, a few steps away from Freud's door. Only his act had changed. After Mayerling he stopped staging plays with the parrots — onlookers no longer responded so freely with their coins. Now he had his birds bring each paying customer an envelope from a shelf of horoscopes as they had at New Year's. He knew how to give each prediction a funny twist. And his customers enjoyed that. The Viennese liked to interpose at least a joke between themselves and the future.

His problem was the lack of passers-by. The Ringstrasse did not make a comfortable strolling mall in the March of '89. The mood remained too blighted, the weather too dismal. At the day's end, the little heap of change the King had garnered was still not quite enough to nourish a family of five humans and seven birds.

Still the King did not abandon his jolliness or his daily stand on the Ringstrasse. But now he worked nights too. In late February he began to visit taverns. He gave humorous impersonations of

Napoleon at a Viennese coffeehouse or of Frederick the Great playing a gypsy violin. He distributed home-made imitations of a fifty-gulden note on which was written, *A fifty-gulden fine for all those not watching my performance.* When that didn't bring in enough money, he searched out dog owners among the more good-natured drinkers in the pubs and taught the pets comic tricks. He performed farcical operas with his shadow-playing fingers, and, after one long such evening at the beginning of March, he went home whistling; climbed up three evil-smelling floors in the Castelezgasse; tiptoed past his family whose members, feathered and unfeathered, were sleeping crammed together in the narrow apartment; opened its single window; and jumped out.

When they found him, dead, he still clutched his case of masks on which was written in gold letters: LIFE IS SERIOUS BUT ART IS GAY — VIENNESE SPECIALITIES

His funeral was marvelous. Truly *eine schöne Leich'* — a beautiful corpse — as the Viennese called successful occasions of the sort. Most newspapers noted his passing. The city which could not keep him alive showered him with fond obituaries and provided populous company on his last ride. After all, he had been a fixture on the Ringstrasse, its most charming landmark and the first to perish. The policeman on his corner there joined the cortege; so did the mailman and the *Dienstmann* and the chestnut vendor and the wine lovers whose taverns had been part of Pfeiffer's nightly rounds.

When he had been laid to rest, they all returned to their pubs and the corpse became very beautiful indeed. It made up for that other, bewildering, tragic body still in its temporary coffin at the Capuchin crypt. Rudolf had conjured the glistening anticipation of greatness, only to dissolve into black bafflement. Johann Pfeiffer, King of the Birds, had offered never more than a moment's diversion. And in one moment he was, quite logically, gone. He reminded the Viennese of one of their specialties: the art of making life unserious.

Chapter 29

Johann Pfeiffer's *schöne Leich'* marked in some ways the beginning of a turning point. The same week in mid-March Prime Minister Taaffe appeared before Parliament to deny that he had ever termed his government's policy "*fortwursteln*" (slogging on). Quite the contrary, he would characterize that policy as "*durchfretten*" (muddling through). He said it with a solemn stern twitch of mustaches which rendered the playfulness all the more masterful. Somehow his pronouncement signaled the end of government mourning.

One began to hope that Mayerling might not be a world-devouring misfortune after all. The city could even give thought to ills elsewhere. London, for example, was still trembling before Jack the Ripper. In Paris, General Boulanger was degenerating rapidly from a new Bonaparte into a catastrophic blusterer. And an event on Russian territory made Viennese anti-Semitism look like a quaint peccadillo. Adolf Baron von Sonnenthal, the Court Theater's foremost classic actor and the capital's avatar of sartorial elegance; von Sonnenthal, whom Franz Joseph had called "Jupiter" in his letters to Frau Schratt — *this* fastidious Austrian luminary was nearly arrested by the Tsarist police during an engagement in Riga. Why? He had failed to apply for a special permit to stay on holy Russian soil, as required of all foreign "Israelites." Only a protest by Franz Joseph's ambassador saved Sonnenthal from deportation.

The incident helped Vienna recover some self-esteem. Austria's feudal coloring might rival Russia's; but — Lueger and Schönerer notwithstanding — it was at the same time democratic enough to champion its Jewish Jupiter.

Gradually the Viennese were regaining their happy sense of singularity. Toward the end of March even the weather mellowed. Overnight the Vienna Woods became snow-dappled undulations of sweet baby-green; birches, willows, poplars leafed; pussywillows pearled up and down the slopes. The trams ran again, during a truce in the strike, and carried thousands out into the spring. And the poor, most of whom lived in the outer districts, often had no need of transportation. Many discovered once again that only a few steps led from fetid tenement to freshness. As soon as school and factory let out, the sprint was on to the hills — the Kahlenberg, Kobenzl and Leopoldsberg — for meadows, for freedom and for flowers. Everybody luxuriated and gathered. The grime of ten thousand windowsills was soon covered by clusters of crocuses and lilacs, by lovely scents and petals. Sunday noon saw Vienna's lower million sunning, basking, sipping wine in the groves; all around them the vineyards budded, and new-born foliage did its first rustling to a breeze. What other city offered such easy solace to its underprivileged?

And where else could you find aristocrats returning with such style from their delinquency? For them the Mayerling dreariness was over. The chill had passed. The horsy turf at Freudenau beckoned to the Esterházys and the Schwarzenbergs. His Highness had to inspect his yearlings. Her Highness had to renew her wardrobe. The May 1st fashion promenade in the Prater lay ahead. Every day another quartered ensign rose on the flagpole of another town palais to announce that Their Lordships were once more in residence. The initial spring event, a roller-skating gala held by Princess Pauline Metternich, was a hilarious success.

Vienna's surface was being smoothed and prettied. Rudolf was gone, yes. But — behold! — life went on, to a general firming of prices. The stock market remained buoyant, the interest rate showed rather serene moderation. The death of this firebrand fairytale liberal had, come to think of it, removed an element of volatility and radical caprice. One might perhaps begin to feel a bit of hope again.

And someone was already waiting in the wings to tickle away the last sheath of numbness. Theodor Herzl set out to cause a pleasant citywide buzz. For the first time, he sharpened his skill as an inspiriting genius and an attention-getter. The man who would in the next decade turn the whole world's eyes to Zionism, in March 1889 learned how to fire up the Vienna public. Not in order to found a Jewish homeland — but to inveigle ticket-buyers to the box office.

The comedy Herzl had written with Hugo Wittmann, purified of all references to sleeping cars, neared production. It went into rehearsal at the Court Theater just when the management again rejected Ibsen and his "problem plays." In terms of literature the Court Theater's decision was a felony. In terms of social therapy it was a boon. Vienna badly needed some nice safe titillation. Couldn't it be provided by something called *Love Poachers*, a pseudo-risqué farce with a question mark for an author? Herzl quickly realized that the city, still ailing from a great evil mystery, would adore curing itself with a juicy little mystification.

"We are fully determined," he wrote in his own and his collaborator's name to the Director of the Court Theater. "We are fully determined not to reveal ourselves even after a success (which the Lord may grant). Only after the play succeeds abroad will we emerge from the mystic clouds."

And very soon Herzl managed to generate some tantalizing vapors, through his burgeoning public-relations virtuosity. Of course he and his partner were fortunately placed. Wittmann controlled the cultural news columns (though not the critics) of the *Neue*

FROM *Herzl, Seer of the State*, EDITED BY I. KLINOV

*Theodor Herzl at twenty-eight, drawing-room
playwright*

Freie Presse where Herzl himself was a power. In addition, Herzl had just become feuilleton editor of the *Wiener Allgemeine Zeitung*. He had big drums to beat with. But the point was not to let the public know the source from which came all that appetizing noise, all those intriguing mists.

"We received the following item from Berlin," read an item in the *Neue Freie Presse* on March 7. "A new comedy, a work of special interest, will receive its premiere at the Deutsches Theater there. *Love Poachers* is the name of the play which has caused a certain excitement in literary circles for the past few weeks. As is well known, it arrived at the Vienna Court Theater anonymously by mail from Berlin, but the very first glance at the manuscript dispelled the mistrust usually inspired by anonymous plays. The work was accepted immediately in Vienna. The parts have already been assigned. We are close to the premiere, and one guesses curiously who the author might be. . . ."

During the next few days both the *Neue Freie Presse* and the *Wiener Allgemeine Zeitung* sprinkled casting news about *Love Poachers* into their pages, noting that the Court Theater elite such as Adolf von Sonnenthal (the Jewish Jupiter) and Hugo Thimig filled major roles, while the play's by-line remained a magnetic vacuum. The coffeehouses and the high-tea gossip congregrations could now buzz about a riddle that was comfortable and toothsome for a change. Herzl & Co. candied and spiced it further.

On March 14, there were yet other stories about interest abroad not only in *Love Poachers* but in its enigmatic authorship. On March 17, Herzl published nonchalantly, under his name, a vignette about the foibles and fascinations of literary life. On March 19, the play opened to an absolutely sold-out house.

"Is it a success? Is it a failure?" Herzl wrote a day later to the Director of the Court Theater. "We anonymous ones don't know for sure."

The critics were quite sure and nearly unanimous. "Yesterday the much-discussed anonymous comedy *Love Poachers* opened," wrote the reviewer of Herzl's own paper. "The public commotion about it is as ill-justified as the speed with which the management produced it. The play is cleverly nailed together but coarse in character and contains some very questionable borrowings from familiar French drama. Herr Förster, the Court Theater Director, must have decided to accept it as a former actor; the piece gives him a chance to display his thespians though it is literarily worthless."

The *Neue Freie Presse* discussed *Love Poachers* not only in the same issue but on the same page with a Hugo Wittmann feuilleton (about the memoirs of a former American Ambassador in Vienna). "Too broad," said the reviewer, and then bent over backward to his *Presse* colleague until he could call the play "a bad comedy but a pretty good farce."

"Do you know a Theodor Herzl? Or a Frau Baumgartner? Or a Herr Hugo Wittmann? Or a Herr Hugo Lubliner?" asked the *Salonblatt*. "These and other unknown and well-known names are being bandied about in connection with *Love Poachers*, which just opened at the Court Theater. If you suppose that the author tried to increase the public's suspense by leaving out his name, you must be wrong. I would think he follows with mixed feelings the hunt for his by-line. . . . The play does not possess the literary significance to deserve special attention or satisfy special expectations. The author will not get much honor from the play, but, judging from its local success here, much gold."

The *Salonblatt* was both right and wrong. Right about the gold. *Love Poachers* played to packed houses. Wrong about "the author's" doubts concerning the curiosity about "his" name. Herzl & Wittmann kept fanning the flames.

Actually that required resourcefulness of a high order. The premiere coincided with those City Council elections revolving to a large degree around the pros and cons of anti-Semitism, a hot controversy. In terms of news space, Herzl & Co. had to compete against the Jewish issue.

Still, the *Love Poachers* boys did well. The *Wiener Allgemeine Zeitung*, for example, reported on Dr. Karl Lueger's rough and successful electioneering on behalf of his Jew-baiting Christian

Socialist Party. But even more space was given — on the same page — to a feuilleton by Herzl's best friend and confidant Heinrich Kana. It was called "How I discovered the Author of *Love Poachers*" and began as follows:

> The mania to ferret out the author of *Love Poachers* has now spread to the editorial offices of this newspaper. At 9 A.M. today the editor-in-chief instructed me to identify the man. I went to the Court Theater and encountered a huge crowd of people, all of whom — men, women and children — were secretly hoping to be pointed out as the author of *Love Poachers*. . . . Inside the theater an attendant told me that the manuscript had been handed in by a man with a full blond beard and an upward-tilted nose [an aryanized cartoon of Herzl]. His name is Johannes Hawranek and he lives in the Johannesgasse. . . . Walking out of the theater I called out to the crowd, "Gentlemen, none of you wrote *Love Poachers*." A tremendous noise started but luckily a fiacre carried me away.

The noise didn't stop. In City Council elections, conservatives, clericals and anti-Semites made gains against the liberals; all along Herzl's *Love Poachers* promotion continued merrily. On April 5, the cultural page of the *Neue Freie Presse* reported that a Herr Kadelsburg of the Deutsches Theater in Berlin had been named "with the greatest certainty" as the author of *Love Poachers*. On April 9, the *Neue Freie Presse* printed Herr Kadelsburg's categorical denial. New puzzlement flowered, the box office prospered. The Viennese were grateful that they could guess at frivolities — no longer about other, darker things.

Even Olga Waissnix, Arthur Schnitzler's flirtatious pen pal, joined the craze. Usually she tried to impress the intellectualizing young doctor with her profundity; but at the end of March she sent him a visiting card on which was written a single sentence: "Did you, perhaps, write *Love Poachers*?" Poor Schnitzler had to answer: "No, gracious lady, *Love Poachers*, like so many other plays, was not written by me. In fact, I haven't even seen it."

Everybody else, though, saw it or intended to. The promotion continued. On April 14, a Herzl feuilleton in the *Wiener Allgemeine Zeitung* quite unembarrassedly savaged Paul Déroulède who had drummed up a tumult to make his book of ultramilitaristic verse a best-seller in France. "These poems are not the result of a genuine inspiration," wrote Herzl. "Not the sort from which a new 'Marseillaise' can be created. What will remain of Junker Déroulède? At the most, his name, like that of the inventor of a famous patent medicine. An artist in publicity, he has caused talk for a while."

Herzl knew whereof he criticized. Himself a first-rank artist in publicity, he would later harness that art to a genuine inspiration. When the Dreyfuss Affair jolted him into his Jewishness in 1895 — he was by then Paris correspondent for the *Neue Freie Presse* — his call would find him fully armed. He knew how to mobilize and politicize the Jews' ancient hunger for Zion. Only a Herzl could have accoutered it in fashionable dramatics. It would take a Viennese maestro of sheer manner to insist that all delegates to the First Zionist Congress in 1897 wear formal attire, top hats and tailcoats, for the benefit of reporters and cameras. Herzl led his people toward Jerusalem with a nearly Christian lordliness taught him by his very self-disdain as a Jew in Schönerer's and Lueger's Vienna. Before he took it over, Zionism had been considered a messy ghetto zealotry. Herzl's public relations would raise it to the glamour of a great "Westernized" international movement.

Meanwhile in 1889 the Court Theater appreciated a playwright who could "cause talk for a while." Additional performances of *Love Poachers* were scheduled throughout the year. Indeed the management informed Herzl that his one-act comedy *Der Flüchtling* (The Refugee) would be produced in May. This time his work would be put on under his own name. Herzl had fulfilled his vow to his friend Schnitzler. He had arrived at the new Court Theater, in its very first season. Now he had the prestige and the means to make definite wedding plans. In June he would slide a gold band over one of those flossy fingers that had been first in Vienna to sport painted nails — his darling Julie's.

Rosiness seemed to break out like a rash in an Austria so recently emerged from woe. A long, freshening, April night rain helped Johann Strauss pull entirely out of his "phase." In a fit of optimism he decided to move to his country seat Schönau in the Vienna Woods earlier than usual in the year, to begin his final assault on his one and only opera.

Gustav Klimt shook off the doldrums which had set in after the completion of the Court Theater paintings. He shook them off not to work, but "to go to Trieste." He resumed his so-called fight-hikes on the roughneck Triesterstrasse, leading south from Vienna. With friends he trudged along the highway's spring mud and looked for horses getting stuck and drivers working brutal whips. Klimt would shout a command to stop the maltreatment, names would be called, fists would fly, and though Klimt's side did not necessarily win, he did manage to flail away the sulks of idleness.

Out of town, Gustav Mahler's directorship at the Budapest Opera had now so thoroughly triumphed over all Magyar troublemakers that even the Viennese newspapers began to applaud. "Herr Director Mahler has made the impossible come true," Hanslick had to admit in the *Neue Freie Presse*.

Franz Joseph, too, harvested an overdue victory. He had gone to the Hungarian capital not only to remove himself from his son's death but also to help fight a bill through the Budapest Parliament; the one that would preserve German as the Army's unitary language of command throughout the many-tongued Monarchy. After many weeks of negotiations and demonstrations, Parliament passed the law on April 3. A new ministry was formed, acceptable to both the nationalists and the Crown. Gratefully Franz Joseph ended a long onerous stint.

Meanwhile Elisabeth, his Empress, had been inching out of her depression over Rudolf. The doctors pronounced her well enough for a stay at Ischl in the Salzburg Alps. Franz Joseph traveled with her and at Ischl he met — after a two-month separation — his beloved Frau Schratt. With him he carried a secret new testament which bequeathed a considerable sum to the actress and her son. Franz Joseph had long wanted to take this step and had long hesitated. Now he had gone through with it, to reward himself, as it were, for sticking out a difficult time.*

Even Dr. Freud seemed to have left behind him a long arid stretch. By now he was beginning to feel almost at home in the pinched cocoon of isolation which his writings on hysteria and hypnosis would not make any more opulent. But on April 15 he opened the *Neue Freie Presse* to a surprise. Here, for the first time in his life, his name was mentioned on the science page. Vienna's leading paper devoted nearly a whole page to a review of his German rendition of Hyppolite Bernheim's treatise on hypnosis, *De la Suggestion.* The review lauded the translator's "measured and sensitive" preface. Such recognition was something new and heady. More important still was the friendly tenor of the theoretical part of the article. It welcomed new approaches in psychiatry. Of course Freud's pet subjects — hypnosis, hysteria, repression and suggestion — remained *themata non grata* at the University. Just the same, their serious discussion by the *Neue Freie Presse* lent them, for a while at least, a film of respectability.

For others in Vienna there were other ameliorations that spring. The Wagner Society made amends for its February rudeness to Hugo Wolf. In late March it gave his Mörike songs a tremendous reception. What he had sworn off a few weeks earlier, Wolf now embraced once again: vanity and society. Unto another familiar temptation he cleaved as well. The good weather let the Köcherts use their country villa in Rinnbach once more, thus easing his trysts with the lady of the house.

But the happiest event in musical Vienna occurred one April evening at the Rothen Igel restaurant. At 7 P.M. Professor Bruckner appeared with two friends. The waiters were astonished. Usually the peasant maestro ate elsewhere, at the restaurant Zur Kugel on Am Hof Square. And the wonders of the night had only begun. A few minutes later Johannes Brahms marched in, complete with white beard, nimbus and a retinue of three. After a stiff greeting

---

* Franz Joseph was to change his will again. Frau Schratt was not mentioned in his final testament, having been provided for — handsomely and discreetly — during his later years.

he took a seat at the opposite end of a long table. Even though this was his regular restaurant, whose dishes he knew by heart, Brahms demanded the menu, quick!! Bruckner tried to match the other man's fierceness by yelling for the same thing in his Upper Austrian dialect.

For long minutes the two masters frowned up and down the list of dishes. Mutual acquaintances had arranged this "conciliation dinner." Obviously they had engineered a debacle. And then, at the very same second, both geniuses shouted the same phrase at the waiter. *"Roast pork and sauerkraut!"*

The table dissolved into laughter. The impossible ensued: an amiability between opposites, feeding on small talk about pilsner beer and Viennese cuisine. It did not survive long beyond the evening. But for the duration of one dinner the muse knew peace.

A harmony that lasted longer, and whose achievement was even more delicate, came to pass at the Freudenau track on April 7. It was the first day of the spring races. Vienna society showed that it could surmount brilliantly all the past winter's bedevilments.

Just that Sunday the weather had had a setback. The sports crowd found the lawn wilted from the night's rain, the sky a gruff iron, the track sodden. Yet the turnout was copious and the clothes splendid. Limited Mourning remained in force, but the ladies had simply done wonders with black. They had invented clever striations of the color with heavy silks and moiré, displayed vivid transitions in texture from brilliant to matte ebony; they just delighted the fashion columnists with the sable trimmings of their dainty gray jackets.

Naturally the Apponyis put in an appearance, the Lobkowitzes and Hohenlohes, the Larisches, the Duke of Braganza, the Esterházys, the Károlyis (who had another great horse running), and practically all the members of the Jockey Club. "One could not complain of a lack of piquant interludes," the *Wiener Allgemeine Zeitung* winked. "In the boxes lively talk went on about the events of the day as well as developments which can't be discussed publicly."

All eyes, it went without saying, were on the box customarily occupied by Alexander Baltazzi, his brother Aristide, and by his niece, the Baroness Mary Vetsera, alias the Turf Angel. At first the seats were empty. Then, well before the first race, the Messrs. Baltazzi appeared in top hat and morning coat as befitted a Derby-winning family. The Turf Angel was not with them. Eight weeks before, Alexander Baltazzi had jammed a broomstick between her body and her dress, to make the corpse sit upright on its nocturnal ride out of Mayerling.

Today all that was so far past that perhaps it had never occurred at all. Today the Baltazzi brothers lifted hats to Prince Schwarzenberg, they bowed before the Archduke Leopold Salvator, they kissed the hands of Princess Metternich and the two pretty Comtesses Hoyos. Piquant interludes transpired, lively talk bubbled through the boxes, binoculars rose to saucy eyes and dropped back on vibrant bosoms, the bell rang, mounts converged on the paddock, betting windows jammed, the *totalisateur* clattered out odds, the starting gun boomed, hooves surfed along the muddy course, highnesses leaped to stand on their seats, baronesses waved black parasols in fastidious passion . . . and Count Albert (Ali) Károlyi's Sophist placed a close second in the 1600 meter handicap.

The racing season was on, smart as ever.

Mayerling had not happened, and it kept on happening. Just five days before the races opened, an agent of the Court Marshal's Office opened the register of deaths at Alland parish and wrote into it the name of Marie Alexandrine Baroness Vetsera, a very belated, very quiet entry. And the same week, on the night preceding the start of the racing season, a candelabra-lit resurrection took place in the crypt of the Capuchins. Members of Rudolf's Court, dissolved months ago, came together again with full livery and sword. They watched in silence. The wooden coffin enclosing their master was being lifted into a magnificent metal costume. Positioned between the caskets of Empress Maria Theresia and Emperor Maximilian of Mexico, the late-Renaissance sarcophagus lay embossed with laurels framing lion heads, with the Crown Prince's personal escutcheon, and with the inscription: *Rudolphus Princeps Hereditarius Imperii Austriae, Regni Hungariae etc. . . . etc. . . .*

While workmen soldered the lid shut, sealing it forever, the courtiers stood at attention; the Capuchin monks breathed prayers; the candles smoked; the soldering flames hissed. Then they all left. Rudolf had become an exhibit for tourists.

The official Rudolf, that is. The unofficial one was a shadow that climbed up the steps of the crypt and mingled with the world and became a thousand things to millions of people.

His slim figure began to hover here and there, all over the Monarchy and even outside its borders. While alive he had already been half-legend. Now he became all vision, myth, fleet chimera

Chapter 30

and stubborn fable. He was glimpsed with a beautiful blonde *principessa* in the window of a campanile in Florence. Footmen whispered that the Jesuits kept him in a red-silk dungeon deep under the Imperial Palace in Vienna. Vintners by the Danube heard him calling from the keep of Castle Dürnstein, which had shut in Richard the Lionheart seven hundred years before. In Galicia peasants told of meeting him in strange disguises, as he prepared to liberate the people from their suffering. Hungarian shepherds saw him again and again, galloping across the steppe, a skeleton on horseback with shako and Hussar's cape, a headlong specter that would become flesh once more on the stroke of redemption.

The progressive-minded, of course, were haunted by a different Rudolf. They were possessed by the mirage of what might have been. Had Rudolf survived to reach the throne . . . had he at least been given his due voice in the Empire's councils . . . how destiny might have improved! He might have turned Austria away from the Prussian alliance toward ties with France and England; away from the Kaiser's Gothic swagger toward democracy, industry and reason; away from domestic quarrels which the Crown Prince might have mediated better than most Habsburgs; away, ulti- mately, from those Balkan nationalist tensions that exploded with the gunshots at Sarajevo to set off World War I.

All that he might have done *if*. But *if* had an obverse side. What if Rudolf's early death just lent him a nimbus his continued career would have mocked? Franz Joseph did not die until 1916. How could the son have withstood the weight of his father's longevity — the pressure of being the nonsucceeding successor for another twenty-seven years?

More important yet: Could Rudolf have dealt with the mis- fortunes of the cause he championed?

That cause, liberalism, had begun to go wrong palpably toward the end of his lifetime. The liberal intelligence had dreamed the great nineteenth-century dream of equality and riches. There would be greater abundance for all through greater production; there would be freedom perfected through democracy; through

313

science there would be new technology and greater knowledge. That was the promise. This was the delivery: new rootless poverty and new excessive wealth equally rootless; new forms of inner and outer want; new envy, new doubt, and an entirely new furious bewilderment.

It was bewildering because the liberal cause was, after all, the cause of "progress" itself. Even its most intelligent supporters saw its adversities as imposed only from the outside by foes, never as the result of interior dynamics. Like most liberal gallants, Rudolf hoped to save liberalism with its own latest engines. Yet just these —the abstractions of technology, the demands of centralizing efficiency, the absolute ambition inherent in the idea of absolute freedom—all sliced away at life livable on a human scale. They sliced away at the rooted nook, the warm detail, the answering particularity. Whatever was local, familial, personal, had to fall under the steamroller that ground on toward modern greatness.

What happened to the Bohemian tailor whose untidy place was superseded by a sleek factory? He got a rote job in the plant. His hours might be fewer, his wages higher. But before, he'd served the needs of specific men. Now he was a nameless lackey to faceless machines. Having no shop to pass on, he sent his children to Vienna. There his unlettered son, desperately unemployed, became an anti-Semite under Lueger; and the bookish son, teaching school, a pan-Slavist fanatic.

The industrial flowering, into which Rudolf put so much hope, meant in the end the debris of a million hearths. And the hearth-dwellers who had thus lost their sense of home tried to find it, come next generation, as nationalists screaming for the salvation of their race. In obsessive and artificial greatness they tried to recapture the small breathing community that had perished.

If Rudolf misunderstood the consequences of liberalism, others misunderstood his contemporaries in the avant-garde. The Emperor thwarting his heir apparent followed the same impulse as the university professor who would go on ignoring Freud; as the concert manager who would keep refusing Mahler; the theater producer who would turn down Schnitzler's *La Ronde*; the gallery director who would exclude Klimt as soon as he became — Klimt. Each arbiter thought, as did Franz Joseph, that he was defending tried, good values against destructive novelties.

The truth was different. These "destroyers" only rendered audible or visible or thinkable a distress already existing and deepening with the forward march of occidental culture. Their innovations were really alarms of loss, or dreams of restoration. The angst in Mahler's huge surges clutched at primal beginnings. Freud reached for a pre-Puritan libido. Herzl called for a return to the land of milk and honey. Klimt contorted his nudes into ancient Oriental opulence. Bruckner cried out for the freshness that lay forgotten in folk and faith.

All these talents served an intuition maturing first in Vienna; something important and green had turned golden and sick and petrified.

"Nervousness is the modern sickness," the *Tagblatt* said that spring. "It is the sickness of the century. . . . Outside, everything is gleam and gorgeousness. One lives only on the outside, one is led astray by the dancing phosphorescence . . . one no longer expects anything from the inner life, from thinking or believing."

Only in Vienna would a leading liberal journal devote a front-page article to nerves. Only in Vienna had the bourgeoisie, this sustaining class of modernity, been born so psychically frail. Here it sickened faster of the machines and the depersonalizing schemes of its own making. And here it became especially nervous at those rooting about in the malaise, namely artists and thinkers. It had to be in Vienna that a predominant psychiatrist like Theodor Meynert denounced young Freud's concept of male hysteria as being by definition nonsensical; only to make a deathbed confession to Freud in 1891 that he, Meynert, had fought so hard because he himself had been a classic case of a male hysteric.

In Vienna the middle class had no rugged burgher hide which could resist, at least for the time being, the rough gusts ahead. In these streets nerves were exposed dangerously and stung prophetically; the future evoked clairvoyant expression and pathological revulsion at once. Here stood the baroque hospital that saw the birth of the twentieth century. Of all Western capitals it was *Alt Wien* which telegraphed the crisis of the New Man.

By such a paradox Vienna attained greatness after all. It bred the geniuses who foretold the modern wound. And Rudolf, too, became in time a sad but significant precursor. He was the herald of an alienation common to the youth of our day. Over him loomed Franz Joseph, a storybook incarnation of The Establishment. Today The Emperor has been computerized into a system willing to grant its children lordly perquisites and sexual license while remaining resistant to all essential reform. Under today's system the young often appear to be a generation of Rudolfs: free and glamorous in theory, crushingly impotent in action; freely skeptical yet unable to establish one skeptic-proof premise; free to see themselves as unbounded individuals without ever arriving at successful individuality; free to press pleasure to numb excess; free to demand the absolute of their senses and their ideals only to be failed by both, overprivileged and hapless at once; free to sound the depths of sophisticated frustration.

The shots in the Vienna Woods were fired in 1889. Today and every day hundreds of other unnerved fingers are already crooked into hundreds of other triggers. Each time we hear of another strange young death in a "good" house we hear of another Mayerling.

In the spring of 1889 none of that seemed to weigh on Vienna's mind. Everything swelled and brightened toward Easter. By the second week of April, Dr. Schnitzler's diary recorded, for all his jadedness, the four hundred seventy-fourth sex act with his Sweet Girl Jeanette. On the Kahlenberg hill, innkeepers dusted off the terraces that looked down over the vineyards into the beautiful city. At the peak, pyrotechnicians labored. They were readying something special for Easter Sunday: a symphonic fireworks in four movements whose crescendo would be the explosion of a crenellated ammunitions tower, high up in the Pleiades.

The price of sugar was rising again. But it didn't matter; the city was launched into Easter, the theater of Resurrection. There was not a branch in the Vienna Woods that wasn't greening. Perhaps nothing was irretrievable, not even the Crown Prince. His ghosts teemed everywhere, his legends bestrode the realm. Some even believed that Rudolf might be reborn as a child entering the world at Eastertide.

On Saturday, April 20, the day before Easter, at 4 P.M., Mozart's "Te Deum" was sung in the Court Chapel, a few yards from Rudolf's old apartment. Professor Anton Bruckner drew great chords and holy harmonies from the organ to celebrate the Resurrection. While the master's august music rose among the vaultings, a different sound was heard in Bruckner's native Upper Austria at Braunau. It was the thin cry of a baby born that afternoon. The parents were Alois and Klara Hitler. They named their little one Adolf.

Acknowledgments

֍ ֍

Marcia Colman Morton has participated decisively in the researching and shaping of this book. There is no way to thank her adequately for her collaborative skill and her mysterious good humor.

I have, of course, been aided by many other people. At the Austrian National Library (Österreichische Nationalbibliothek) in Vienna, Hofrat Dr. Franz Steininger smoothed my way. Dr. Hermann Frodl has been exceptionally resourceful and prompt in his response to fact queries. Professor Dr. Franz Grasberger and Dr. Günther Brosche of the Music Division of that library have been very helpful, as have Professor Otto Mazal of the Holograph Division, Dr. Kurt Broer of the Austrian National Tourist Board, and Dr. Anna Benda of the Austrian Court and State Archives.

A number of Austrian diplomats have provided me with valuable advice and liaison. Among them are Ambassador Peter Jankowitsch (formerly at the United Nations in New York, now in Paris); Consul General Thomas Nowotny in New York; and, in the New York Consulate, Dr. Peter Marboe and Dr. Erich Fenkart. At the Austrian Institute in New York, I'd like to mention its director, Dr. Fritz Cocron; his deputy, Miss Gertrude Kothanek; and the tireless librarian of the Institute, Miss Friederike Zeitelhofer. My thanks go to them all.

I am very indebted to Professor Heinrich Schnitzler and to Mrs. Therese Nickl for giving me access to the Arthur Schnitzler diaries and for their comments on Arthur Schnitzler. The Arthur Schnitzler photograph in this book was furnished by Professor Heinrich Schnitzler from his family album, and this kindness deserves separate mention.

Dr. Frederick Hacker of Beverly Hills and Vienna has been most helpful to me through his essays and his private advice. He has introduced me to Dr. Anna Freud, to whom I tender my respectful thanks for her cooperation and especially for permission to use the hitherto unpublished photograph of her father, Sigmund Freud. Herr Hans Lobner of the Freud Haus in Vienna has been unfailingly forthcoming.

I have yet others to thank. In Vienna, Ernst Haeusserman, director of the Theater in der Josefstadt, for being so encyclopedically, informatively and wittily Viennese; Dr. Wolfgang Kraus, head of the Austrian Society for Literature, and his associate, Dr. Günther Frühwirth, for being such versatile resources; Dr. Gottfried Heindl of the Austrian State Theater for sharing his scholarship in Viennensa and his treasures as an anecdotalist; Professor Hilde Spiel for letting me profit from her insights; Thomas Weyr (of New York and Vienna) and Traudl and Erich Lessing for the books they lent me; Georg Eisler for putting at my disposal his expertise as well as his rare book, *Wienerstadt*, source of the drawings in these pages.

In New York, Dr. Erika Freeman has let me loot her large psychoanalytic library; I have benefited from her gifts as analyst and social commentator. Mrs. Sylvia Landress, director of the Zionist Archives and Library of the Herzl Institute, has been of valuable service. George Marek has also been a great help, and not only through his published works. He has let me draw on his library and the full scope of his knowledgeability.

Last not least, I want to thank Peter Davison, director of the Atlantic Monthly Press, for his editorial acumen and for his faith in this project. He has seen it splendidly through several nervousnesses.

F. M.

Bibliography

This list is limited to primary sources.

❧ ❧

❧ AUSTRIA AND VIENNA ❧

Books

Apponyi, Albert. *The Memoirs of Count Apponyi*. New York, 1935.

Barea, Ilsa. *Vienna*. New York, 1966.

Beatty-Kingston, William. *A Wanderer's Notes*, Vol. 1. London, 1888.

Bloch, Josef Samuel. *Erinnerungen aus meinem Leben*. Vienna, 1922.

Chiavacci, Vinzens. *Aus dem Kleinleben der Grossstadt: Wiener Genre-bilder*. Vienna, 1884.

Crankshaw, Edward. *The Fall of the House of Habsburg*. New York, 1963.

Die österreichisch-ungarische Monarchie in Wort und Bild. 24 vols. Vienna, 1886–1902. (Encyclopedia.)

Eisenberg, Ludwig, and Groner, Richard. *Das geistige Wien: Künstler und Schriftsteller-Lexikon*. Vienna, 1890.

Elmayer-Vestenbrugg, Rudolf. *Georg Ritter von Schönerer*. Munich, 1936.

Friedlaender, Otto. *Wolken drohen über Wien*. Vienna, 1949.

———. *Letzter Glanz der Märchenstadt*. Vienna, 1969.

Gainham, Sarah. *The Habsburg Twilight: Tales from Vienna*. London, 1979.

Greve, Ludwig, and Volke, Werner. *Jugend in Wien: Literatur um 1900*. Catalogue for Schiller National Museum. Munich, 1974.

Groner, Richard, and Czeike, Dr. Felix. *Wien wie es War*. Vienna, 1965.

Hanslick, Eduard. *Aus meinem Leben*. Berlin, 1894.

Hennings, Fred. *Ringstrassen Symphonie*. 3 vols. Vienna, 1963–64.

———. *Solange er Lebt*. Vienna, 1968.

Hitler, Adolf. *Mein Kampf*. Berlin, 1938.

Höfler, Rudolf. *Der schriftliche Verkehr des Offiziers und Militärbeamten*. Vienna, 1909.

Janik, Allan, and Toulmin, Stephen. *Wittgenstein's Vienna*. New York, 1973.

Jászi, Oscar. *The Dissolution of the Habsburg Monarchy*. Chicago, 1971.

Jenks, William A. *Austria under the Iron Ring 1879–1893*. Charlottesville, Va., 1965.

Johnston, William M. *The Austrian Mind*. Berkeley, Calif., 1972.

Kann, Robert A. *The Multinational Empire: Nationalism and National Reform in the Habsburg Monarchy 1848–1918*. New York, 1964.

Lehmanns Allgemeine Wiener Wohnungs Anzeiger. Vienna, 1888, 1889, 1890.

Lesky, Erna. *Die Wiener medizinische Schule im 19. Jahrhundert*. Graz, 1965.

Macartney, C. A. *The Habsburg Empire, 1790–1918*. London, 1969.

McGrath, William J. *Dionysian Art and Populist Politics in Austria*. New Haven, Conn., 1974.

Marek, George. *The Eagles Die*. New York, 1974.

May, Arthur J. *The Hapsburg Monarchy: 1867–1914*. New York, 1968.

Mayer, Sigmund. *Ein jüdischer Kaufmann, 1831 bis 1911: Lebenserinnerungen*. Leipzig, 1911.

———. *Die Wiener Juden — 1700–1900*. Vienna, 1918.

Mazakarini, Leopold. *Historische Adressen — Wien*. Vienna, 1973.

Mikulas, Karl, ed. *Ewiges Wien — Ein Band schönster Wiener Lieder*. Berlin, n.d.

Österreich Lexikon. Vienna, 1966.

Palmer, Francis H. E. *Austro-Hungarian Life in Town and Country*. New York, 1903.

Pemmer, Hans. *Der Prater*. Vienna, 1974.

Perfahl, Jost, ed. *Wien Chronik*. Salzburg, 1961.

Powell, Nicolas. *The Sacred Spring*. Greenwich, Conn., 1974.

Pulzer, Peter G. J. *The Rise of Political Anti-Semitism in Germany and Austria*. New York, 1964.

Ritschel, Karl-Heinz. *Stichwort Österreich*. Vienna, 1978.

Schierbrand, Wolf von. *Austria-Hungary: Polyglot Empire*. New York, 1917.

Schlögl, Friedrich, and Karmel, Franz, eds. *Wiener Skizzen*. Vienna, 1946.

Smith, Bradley F. *Adolf Hitler: His Family, Childhood and Youth*. Stanford, Calif., 1967.

Spitzer, Daniel. *Wiener Spaziergänge*. Vienna, 1886.

———. *Letzte Wiener Spaziergänge*. Vienna, 1894.

———. *Hereinspaziert ins alte Wien*. Vienna, 1967.

Steed, Henry Wickham. *The Habsburg Monarchy*. London, 1913.

Suttner, Bertha von. *Memoiren*. Bremen, 1965.

Szeps, Berta. *My Life and History*. New York, 1939.

Taylor, A. J. P. *The Habsburg Monarchy: 1809–1918*. London, 1948.

Taylor, Edmond. *The Fall of the Dynasties*. New York, 1963.

Uhl, Friedrich. *Aus meinem Leben*. Stuttgart, 1908.

Vasili, Comte Paul. *La société de Vienne*. Paris, 1885.

Vergin, Fedor. *Das unbewusste Europa*. Vienna, 1931.

Waldegg, Richard. *Sittengeschichte von Wien*. Stuttgart, 1957.
Wallersee-Larisch, Countess Marie. *My Past*. New York and London, 1913.
Wallersee, Marie Louise von, vormais Gräfin Larisch. *Kaiserin Elisabeth und ich*. Leipzig, 1935.
Wandruszka, Adam. *Geschichte einer Zeitung: Das Schicksal der "Presse" und der "Neuen Freien Presse" von 1848 bis zur zweiten Republik*. Vienna, 1958.
Wassilko, Theophilia. *Fürstin Pauline Metternich*. Vienna, 1959.
Weigel, Hans. *Flucht vor der Grösse*. Vienna, 1960.
Wien 1848–1888. 2 vols. Vienna, 1888. (A municipal survey.)
Wiener Salon Album. Vienna, 1887. (Anthology of magazine illustrations and excerpts.)
Wienerstadt: Lebensbilder aus der Gegenwart. Vienna, 1895. (Anthology.)
Wilczek, Count Hans. *Happy Retrospect: The Reminiscences of Count Wilczek, 1837–1922*. London, 1934.
Zweig, Stefan. *Die Welt von Gestern*. Stockholm, 1947.

Periodicals

Die bildende Künste. Vienna, 1919.
Schnitzler, Henry. " 'Gay Vienna' — Myth and Reality." *Journal of the History of Ideas*, Vol. 15, No. 1, Jan. 1954.
Schorske, Carl E. "Politics and the Psyche in *fin de siècle* Vienna, Schnitzler and Hofmannsthal." *American Historical Review* 66, July 1961.
———. "The Transformation of the Garden: Ideal and Society in Austrian Literature." *American Historical Review* 72, July 1967.
———. "Politics in a New Key: An Austrian Triptych." *The Journal of Modern History*, Vol. 39, No. 4, Dec. 1967.
———. "Cultural Hothouse." *The New York Review*, Dec. 11, 1975.
———. "General Tension and Cultural Change: Reflections on the Case of Vienna." *Daedalus*, Fall 1978.
"Selbstmorde in Wien." *Statistische Monatschrift* 21, Vienna, 1895.

The daily newspapers in Vienna from July 1, 1888 through April 30, 1889: *Abendpost, Illustriertes Wiener Extrablatt, Neue Freie Presse, Neuigkeits-Weltblatt, Wiener Allgemeine Zeitung, Wiener Fremdenblatt, Wiener Tagblatt, Wiener Zeitung*.
The weeklies: *An der schönen blauen Donau, Der Floh, Kikeriki, Österreichische Wochenpresse, Wiener Salonblatt*.

JOHANNES BRAHMS

Billroth im Briefwechsel mit Brahms. Munich, 1964.
Billroth und Brahms im Briefwechsel. Vienna, 1935.
Brahms, Briefe. Berlin, 1915.
Brahms, Johannes, *Im Briefwechsel mit Heinrich und Elisabeth von Herzogenberg*. Berlin, 1907.
Brahms, Johannes, *Im Briefwechsel mit Philipp Spitta*. Tutzing, 1971.
Brahms, Johannes, *Im Briefwechsel mit Franz Wüllner*. Berlin, 1922.
Brahms, Johannes, *In seiner Familie, der Briefwechsel*. Hamburg, 1973.
Geiringer, Karl. *Brahms, His Life and Work*. London, 1948.
Grassberger, Franz. *Johannes Brahms*. Vienna, 1952.
Kalbeck, Max. *Johannes Brahms*. Berlin, 1914.
May, Florence. *The Life of Johannes Brahms*. London, 1905.
Schumann, Clara–Brahms, Johannes. *Briefe aus den Jahren 1853–1896*. Leipzig, 1927.

ANTON BRUCKNER

Auer, Max. *Anton Bruckner*. Leipzig, 1941.
Bruckner, Anton, *Gesammelte Briefe*. Regensburg, 1924.
Doernberg, Erwin. *The Life and Symphonies of Anton Bruckner*. London, 1960.
Eckstein, Friedrich. *Erinnerungen an Anton Bruckner*. Vienna, 1927.
———. *Alte unnennbare Tage*. Vienna, 1936.
Göllerich, August. *Anton Bruckner*. Regensburg, 1974.
Hruby, Carl. *Meine Erinnerungen an Anton Bruckner*. Vienna, 1901.
Louis, Rudolf. *Anton Bruckner*. Munich, 1905.
Nowak, Leopold. *Anton Bruckner — Musik und Leben*. Linz, 1973.
r. "Die volle Wahrheit über Anton Bruckner." *Die Presse*, Vienna, Sept. 24–25, 1977.
Schönzeler, Hans-Hubert. *Bruckner*. New York, 1970.
Wolff, Werner. *Anton Bruckner, Rustic Genius*. New York, 1942.

EMPEROR FRANZ JOSEPH AND EMPRESS ELISABETH

Corti, Count Egon. *Elizabeth Empress of Austria*. New Haven, 1936.
———, and Sokol, Hans. *Der alte Kaiser*. Graz, 1955.
de Bourgoing, Jean, ed. *Briefe Kaiser Franz Josephs an Frau Katharina Schratt*. Vienna, 1964.

Ernst, Otto, ed. *Francis Joseph as Revealed by His Letters*. New York, 1927.

Harding, Bertita. *Golden Fleece*. Indianapolis, 1937.

Haslip, Joan. *The Lonely Empress: A Biography of Elizabeth of Austria*. London, 1965.

———. *The Crown of Mexico: Maximilian and His Empress Carlota*. New York, 1971.

Janetschek, Ottokar. *Kaiser Franz Joseph*. Zurich, 1949.

Korty, Raoul, ed. *Franz Joseph I. in 100 Bildern*. Vienna, 1935.

Nostitz-Rieneck, Georg, ed. *Briefe, Kaiser Franz Joseph und Kaiserin Elisabeth*. Vienna, 1966.

Redlich, Josef. *Emperor Franz Joseph of Austria: A Biography*. New York, 1929.

Tschudi, Clara. *Elisabeth, Kaiserin von Österreich und Königin von Ungarn*. Leipzig, n.d.

Tschuppik, Karl. *Franz Joseph I: Der Untergang eines Reiches*. Dresden, 1928.

———. *Elisabeth, Kaiserin von Österreich*. Vienna, 1929.

᠅ SIGMUND FREUD ᠅

Books

Bonaparte, Marie; Freud, Anna; and Kris, Ernst; eds. *The Origins of Psychoanalysis: Letters to Wilhelm Fliess, Drafts and Notes: 1887–1902*. New York, 1954.

Freud, Martin. *Glory Reflected: Sigmund Freud — Man and Father*. London, 1957.

Freud, Sigmund. *Briefe, 1873–1939*. Frankfurt, 1968.

———. *The Standard Edition of the Complete Psychological Works of Sigmund Freud*. 23 vols. London, 1953–66.

Grubrich-Simitis, Ilse. *Sigmund Freud "Selbstdarstellung" — Schriften zur Geschichte der Psychoanalyse*. Frankfurt am Main, 1971.

Jones, Ernest. *The Life and Work of Sigmund Freud*. 3 vols. New York, 1953–57.

Leupold-Löwenthal, Harald, and Lobner, Hans. *Sigmund Freud — Haus Katalog*. Vienna, 1975.

Mannoni, Octave. *Sigmund Freud in Selbstzeugnissen und Bilddokumenten*. Hamburg, 1971.

Miller, Jonathan. *Freud*. Boston, 1972.

Periodicals

Bernays, Anna Freud. "My Brother, Sigmund Freud." *American Mercury*, Vol. 51, No. 203, Nov. 1940.

Hacker, Frederick J., M.D. "The Living Image of Freud." *Bulletin of the Menninger Clinic*, Vol. 20, No. 3, May 1956.

———. "Psychologia Austriaca: Der österreichische Anteil an der Lehre Sigmund Freuds." *Forum* 50, Feb. 1958.

Leupold-Löwenthal, Harald. "Das Wien Sigmund Freuds." *Das Jüdische Echo*, Sept. 1976.

Schick, Alfred. "The Vienna of Sigmund Freud." *The Psychoanalytic Review*, Vol. 55, No. 4, Winter 1968–69.

———. "Psychotherapy in Old Vienna and New York: Cultural Comparisons." *The Psychoanalytic Review*, Vol. 60, No. 1, 1973.

Schorske, Carl E. "Politics and Patricide in Freud's *Interpretation of Dreams*." *American Historical Review* 78, April 1973.

𝒮 THEODOR HERZL 𝒮

Bein, Alex. *Theodore* [sic] *Herzl*. New York, 1941.

Cohen, Israel. *Herzl*. New York, 1960.

de Haas, Jacob. *Theodor Herzl*. Chicago and New York, 1927.

Elon, Amos. *Herzl*. New York, 1975.

Fraenkel, Josef. *Theodor Herzl, des Schöpfers erstes Wollen*. Vienna, 1934.

Georg, Manfred, ed. *Herzl Briefe*. Berlin, n.d.

Herzl, Theodor. *Letters, unpublished*. Zionist Archives and Library, New York.

———. *Jugendtagebuch*. Yivo Institute for Jewish Research, New York.

———. *Tagebücher*. 3 vols. New York, 1960.

———. *Neues von der Venus*. Leipzig, 1887.

———. *Das Buch der Narrheit*. Leipzig, 1888.

———. *Feuilletons*. 2 vols. Vienna, 1911.

———. *Altneuland*. Berlin and Vienna, 1921.

———, and Wittmann, Hugo. *Wilddiebe*. Berlin, 1889.

Kellner, Leon. *Theodor Herzls Lehrjahre*. Vienna, 1920.

Klinov, I., ed. *Herzl: Seer of the State*. Tel Aviv, 1950.

Patai, Josef. *Star Over Jordan*. New York, 1946.

Stewart, Desmond. *Theodor Herzl*. New York, 1974.

Unger, Imanuel, ed. *Theodor Herzl: der Wiener*. Vienna, 1965.

GUSTAV KLIMT

Dobai, Johannes. "Das Frühwerk Gustav Klimts." Doctoral dissertation, University of Vienna, 1958.

Giese, Herbert. "Franz Matsch — Leben und Werk." Doctoral dissertation, University of Vienna, 1976.

Guggenheim Museum. *Gustav Klimt and Egon Schiele*. New York, 1965.

Hanak, Anton. "Gustav Klimt — Die Triesterstrasse." *Der Wiener Kunstwanderer*, Feb. 1934.

Nebehay, Christian. *Gustav Klimt Dokumentation*. Vienna, 1969.

———. *Gustav Klimt — Sein Leben nach zeitgenössischen Berichten und Quellen*. Munich, 1976.

Novotny, Fritz, and Dobai, Johannes. *Gustav Klimt*. Salzburg, 1967.

Pirchan, Emil. *Gustav Klimt*. Vienna, 1956.

Rochowanski, L. W. "Gustav Klimt — Intim: Ein Besuch bei Georg Klimt." *Neues Wiener Journal*, Jan. 13, 1929.

GUSTAV MAHLER

Blaukopf, Kurt. *Mahler*. New York, 1973.

———, ed. *Mahler — A Documentary Study*. New York, 1976.

de la Grange, Henry-Louis. *Mahler*. New York, 1973.

Mahler, Gustav. *Briefe*. Vienna, 1925.

Mahler-Werfel, Alma. *Mein Leben*. Frankfurt, 1960.

Walter, Bruno. Notes for his record with the New York Philharmonic of Mahler's Symphony No. 2. Columbia, #Ys 30848.

———. *Gustav Mahler*. New York, 1958.

Wessling, Berndt W. *Gustav Mahler*. Hamburg, 1974.

CROWN PRINCE RUDOLF AND MAYERLING

Books

Barkeley, Richard. *The Road to Mayerling*. New York, 1958.

Dobrowski, Raoul Ritter von (anonymously). *Rudolf, Kronprinz von Österreich-Ungarn als Forscher und Weidmann*. Gedenkblätter, Vienna, 1889.

Egger-Fabritius, Friedrich. "Kronprinz Erzherzog Rudolf von Österreich als Journalist und Schriftsteller." Doctoral Dissertation, University of Vienna, 1954.

Franzel, Emil. *Kronprinzen-Mythos und Mayerling-Legenden*. Vienna, 1973.

Hamann, Brigitte. *Rudolf: Kronprinz und Rebell*. Vienna, 1978.

Judtmann, Fritz. *Mayerling: The Facts behind the Legend*. London, 1971.

Lonyay, Count Carl. *Rudolph, The Tragedy of Mayerling*. New York, 1949.

Mayerling: Der Polizeibericht — No. 1 Reservat 1889. Vienna, 1955.

Mitis, Oskar Freiherr von, and Wandruszka, Adam, ed. *Das Leben des Kronprinzen Rudolf. Mit einem Anhang: Kronprinz Rudolf und Theodor Billroth*. Vienna, 1971.

Polzer, Wilhelm. *Licht über Mayerling*. Graz, 1954.

Richter, Werner. *Kronprinz Rudolf von Österreich*. Zurich, 1941.

Rudolf, Crown Prince. *Der österreichische Adel und sein konstitutioneller Beruf. Mahnruf an die aristokratische Jugend, von einem Österreicher*. (Anonymous pamphlet.) Munich, 1878.

Stephanie, H.R.H., Princess of Belgium, Fürstin of Lonyay, Ex–Crown Princess of Austria-Hungary. *I Was to Be Empress*. London, 1937.

Stockhausen, Juliana von. *Im Schatten der Hofburg — Gestalten, Puppen und Gespenster*. Vienna, 1952.

Szeps, Julius, ed. *Politische Briefe an einen Freund, 1882–1889*. Vienna, 1922.

Vetsera, Baronin-Mutter Helene. *Denkschrift: Das Drama von Mayerling*. Reichenberg, 1921.

Periodicals

Antonius, Dr. Fritz. "Kaiserhaus und Polizei." *Wochen Ausgabe, Neues Wiener Tagblatt*, Nov. 20, 1926.

Bader, Emil. "Das überwachte Kaiserhaus." *Wochen Ausgabe, Neues Wiener Tagblatt*, Nov. 24, 1923.

Binyon, Rudolph. "Mayerling." *Journal of Modern History*, July 1975.

Broucek, Peter. "Kronprinz Rudolf und k. u. k. Oberstleutnant im Generalstab Steininger." *Mitteilungen des Österreichischen Staatsarchivs* 26, 1973.

Fischer, Michael. "Wie Kronprinz Rudolf Mayerling erwarb." *Sonntags Beilage, Neues Wiener Tagblatt*, July 5, 1925.

Frischauer, Berthold. "Kronprinzenlegenden — aus meinen Erinnerungen an den verstorbenen Kronprinzen Rudolf." *Neue Freie Presse*, Aug. 21, 1921.

———. "Kronprinz Rudolf und Graf Taaffe — eine Erinnerung." *Neue Freie Presse*, April 23, 1922.

Hummelberger, Walter. "Maria Caspar und Josef Bratfisch." *Mitteilungen des Österreichischen Staatsarchivs* 19–20, 1963–64.

Loschek, Johann. "Was ich von Mayerling weiss." *Sonntags Beilage, Neues Wiener Tagblatt*, April 24, 1932.

Niel, Dr. Alfred. "Nach Mayerling der Liebe wegen." *Die niederösterreichische Wirtschaft*, Jan. 31, 1975.

Püchel, Rudolf. "Die letzten Stunden des Kronprinzen Rudolf in der Wiener Hofburg — Persönliche Erinnerungen an den 30. Jänner 1889." *Reichspost*, Vienna, Jan. 31, 1926.
Slatin, Dr. Heinrich von. "Die Wahrheit über Mayerling — Der Tod des Kronprinzen Rudolf und der Baronesse Mary Vetsera." *Neues Wiener Tagblatt*, Aug. 15, Aug. 23, Aug. 30, Sept. 6, Sept. 13, 1931.
Sternberg, Graf Adalbert. "Das Martyrium der Baronin Vetsera. Die Nemesis von Mayerling." *Wiener Sonn- und Montags-Zeitung*, Feb. 9, 1925.
Szeps, Dr. Julius. "Kronprinz und Journalist." *Neues Wiener Journal*, Jan. 13, March 2, March 9, 1924.
Zillinger, Eduard. "Streifzüge im verschneiten Wienerwald." *An der schönen blauen Donau*, March 15, 1889.

Austrian National Library, Vienna

Mayerling-Lloyd-Mitis Collection. Microfilm. Washington, D.C., 1950, Rekordak.

Austrian State Archives, Vienna

Crown Prince Rudolf Collection, Boxes 1 through 22.
Protocol of Ceremonies, 1889.

@ ARTHUR SCHNITZLER @

Schnitzler, Arthur. *Diaries*. Unpublished.
———. *Gesammelte Werke*. Berlin, 1922.
———. *My Youth in Vienna*. Foreword by Frederic Morton. New York, 1970.
———, and Waissnix, Olga. *Briefe*. Vienna, 1970.

@ ARNOLD SCHÖNBERG @

"Arnold Schönberg." *Austrian Information Bulletin*, New York, Vol. 29, No. 5, 1976.
Reich, Willi. *Schönberg*. Vienna, 1968.

JOHANN STRAUSS

Decsey, Ernst. *Johann Strauss.* Stuttgart, 1922.
Fantel, Hans. *The Waltz Kings, Father and Son, and Their Romantic Age.* New York, 1972.
Jaspert, Werner. *Johann Strauss, sein Leben, sein Werk.* Vienna, 1939.
Pahlen, Kurt. *Johann Strauss—Die Walzerdynastie.* Munich, 1975.
Prawy, Marcel. *Johann Strauss.* Vienna, 1975.
Schnitzer, Ignatz. *Meister Johann.* Vienna, 1920.
Strauss, Johann, *Schreibt Briefe.* Berlin, 1926.
Wechsberg, Joseph. *The Waltz Emperors.* New York, 1973.
Weigl, Hans. *Das kleine Walzerbuch.* Salzburg, 1965.

HUGO WOLF

Decsey, Ernst. *Hugo Wolf—Das Leben und das Lied.* Berlin, 1921.
Ehrmann, Alfred von. *Hugo Wolf—Sein Leben in Bildern.* Leipzig, 1937.
Hattingberg, Magda von. *Hugo Wolf.* Vienna, 1953.
Walker, Frank. *Hugo Wolf.* London, 1968.
Werner, Heinrich. *Hugo Wolf in Maierling. Eine Idylle.* Leipzig, 1913.
Wolf, Hugo. *Fifty Songs by Hugo Wolf.* Philadelphia, 1909.
———. *Familienbriefe.* Leipzig, 1912.

Index

Index

333

Schönerer, Georg von, 73–74, 162, 199, 301; jailing of, for anti-Semitic activities, 61–62, 74, 99, 272

Schratt, Frau Katharina, 169, 204, 223; Emperor Franz Joseph's letters to, 22, 80, 101, 107, 110, 152, 186–188, 224, 301; her relationship with Emperor Franz Joseph, 23, 47, 92; and *The Refugee*, 26; and opening of Court Theater, 122; and Sarah Bernhardt, 153, 155; visiting Empress after Rudolf's suicide, 237, 239, 240; and suicides of Rudolf and Mary, 245; provision for, in Franz Joseph's will, 308–309, 309n

Schratt, Toni, 186

Schubert, Franz, 20, 97–98, 134–135

Schumann, Clara, 164–166

Schumann, Robert, 20

Schwarzenberg, Prince, 174, 311

Schwarz-Gelb, 112

Simrock (Berlin publisher), 142

Singer, Sigmund, 208

Slatin, Dr. Heinrich, 251, 275

Social Democratic Party, 54, 68, 199–200

Somics, Ella, 114

Sonnenthal, Baron Adolf von, 300–301, 304

Speidel, Ludwig, 190

Steininger, Lt. Karl von, 113

Stephanie, Crown Princess, 46, 63, 119, 215, 220, 286; on change in behavior of Rudolf, 115–116; her last Christmas Eve with Rudolf, 179; and Mary Vetsera, 224–225; Rudolf's good-bye to, 226; Rudolf's last telegram to, 232; receives news of Rudolf's and Mary's suicides, 240; Rudolf's last letter to, 245; absence of, from Rudolf's funeral, 266; her stay at Miramar, 268

Stockau, Count Georg, 249, 251–252

Strauss, Adele, 24, 141, 144, 201

Strauss, Eduard (Edi), 108, 144, 193, 194, 201

Strauss, Johann, Sr., "Radetsky March," 57

Strauss, Johann, Jr., 23–25, 108, 123, 166, 200–201; *Ritter Pazman*, 25, 47, 141, 142, 201; *The Gypsy Baron*, 101; conducting engagements of, in Prague, 141; his visit to Franzensbad, 141–142; Emperor Waltz of, 142;

"phase" suffered by, 142–145, 201; and Anton Bruckner, 201–202; his move to Schönau in Vienna Woods, 308

suicide, prevalence of, in Vienna (1888–1889), 65–66, 67, 124, 133–134, 280

Suppé, Franz von, *La Vie Parisienne*, 221

Szeps, Bertha, 36

Szeps, Moritz, 46, 83, 112, 169, 196; Rudolf's correspondence with, 9, 33–34; 64–65, 99, 116, 154, 188–189; and Rudolf's articles in *Wiener Tagblatt*, 36, 100, 102; founding of *Neues Wiener Tagblatt* by, 62n; on aftertaste of Wilhelm II's visit to Vienna, 111; and Georges Clemenceau, 113; and diaries of Crown Prince Friedrich, 171; and attacks on Rudolf in Prussian newspapers, 177; and Heine letters, 178

Szögyény (of Foreign Ministry), 114

Taaffe, Count Eduard von, 107, 157–159, 169, 220, 300; and deaths of Rudolf and Mary, 240–241, 247–248

Thimig, Hugo, 190, 304

Tilgner, Viktor, 225

Tisza, Koloman, 107

Tramway Conductors' Ball, 293

Truxa, Frau, 163, 182

Uhl, Herr (Mayor of Vienna), 107, 108

Upper Austrian Foresters' Ball, 202

Valerie (sister of Rudolf), 118, 178–180, 245

Vavrinecz, Maurus, 209–210

Verdi, Giuseppe, 209

Vetsera, Baroness Hanna, 123, 130

Vetsera, Baroness Helene, 77–78, 82, 123, 129; and Mary's affair with Rudolf, 132, 175; and Mary's disappearance, 228; and death of Mary, 247–248

Vetsera, Baroness Mary (Marie), 76, 85, 88, 116; ambition of, 78, 79, 81–82; her pursuit of Rudolf, 82, 118–120; furs worn by, 82–83; her first introduction to Rudolf, 83–84; appearance of, at opening of Court Theater, 123; first meetings between

The Rathaus and Ringstrasse